LONDON WASPS

OFFICIAL YEARBOOK 2006/07

Editorial
Fiona Hackett, Andrew Sleight

Sidan Press Team
Simon Rosen, Julian Hill-Wood, Marc Fiszman, Mark Peters, Karim Biria, Robert Cubbon, Marina Kravchenko, Anette Lundebye, Katie L Fiszman, Gareth Peters, Janet Callcott, Trevor Scimes, John Fitzroy, Anders Rasmussen, Lim Wai-Lee, Zoe Westbourne, Charles Grove, Carla Atkins, Humphrey Badia

Statistics
Stuart Farmer Media Services, OPTA

Kick Off Editorial
Amanda Chatterton

Photography
Action Images

Sidan Press, 63-64 Margaret St, London W1W 8SW
Tel: 020 7580 0200
Email: info@sidanpress.com

sidanpress.com

Club Directory

Stadium

Adams Park
Hillbottom Rd, Sands,
High Wycombe
HP12 4HJ

Training Ground

Twyford Avenue Sports Ground
Twyford Avenue
Acton, London
W3 9QA

Phone 020 8993 8298
Fax: 020 8993 2621
Email: enquiries@wasps.co.uk

Chairman and Directors

Chairman
Chris Wright

Vice Chairman
John O'Connell

Directors
Nigel Butterfield, Bob Collier, Ivor Montlake

Company Secretary
Graham Wynde

Chief Executive
David Davies

Contacts

Director of Rugby
Ian McGeechan

Operations & Events
Gloria Sennitt
Tel: 020 8896 4872
Email: gloria.sennitt@wasps.co.uk

Commercial
Samantha Taylor
Tel: 020 8896 4875
Email: samantha.taylor@wasps.co.uk

Community Dept
David Larham
Tel: 020 8896 4886
Email: dave.larham@wasps.co.uk

Communications
Fiona Hackett
Tel: 020 8896 4890
Email: fiona.hackett@wasps.co.uk

Corporate & Hospitality
Rachel Bayes
Tel: 020 8896 4873
Email: rachel.bayes@wasps.co.uk

Ticket Office
0870 414 1515

Merchandise
Ben Brooke
Tel 020 8993 8372
Mail Order: 0870 428 7910
Email:ben.brooke@wasps.co.uk

Supporters Club
Alistair Beynon
Tel: 020 8996 4874
Email: alistair.beynon@wasps.co.uk

Contents

Chairman's message

Chris Wright

Welcome to the first edition of the London Wasps Official Yearbook. This is a new venture, and hopefully a souvenir that all Wasps' supporters will value.

Your yearbook is a mine of information about Wasps that includes a match-by-match review of the season with analysis and statistics, player biographies and a guide to all the away grounds in the Premiership, which I am sure our travelling supporters will find very handy.

As well as being a source of information, your yearbook will hopefully also rekindle some memories from last year, including our successfu run in the Powergen Cup that saw us secur silverware for the club for the fourth season i succession.

This season Wasps will be striving to continu this, the most successful era of the club. We hop that this book will help to whet your appetite fc the challenge ahead of us.

Thank you for your continued support of Londc Wasps.

Chris Wright

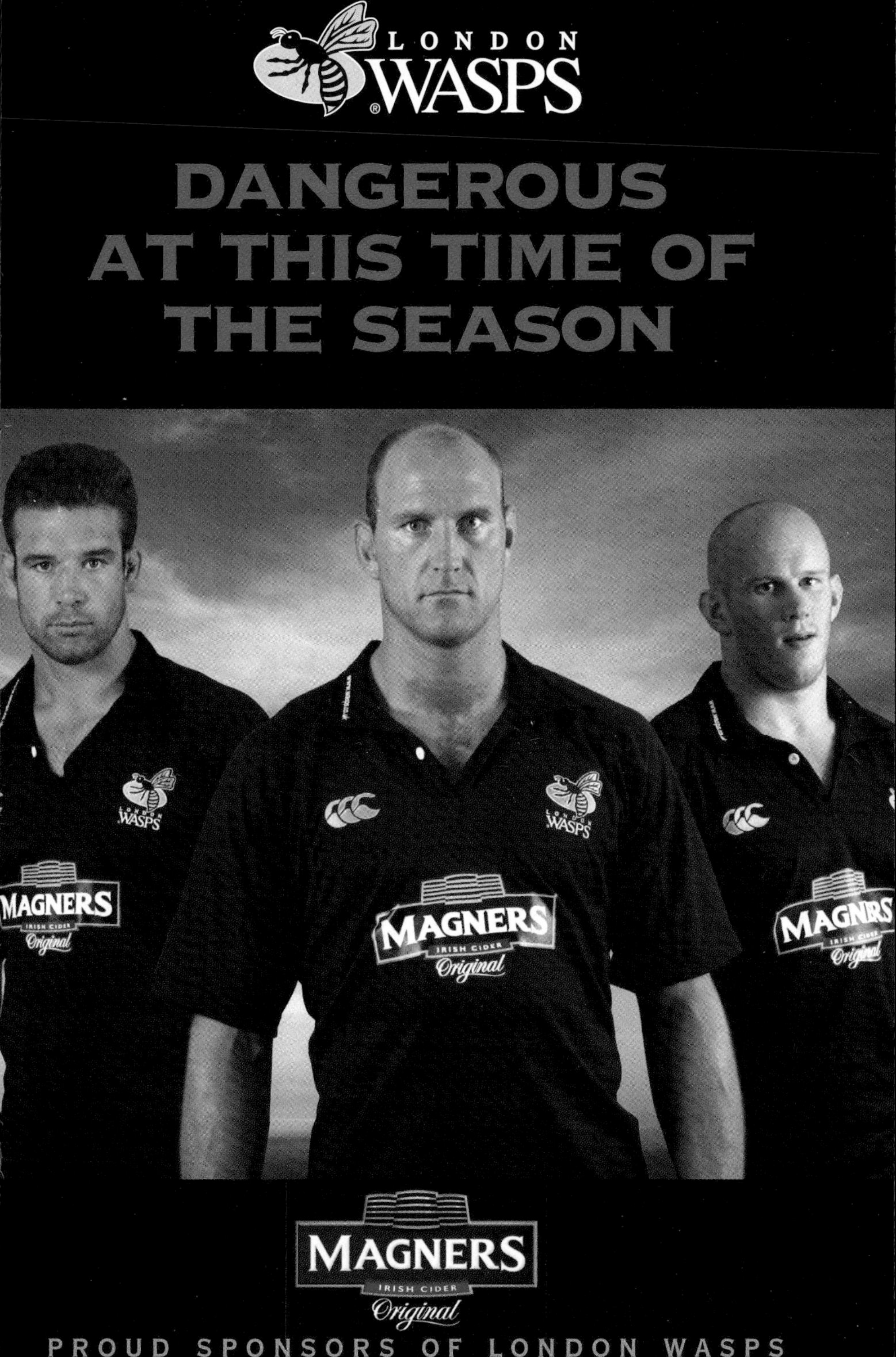

Season Review 2005/06

WASPS

London Wasps 23
Saracens 11

Guinness Premiership

03.09.05

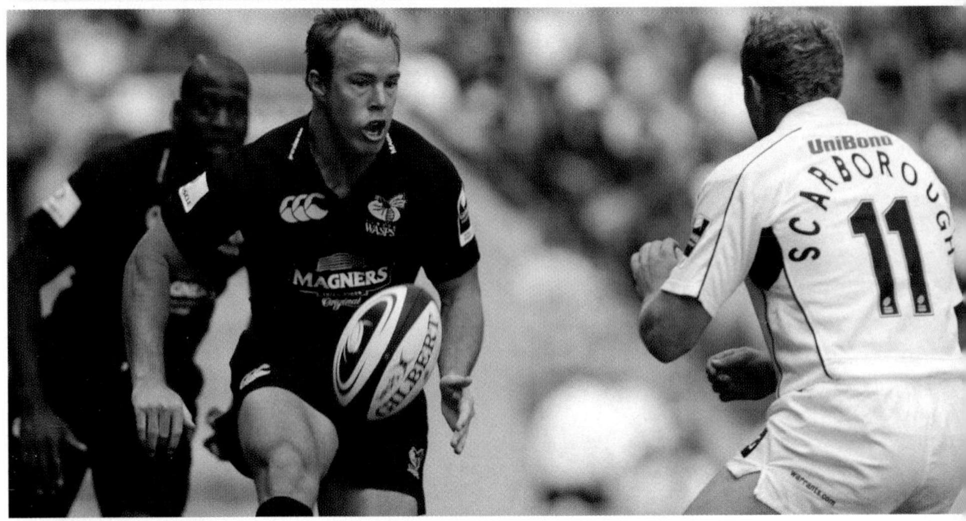

Premiership Home Record vs Saracens

Played	Won	Drawn	Lost	For	Against
9	7	1	1	268	123

The season began in bizarre fashion for the champions – with a win! – in the annual curtain raiser at Twickenham.

Quote

Ian McGeechan

I thought the attitude of the players out there today was superb, they worked hard in some very hot conditions.

After losing against neighbours Saracens the previous September, it looked like being a case of déjà vu at HQ for Wasps, with Saracens racing into an early 6-0 lead via Glen Jackson penalties. Wasps' lock Martin Purdy was an early casualty, with a head injury, after he collided with Saracens' prop Cobus Visagie.

But the champions hit back with Mark Van Gisbergen slotting a penalty over – the first of five beautifully struck place kicks taken by the full-back. On the half hour concerted pressure resulted in Tom Voyce darting through for the first try.

After the break, Saracens came out fighting, No8 Ben Skirving bolting through to score in the corner. Van Gisbergen countered with a penalty shortly afterwards to restore Wasps' narrow lead, and put over another expertly-taken kick to stretch the gap to a 16-11.

The final act of the game was Stuart Abbott's perfectly-timed off-load, that allowed his centre partner Fraser Waters to slide underneath the posts and seal victory. Alex King was the stand-out performer winning the Man of the Match award in Director of Rugby Ian McGeechan's inaugural win in charge.

Venue:	Twickenham	Referee:	David Rose - Season 05/06	**London Wasps**
Attendance:	35,000	Matches:	0	**Saracens**
Capacity:	75,000	Yellow Cards:	0	
Occupancy:	47%	Red Cards:	0	

Starting Line-Ups

London Wasps		Saracens
Van Gisbergen	15	Castaignede
Sackey	14	Haughton
Erinle	13	Johnston
Abbott	12	Sorrell
Voyce	11	Scarbrough
King	10	Jackson
Reddan	9	Dickens
Payne	1	Yates
Ibanez	2	Cairns
Bracken	3	Visagie
Purdy	4	Chesney
Birkett	5	Vyvyan (c)
Hart (c)	6	Russell
O'Connor	7	Seymour
Worsley	8	Skirving

Replacements

Waters	22	Harris
Brooks	21	Russell
M Dawson	20	Rauluni
Lock	19	Sanderson
Rees	18	Fullarton
J Dawson	17	Lloyd
Gotting	16	Byrne

Match Stats

	London Wasps	Saracens
Tackles	102	136
Missed Tackles	12	22
Ball Carries	124	91
Metres	668	398
Defenders Beaten	20	12
Passes	134	98
Clean Breaks	16	8
Pens Conceded	13	15
Turnovers	28	19
Breakdowns Won	81	64
% Scrums Won	86%	100%
% Line-Outs Won	95%	89%

Premiership Table

Team	P	W	D	L	F	A	BP	Pts
2 London Irish	1	1	0	0	27	11	1	5
3 London Wasps	1	1	0	0	23	11	0	4
4 Sale Sharks	1	1	0	0	26	25	0	4

Event Line

TC Try Converted — P Penalty
T Try — DG Drop Goal

Min	Score Progress		Event	Players
8	0	3	P	Jackson
15	0	6	P	Jackson
20	0	6	⇄	Rees > Purdy
21	0	6	⇄	Sanderson > Russell
28	3	6	P	Van Gisbergen
29	3	6	⇄	Dawson > Bracken
32	10	6	TC	Voyce / Van Gisbergen
38	10	6	⇄	Brooks > King
40	10	6	⇄	King > Brooks
40	10	6	⇄	Lloyd > Yates
Half time 10-6				
43	10	11	T	Skirving
46	13	11	P	Van Gisbergen
47	13	11	⇄	Fullarton > Chesney
52	13	11	⇄	Byrne > Cairns
52	16	11	P	Van Gisbergen
57	16	11	⇄	Gotting > Ibanez
59	16	11	⇄	Rauluni > Dickens
60	16	11	⇄	Dawson > Reddan
66	16	11	⇄	Waters > Erinle
66	16	11	⇄	Harris > Johnston
72	16	11	⇄	Yates > Visagie
77	16	11	■	Yates
79	16	11	⇄	Ibanez > Gotting
80	16	11	⇄	Lock > Dawson
81	23	11	TC	Waters / Van Gisbergen
Full time 23-11				

Scoring Statistics

London Wasps

by Situation		by Half	
TC:	14	first:	43%
T:	0	second:	57%
P:	9		
DG:	0		

Saracens

by Situation		by Half	
TC:	0	first:	55%
T:	5	second:	45%
P:	6		
DG:	0		

London Wasps 29
Leicester Tigers 29

Guinness Premiership

10.09.05

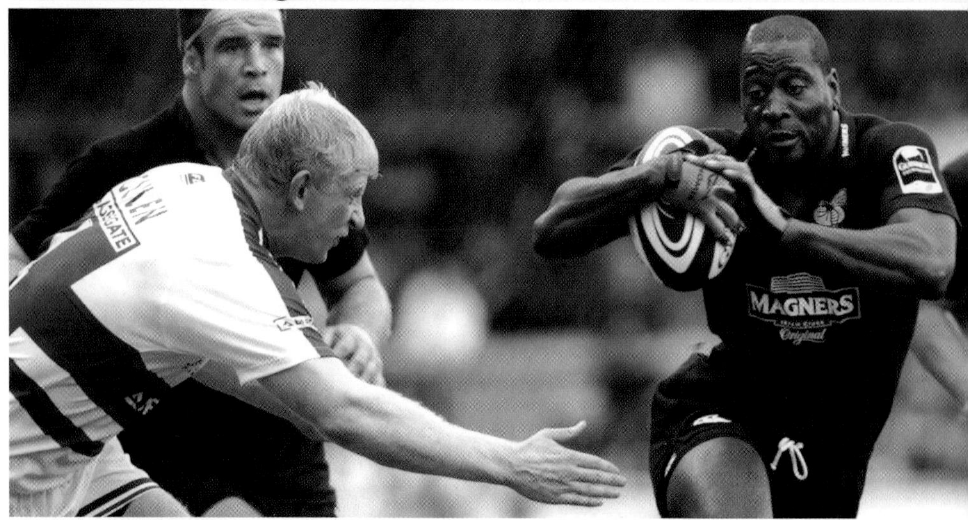

Premiership Home Record vs Leicester Tigers					
Played	Won	Drawn	Lost	For	Against
9	4	2	3	229	214

Back rower Tom Rees deservedly scooped the Man of the Match award, scoring two tries in an adrenaline-charged draw against Leicester.

Quote

Ian McGeechan

We are disappointed. We defended the line well and I thought the referee was harsh with us, but you can't afford to give away points like that to a team like Leicester.

A thrilling first half saw two spectacular tries from Rees and two opportunistic scores for Leicester from Tom Varndell and Harry Ellis. Mark Van Gisbergen and Andy Goode matched each other kick for kick, and the match was locked at 23-23 at the interval.

Rees scored his first try following a purposeful run from Tom Voyce. The prolific wing was brought down five yards short and, with Wasps producing quick ball, Rees evaded two tackles before touching down. His second effort was also eye-catching as he sliced through Leicester's covering defence, stepping through tackles in another inexorable advance to the whitewash.

Unfortunately Rees withdrew with an ankle problem seven minutes later and, in torrential rain, Wasps could only score points via Van Gisbergen's boot, Goode responded with six points for Leicester. Wasps had a chance to win it late on, but Alex King's drop goal was wide of the target while Goode missed with a similar effort from close range at the death.

Venue:	Causeway Stadium	Referee:	Dave Pearson - Season 05/06
Attendance:	8,459	Matches:	1
Capacity:	10,200	Yellow Cards:	1
Occupancy:	83%	Red Cards:	0

London Wasps
Leicester Tigers

Starting Line-Ups

London Wasps		Leicester Tigers
Van Gisbergen	15	Murphy
Sackey	14	Tuilagi
Waters	13	Lloyd
Abbott	12	Gibson
Voyce	11	Varndell
King	10	Goode
Reddan	9	Ellis
Payne	1	Holford
Ibanez	2	Chuter
J Dawson	3	Moreno
Shaw	4	Cullen
Birkett	5	Kay
Rees	6	Deacon
O'Connor	7	Jennings
Worsley (c)	8	Corry (c)

Replacements

Hoadley	22	Cornwell
Brooks	21	Broadfoot
M Dawson	20	Healey
Lock	19	Abraham
Hart	18	Deacon
Bracken	17	White
Gotting	16	Taukafa

Match Stats

	London Wasps	Leicester Tigers
Tackles	59	69
Missed Tackles	7	15
Ball Carries	57	49
Metres	314	357
Defenders Beaten	15	8
Passes	62	42
Clean Breaks	4	3
Pens Conceded	13	10
Turnovers	17	16
Breakdowns Won	44	42
% Scrums Won	93%	91%
% Line-Outs Won	67%	77%

Premiership Table

Team	P	W	D	L	F	A	BP	Pts
1 Leicester Tigers	2	1	1	0	61	29	1	7
2 London Wasps	2	1	1	0	52	40	0	6
3 Gloucester Rugby	2	1	1	0	36	33	0	6

Event Line

TC Try Converted — P Penalty
T Try — DG Drop Goal

Min	Score Progress		Event	Players
3	0	3	P	Goode
5	7	3	TC	Rees / Van Gisbergen
9	7	10	TC	Varndell / Goode
12	7	13	P	Goode
17	10	13	P	Van Gisbergen
24	13	13	P	Van Gisbergen
27	13	16	P	Goode
28	13	16		Jennings
29	16	16	P	Van Gisbergen
30	23	16	TC	Rees / Van Gisbergen
32	23	16	⇄	Healey > Murphy
36	23	23	TC	Ellis / Goode
38	23	23	⇄	Cornwell > Ellis
Half time 23-23				
41	23	23	⇄	Ellis > Cornwell
41	23	23	⇄	White > Holford
41	23	23	⇄	Murphy > Healey
44	23	23	⇄	Gotting > Ibanez
45	23	26	P	Goode
48	23	26	⇄	Hart > Rees
48	26	26	P	Van Gisbergen
49	26	26	⇄	Bracken > Dawson
50	26	26	⇄	Deacon > Cullen
52	26	26	⇄	Dawson > Reddan
63	29	26	P	Van Gisbergen
66	29	26	⇄	Abraham > Deacon
70	29	26	⇄	Healey > Varndell
72	29	26	⇄	Lock > Shaw
76	29	29	P	Goode
77	29	29	⇄	Broadfoot > Gibson
79	29	29	⇄	Hoadley > Abbott
82	29	29	⇄	Dawson > Bracken
Full time 29-29				

Scoring Statistics

London Wasps

by Situation — by Half

by Situation		by Half	
TC:	14	first:	79%
T:	0	second:	21%
P:	15		
DG:	0		

Leicester Tigers

by Situation — by Half

by Situation		by Half	
TC:	14	first:	79%
T:	0	second:	21%
P:	15		
DG:	0		

Leeds Tykes 23
London Wasps 47

Guinness Premiership

18.09.05

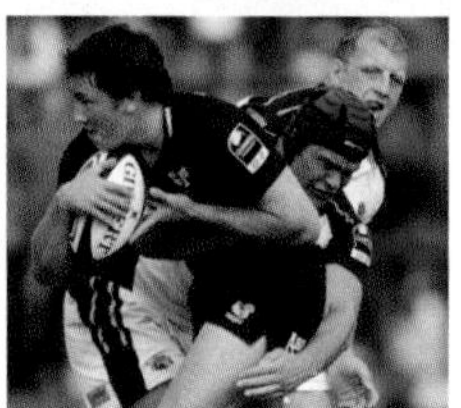

Premiership Away Record vs Leeds Tykes

Played	Won	Drawn	Lost	For	Against
5	5	0	0	117	72

The champions produced an outstanding display at Headingley and ran in five tries to brush aside Leeds.

However, London Wasps had found themselves 16-12 down after Ian Balshaw had crossed over just before half-time. But in the second-half it was all Wasps as a Tom Voyce try soon after the restart put the Londoners ahead. An inspired treble substitution followed which determined the outcome of the game, replacements Raphael Ibanez, Simon Shaw and Ayoola Erinle making the difference. Three tries in ten minutes plus Mark Van Gisbergen's flawless kicking display enabled Wasps to sail on to victory.

After only being on the pitch for 10 minutes, Ibanez had struck twice. Popping up in support, he was on hand to take the final pass for both scores – the second try coming after a characteristic Erinle break through the midfield.

Scrum-half Matt Dawson was able to dictate play from behind his confident-looking pack and the bonus point arrived with five minutes remaining, courtesy of stand-in captain John Hart, who touched down from close range to underline a classy display from the champions.

Leeds grabbed a late consolation try from Stuart Hooper prior to wing Paul Sackey running in Wasps' fifth try of the game. Van Gisbergen's conversion gave the full-back a perfect kicking record of nine from nine on the day.

Venue:	Headingley Carnegie	Referee:	Martin Fox - Season 05/06
Attendance:	4,544	Matches:	1
Capacity:	24,000	Yellow Cards:	3
Occupancy:	19%	Red Cards:	0

Leeds Tykes
London Wasps

Starting Line-Ups

Leeds Tykes		London Wasps
Balshaw (c)	**15**	Van Gisbergen
Biggs	**14**	Sackey
Jones	**13**	Waters
Snyman	**12**	Abbott
Doherty	**11**	Voyce
De Marigny	**10**	King
Marshall	**9**	M Dawson
Shelley	**1**	Payne
Rawlinson	**2**	Gotting
Kerr	**3**	J Dawson
Murphy	**4**	Purdy
Palmer	**5**	Birkett
Dunbar	**6**	Hart (c)
Parks	**7**	O'Connor
Crane	**8**	Worsley

Replacements

Ross	**22**	Erinle
Stimpson	**21**	Brooks
Care	**20**	Reddan
Morgan	**19**	Lock
Hooper	**18**	Shaw
Bulloch	**17**	Bracken
Cusack	**16**	Ibanez

Match Stats

	Leeds Tykes	London Wasps
Tackles	122	83
Missed Tackles	13	5
Ball Carries	77	114
Metres	300	551
Defenders Beaten	5	13
Passes	80	132
Clean Breaks	7	7
Pens Conceded	11	15
Turnovers	14	15
Breakdowns Won	52	82
% Scrums Won	95%	100%
% Line-Outs Won	90%	80%

Premiership Table

Team	P	W	D	L	F	A	BP	Pts
1 Leicester Tigers	3	2	1	0	101	55	2	12
2 London Wasps	3	2	1	0	99	63	1	11
3 Gloucester Rugby	3	2	1	0	77	42	1	11

Event Line

TC Try Converted
T Try
P Penalty
DG Drop Goal

Min	Score Progress		Event	Players
4	0	3	P	Van Gisbergen
12	0	3	⇄	Bracken > Payne
12	3	3	P	De Marigny
16	6	3	P	De Marigny
17	6	3	⇄	Payne > Bracken
18	6	6	P	Van Gisbergen
27	6	9	P	Van Gisbergen
32	9	9	P	De Marigny
38	9	12	P	Van Gisbergen
40	16	12	TC	Balshaw / De Marigny
Half time 16-12				
47	16	12	⇄	Cusack > Shelley
47	16	19	TC	Voyce / Van Gisbergen
57	16	19	⇄	Erinle > Waters
57	16	19	⇄	Ibanez > Gotting
57	16	19	⇄	Morgan > Dunbar
57	16	19	⇄	Hooper > Murphy
57	16	19	⇄	Shaw > Purdy
57	16	19	⇄	Bulloch > Rawlinson
61	16	26	TC	Ibanez / Van Gisbergen
62	16	26	⇄	Ross > De Marigny
63	16	26	⇄	Shelley > Cusack
67	16	33	TC	Ibanez / Van Gisbergen
72	16	33	⇄	Brooks > King
75	16	40	TC	Hart / Van Gisbergen
76	16	40	⇄	Reddan > Dawson
76	16	40	⇄	Lock > O'Connor
76	16	40	⇄	Bracken > Payne
79	23	40	TC	Hooper / Ross
83	23	47	TC	Sackey / Van Gisbergen
Full time 23-47				

Scoring Statistics

Leeds Tykes

by Situation | by Half

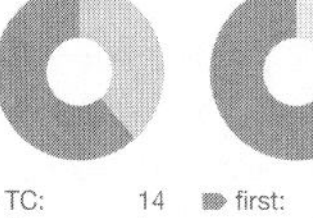

TC:	14	first:	70%
T:	0	second:	30%
P:	9		
DG:	0		

London Wasps

by Situation | by Half

TC:	35	first:	26%
T:	0	second:	74%
P:	12		
DG:	0		

London Wasps 34
Worcester Warriors 20

Guinness Premiership

25.09.05

Premiership Home Record vs Worcester Warriors					
Played	Won	Drawn	Lost	For	Against
2	2	0	0	66	37

London Wasps retained second place in the Premiership, on try difference, after a bruising 34-20 victory over Worcester.

Quote

Ian McGeechan

They made it hard for us for forty minutes, but we kept to our task – to play some rugby. That's what the supporters want to see us do, and that's what we try to deliver.

The Warriors lived up to their name with an awesome show of physicality, but in the Wasps' pack they met their match. Despite trailing by three at half time, Wasps showed their pedigree from 1 to 15 in the second half to secure the bonus point and send the Midlanders home disappointed.

Wasps drew first blood, with Raphael Ibanez touching down, but Worcester countered with a Pat Sanderson try. Worcester's Shane Drahm began to influence the game and kicked a penalty on 29 minutes. Wasps were given a route back into the game just before half-time with a Mark Van Gisbergen penalty opportunity to rewrite history. Success would have seen the full-back surpassing Jonny Wilkinson's record streak of 27 consecutive kicks at goal, but he scuffed his shot.

After the break, Wasps raced ahead via a Tom Voyce score and two Van Gisbergen penalties, although Drahm kept Worcester in touch with a penalty. On the hour mark, Joe Worsley fended off two tackles to cross the whitewash and Van Gisbergen added the conversion.

Nicholas Le Roux responded with Worcester's second try before Wasps' prop Tim Payne scored from a fine driving move to round off an ultra-professional show from the champions.

Venue:	Causeway Stadium	Referee:	Sean Davey - Season 05/06
Attendance:	8,720	Matches:	1
Capacity:	10,200	Yellow Cards:	1
Occupancy:	85%	Red Cards:	0

London Wasps
Worcester Warriors

Starting Line-Ups

London Wasps		Worcester Warriors
Van Gisbergen	15	Le Roux
Sackey	14	Hylton
Erinle	13	Rasmussen
Abbott	12	Lombard
Voyce	11	Hinshelwood
King	10	Drahm
M Dawson	9	Gomarsall
Payne	1	Windo
Ibanez	2	Van Niekerk
J Dawson	3	Horsman
Purdy	4	Murphy
Birkett	5	Gillies
Hart (c)	6	Vaili
Worsley	7	Sanderson (c)
Lock	8	Horstmann

Replacements

Waters	22	Delport
Brooks	21	Trueman
Reddan	20	Powell
O'Connor	19	Tu'amoheloa
Chamberlain	18	Collier
Bracken	17	C Fortey
Gotting	16	Taumoepeau

Match Stats

	London Wasps	Worcester Warriors
Tackles	88	101
Missed Tackles	11	28
Ball Carries	87	79
Metres	414	305
Defenders Beaten	28	11
Passes	93	69
Clean Breaks	1	0
Pens Conceded	11	17
Turnovers	17	9
Breakdowns Won	73	70
% Scrums Won	83%	75%
% Line-Outs Won	82%	100%

Premiership Table

Team	P	W	D	L	F	A	BP	Pts
1 Leicester Tigers	4	3	1	0	129	75	2	16
2 London Wasps	4	3	1	0	133	83	2	16
3 Gloucester Rugby	4	3	1	0	105	66	1	15

Event Line

TC Try Converted — P Penalty
T Try — DG Drop Goal

Min	Score Progress		Event	Players
2	7	0	TC	Ibanez / Van Gisbergen
5	7	7	TC	Sanderson / Drahm
30	7	10	P	Drahm
36	7	10	⇄	Gotting > Ibanez
Half time 7-10				
43	14	10	TC	Voyce / Van Gisbergen
48	17	10	P	Van Gisbergen
50	20	10	P	Van Gisbergen
54	20	13	P	Drahm
55	20	13	⇄	Fortey > Van Niekerk
57	20	13	⇄	Taumoepeau > Horsman
57	20	13	⇄	O'Connor > Lock
59	20	13	⇄	Powell > Gomarsall
59	27	13	TC	Worsley / Van Gisbergen
63	27	13	⇄	Collier > Murphy
68	27	13	⇄	Brooks > King
70	27	13	⇄	Waters > Voyce
70	27	13	⇄	Bracken > Dawson
71	27	13	⇄	Trueman > Lombard
78	27	20	TC	Le Roux / Drahm
82	27	20	⇄	Delport > Hinshelwood
82	34	20	TC	Payne / Van Gisbergen
Full time 34-20				

Scoring Statistics

London Wasps

by Situation		by Half	
TC:	28	first:	21%
T:	0	second:	79%
P:	6		
DG:	0		

Worcester Warriors

by Situation		by Half	
TC:	14	first:	50%
T:	0	second:	50%
P:	6		
DG:	0		

London Irish 26
London Wasps 30

Powergen Cup

02.10.05

It was a case of high drama at the Madjeski Stadium in London Wasps' opening Powergen Cup group game with replacement Alex King sending over a last-minute drop goal to seal victory over the Exiles.

Quote

Shaun Edwards

We needed to play with a lot more passion and aggression today, we didn't play like a Wasps team. I feared a performance like this was coming after the good wins we've had so far.

With both clubs eager to progress through to the next phase of the competition it proved to be a keenly-contested fixture with, ironically, two of Wasps' tries coming from Irishmen, Eoin Reddan and Jonny O'Connor.

The hosts led for the majority of the first half. Shane Geraghty scored the first try after only eight minutes, before both Mark Van Gisbergen and Riki Flutey converted penalty goals to make it 12-12 at the interval.

At the start of the second half, Wasps were awarded a penalty close to the Exiles try line and captain John Hart elected to take a scrum. Scrum-half Reddan exploited the blind side to score his debut try for Wasps and put the club in front.

From the restart, Flutey snatched the lead back with a fourth successful penalty attempt before O'Connor slipped round Irish's cover defence to score.

However, the Exiles were not finished, Topsy Ojo touching down with nine minutes remaining to set up a grandstand finale.

The stage was thus set for King, who had replaced James Brooks, to drop into the pocket and dispatch an expert drop goal to kill off any Irish fightback before a Van Gisbergen penalty closed the scoring.

Venue: Madejski Stadium
Attendance: 6,829
Capacity: 24,104
Occupancy: 28%

Referee: Ashley Rowden

London Irish
London Wasps

Starting Line-Ups

London Irish		London Wasps
Armitage	15	Van Gisbergen
Staniforth	14	Sackey
Penney	13	Waters
Geraghty	12	Erinle
Bishop	11	Voyce
Flutey	10	Brooks
Hodgson	9	Reddan
Collins	1	Payne
Paice	2	Gotting
Hardwick	3	Bracken
Casey (c)	4	Hart (c)
Kennedy	5	Birkett
Gustard	6	Worsley
Danaher	7	O'Connor
Leguizamon	8	Lock

Replacements

Storey	22	Lewsey
Willis	21	King
Ojo	20	M Dawson
Murphy	19	Chamberlain
Strudwick	18	Skivington
Flavin	17	J Dawson
Hatley	16	Barrett

Match Stats

	London Irish	London Wasps
Tackles	105	59
Missed Tackles	16	8
Ball Carries	67	97
Metres	174	321
Defenders Beaten	8	21
Passes	78	105
Clean Breaks	0	0
Pens Conceded	17	11
Turnovers	14	16
Breakdowns Won	53	83
% Scrums Won	89%	93%
% Line-Outs Won	93%	65%

Powergen Cup Table

Team	P	W	D	L	F	A	BP	Pts
1 Cardiff Blues	1	1	0	0	37	20	1	5
2 London Wasps	1	1	0	0	30	26	0	4
3 London Irish	1	0	0	1	26	30	1	1
4 Saracens	1	0	0	1	20	37	0	0

Event Line

TC Try Converted | T Try | P Penalty | DG Drop Goal

Min	Score Progress		Event	Players
8	7	0	TC	Geraghty / Flutey
11	10	0	P	Flutey
14	10	0	⇄	Murphy > Danaher
14	10	3	P	Van Gisbergen
19	10	3	⇄	Danaher > Murphy
19	13	3	P	Flutey
22	13	6	P	Van Gisbergen
24	13	6	⇄	Dawson > Bracken
26	16	6	P	Flutey
33	16	6	⇄	Bracken > Dawson
38	16	6	■	Geraghty
39	16	9	P	Van Gisbergen
40	16	9	⇄	Ojo > Bishop
40	16	12	P	Van Gisbergen
Half time 16-12				
41	16	12	⇄	Strudwick > Casey
46	16	17	T	Reddan
49	19	17	P	Flutey
53	19	24	TC	O'Connor / Van Gisbergen
61	19	24	⇄	Lewsey > Waters
63	19	24	⇄	Dawson > Bracken
65	19	24	⇄	Dawson > Reddan
68	19	24	⇄	Murphy > Leguizamon
68	19	24	⇄	Hatley > Collins
69	19	24	⇄	Bracken > Dawson
69	19	24	⇄	Barrett > Gotting
71	26	24	TC	Ojo / Flutey
73	26	24	⇄	King > Brooks
79	26	27	DG	King
82	26	30	P	Van Gisbergen
Full time 26-30				

Scoring Statistics

London Irish

by Situation: TC: 14, T: 0, P: 12, DG: 0

by Half: first: 62%, second: 38%

London Wasps

by Situation: TC: 7, T: 5, P: 15, DG: 3

by Half: first: 40%, second: 60%

London Wasps 40
Cardiff Blues 19

Powergen Cup

07.10.05

London Wasps marked Captain Lawrence Dallaglio's first appearence of the season with a comprehensive Powergen Cup win over Cardiff.

Dallaglio had fractured his ankle on the Lions tour four months earlier, but played the entire 80 minutes as his team stolled to a confident victory.

Wasps raced into a 30-0 lead with winger Paul Sackey and flanker Jonny O'Connor turning in excellent performances. O'Connor earned the Powergen Man of the Match Award whilst Sackey's performance was later described by head coach, Shaun Edwards, as 'absolutely outstanding'.

After an early Alex King penalty, Sackey's electric pace created an opening and his offload enabled Ben Gotting to score, with King adding the extras. Sackey then turned try scorer, with King's conversion adding to an earlier penalty to give Wasps a 20-0 lead at the turnaround.

Within four minutes of the re-start, the death knell had sounded for the Welshmen, Josh Lewsey collected a charged down kick and dived under the posts to score Wasps' third of the night. Cardiff buckled under the pressure and Mark Van Gisbergen, on as a blood replacement for Tom Voyce, exploited the Blues indiscipline by slotting over two penalties to stretch Wasps' lead to 33-0 on the hour.

The visitors staged a late comeback to make the scoreline more respectable - Chris Czekaj, Xavier Rush and Maama Molitika reducing the deficit. However, Wasps rounded off the scoring on the night, with James Brooks exploiting an interception to score.

Quote

Lawrence Dallaglio

I knew this fixture could be lively and I think our performance took it away from them in the first half. We blotted our copy books a bit in the second half however.

Venue: Causeway Stadium
Attendance: 6,427
Capacity: 10,200
Occupancy: 63%

Referee: Chris White

London Wasps
Cardiff Blues

Starting Line-Ups

London Wasps		Cardiff Blues
Voyce	**15**	Williams (c)
Sackey	**14**	Czekaj
Waters	**13**	Robinson
Abbott	**12**	Shanklin
Lewsey	**11**	Morgan
King	**10**	Robinson
M Dawson	**9**	Powell
Bracken	**1**	Yapp
Gotting	**2**	Goodfield
J Dawson	**3**	Jones
Hart	**4**	Jones
Birkett	**5**	Sidoli
Worsley	**6**	Powell
O'Connor	**7**	Williams
Dallaglio	**8**	Rush

Replacements

Van Gisbergen	**22**	Thomas
Brooks	**21**	Molitika
Reddan	**20**	Phillips
Lock	**19**	Sowden-Taylor
Skivington	**18**	Quinnell
Payne	**17**	Johnson
Ibanez	**16**	Evans

Match Stats

	London Wasps	Cardiff Blues
Tackles	60	74
Missed Tackles	14	22
Ball Carries	83	76
Metres	344	366
Defenders Beaten	25	15
Passes	115	96
Clean Breaks	10	10
Pens Conceded	10	14
Turnovers	16	23
Breakdowns Won	75	56
% Scrums Won	100%	82%
% Line-Outs Won	100%	93%

Powergen Cup Table

Team	P	W	D	L	F	A	BP	Pts
1 London Wasps	2	2	0	0	70	45	1	9
2 Saracens	2	1	0	1	52	50	1	5
3 Cardiff Blues	2	1	0	1	56	60	1	5
4 London Irish	2	0	0	2	39	62	1	1

Event Line

TC Try Converted
T Try
P Penalty
DG Drop Goal

Min	Score Progress		Event	Players
9	3	0	P	King
14	10	0	TC	Gotting / King
27	10	0	⇄	Skivington > Birkett
32	13	0	P	King
33	13	0	⇄	Birkett > Skivington
35	13	0	⇄	Thomas > Shanklin
40	20	0	TC	Sackey / King
Half time 20-0				
41	20	0	⇄	Shanklin > Thomas
44	20	0	⇄	Skivington > Birkett
44	27	0	TC	Lewsey / King
52	27	0	⇄	Evans > Jones
52	27	0	⇄	Ibanez > Gotting
52	27	0	⇄	Brooks > King
52	27	0	⇄	Van Gisbergen > Voyce
52	27	0	⇄	Molitika > Powell
56	27	0	⇄	Phillips > Powell
56	30	0	P	Van Gisbergen
60	30	0	⇄	Quinnell > Jones
60	33	0	P	Van Gisbergen
61	33	0	⇄	Lock > Worsley
64	33	0	⇄	Voyce > Van Gisbergen
65	33	0	⇄	Reddan > Dawson
67	33	0	⇄	Sowden-Taylor > Williams
67	33	5	T	Czekaj
70	33	12	TC	Rush / Robinson
73	33	12	■	Ibanez
73	33	19	TC	Molitika / Robinson
77	40	19	TC	Brooks / Brooks
78	40	19	⇄	Johnson > Goodfield
Full time 40-19				

Scoring Statistics

London Wasps

by Situation: TC: 28; T: 0; P: 12; DG: 0

by Half: first: 50%; second: 50%

Cardiff Blues

by Situation: TC: 14; T: 5; P: 0; DG: 0

by Half: first: 0%; second: 100%

Sale Sharks 18
London Wasps 10

Guinness Premiership

14.10.05

Quote

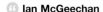

Ian McGeechan

We didn't execute as well as we usually do and the game was played at the wrong end of the field, which was three point territory for Sale - that says it all

Premiership Away Record vs Sale Sharks

Played	Won	Drawn	Lost	For	Against
9	5	1	3	234	198

The Premiership champions suffered their first defeat of the season, an 18-10 loss at Sale thanks to six penalties from Sharks' fly half, Charlie Hodgson.

In a game that lacked fluidity, Hodgson opened the scoring after four minutes with a penalty, but London Wasps applied concerted pressure and Mark Van Gisbergen struck over a simple pot at goal to draw level.

Sebastian Chabal – Sale's huge No8 – was a constant menace at the base of the scrum, but collectively Wasps looked far more purposeful as Sale's Jason White received a yellow card for persistently killing the ball.

Mid-way through the first half, Joe Worsley was replaced by John Hart after sustaining a knee injury that kept him out until December. Further penalties from Hodgson gave Sale a 12-3 lead at half-time – Wasps' frustration resulting in Simon Shaw receiving a yellow card in the 40th minute.

However, when Shaw returned to the pitch, Wasps produced some quick ball for Josh Lewsey, using guile and craft, to slice open Sale's defence to score the only try of the game. Mark Van Gisbergen was his usual reliable self with the conversion that followed Lewsey's moment of brilliance, but two more penalties from Hodgson meant that Sharks kept Wasps at bay until the final whistle.

Venue:	Edgeley Park	Referee:	Sean Davey - Season 05/06
Attendance:	9,916	Matches:	2
Capacity:	10,641	Yellow Cards:	1
Occupancy:	93%	Red Cards:	0

Sale Sharks
London Wasps

Starting Line-Ups

Sale Sharks		London Wasps
Larrechea	15	Van Gisbergen
Cueto	14	Sackey
Taylor	13	Lewsey
Seveali'i	12	Abbott
Robinson (c)	11	Voyce
Hodgson	10	King
Martens	9	M Dawson
Sheridan	1	Payne
Bruno	2	Ibanez
Stewart	3	J Dawson
Jones	4	Shaw
Schofield	5	Birkett
White	6	Worsley
Lund	7	O'Connor
Chabal	8	Dallaglio (c)

Replacements

Hanley	22	Waters
Todd	21	Brooks
Courrent	20	Reddan
Bonner-Evans	19	Hart
Fernandez Lobbe	18	Skivington
Turner	17	Bracken
Titterrell	16	Gotting

Match Stats

	Sale Sharks	London Wasps
Tackles	69	55
Missed Tackles	21	5
Ball Carries	61	80
Metres	193	444
Defenders Beaten	7	27
Passes	65	89
Clean Breaks	2	10
Pens Conceded	10	17
Turnovers	5	17
Breakdowns Won	61	62
% Scrums Won	90%	43%
% Line-Outs Won	83%	76%

Premiership Table

Team	P	W	D	L	F	A	BP	Pts
2 Leicester Tigers	5	3	2	0	145	91	2	18
3 London Wasps	5	3	1	1	143	101	2	16
4 Gloucester Rugby	4	3	1	0	105	66	1	15

Event Line

TC Try Converted — P Penalty
T Try — DG Drop Goal

Min	Score Progress		Event	Players
4	3	0	P	Hodgson
8	3	3	P	Van Gisbergen
14	3	3		White
23	6	3	P	Hodgson
24	6	3	⇄	Hart > Worsley
25	9	3	P	Hodgson
40	9	3		Shaw
40	12	3	P	Hodgson
Half time 12-3				
51	12	10	TC	Lewsey / Van Gisbergen
53	12	10	⇄	Turner > Stewart
54	12	10	⇄	Bracken > Dawson
57	12	10	⇄	Fernandez Lobbe > Schofield
60	12	10	⇄	Titterrell > Bruno
60	15	10	P	Hodgson
63	15	10	⇄	Gotting > Ibanez
74	18	10	P	Hodgson
75	18	10	⇄	Courrent > Martens
77	18	10	⇄	Brooks > King
85	18	10	⇄	Bonner-Evans > Chabal
Full time 18-10				

Scoring Statistics

Sale Sharks

by Situation		by Half	
TC:	0	first:	67%
T:	0	second:	33%
P:	18		
DG:	0		

London Wasps

by Situation		by Half	
TC:	7	first:	30%
T:	0	second:	70%
P:	3		
DG:	0		

Edinburgh Gunners 32
London Wasps 31

Heineken Cup

23.10.05

Quote

Ian McGeechan

We know what we've got to get back to. The problems are fixable, but it is important that we fix them.

London Wasps' Heineken Cup campaign started off inauspiciously with a shock loss to Edinburgh at Murrayfield.

Despite leading 20-13 at half-time, the English champions slid to defeat at the hands of a spirited Gunners side, who staged a remarkable second-half comeback.

Wasps were 13-3 ahead after 20 minutes. Two penalties from Mark Van Gisbergen followed by a try from Jonny O'Connor and Van Gisbergen's ensuing conversion put the visitors 10 points ahead and they looked to be cruising.

But Wasps' stranglehold on the game loosened, allowing Edinburgh to draw level on the half hour through a converted try and penalty from Chris Paterson. Wasps regained the lead after Van Gisbergen's penalty cannoned off the post and Josh Lewsey scooped up the rebound to score. Another conversion from Van Gisbergen secured a seven-point lead at half-time, and the task ahead still looked straightforward.

But after the interval Edinburgh came out fighting with Hugo Southwell getting on the score-sheet prior to Paterson's two successful penalties that put the Scotsmen ahead by 24-20.

Van Gisbergen remained accurate with his boot to reduce Edinburgh's lead, but mistakes plagued Wasps progress and the error-count was alarmingly high. Paterson knocked over another penalty before Wasps hit back with a try from Paul Sackey and a fourth Van Gisbergen penalty to give Wasps a narrow one-point lead with five minutes remaining.

But the game was lost when Edinburgh replacement Simon Webster slid under the posts, his dramatic extra-time score snatching victory for the Celtic League side.

Venue: Murrayfield
Attendance: 4,639
Capacity: 67,500
Occupancy: 7%

Referee: Christophe Berdos

Edinburgh Gunners
London Wasps

Starting Line-Ups

Edinburgh Gunners		London Wasps
Southwell	15	Van Gisbergen
Paterson (c)	14	Sackey
Di Rollo	13	Lewsey
Jorgensen	12	Abbott
Leonelli Morey	11	Voyce
Godman	10	King
Blair	9	M Dawson
Hewett	1	Payne
Hall	2	Ibanez
Smith	3	Bracken
Kellock	4	Shaw
Murray	5	Birkett
Mustchin	6	Hart
Hogg	7	O'Connor
Taylor	8	Dallaglio (c)

Replacements

Webster	22	Staunton
Hodge	21	Brooks
Lawson	20	Reddan
Strokosch	19	Rees
Pringle	18	Skivington
Jacobsen	17	J Dawson
Kelly	16	Barrett

Match Stats

Tackles	87	43
Missed Tackles	13	7
Ball Carries	58	94
Metres	258	374
Defenders Beaten	9	14
Passes	72	89
Clean Breaks	2	3
Pens Conceded	9	11
Turnovers	12	23
Breakdowns Won	37	86
% Scrums Won	93%	100%
% Line-Outs Won	89%	83%

Heineken Cup Table

Team	P	W	D	L	F	A	BP	Pts
1 Toulouse	1	1	0	0	50	28	1	5
2 Edinburgh Gunners	1	1	0	0	32	31	0	4
3 London Wasps	1	0	0	1	31	32	1	1
4 Llanelli Scarlets	1	0	0	1	28	50	0	0

Event Line

TC Try Converted
T Try
P Penalty
DG Drop Goal

Min	Score Progress		Event	Players
7	0	3	P	Van Gisbergen
11	0	6	P	Van Gisbergen
16	3	6	P	Paterson
17	3	13	TC	O'Connor / Van Gisbergen
21	6	13	P	Paterson
29	13	13	TC	Paterson / Paterson
33	13	20	TC	Lewsey / Van Gisbergen
Half time 13-20				
46	18	20	T	Southwell
52	18	20		Bracken
54	18	20		Dawson > Hart
57	18	20		Lawson > Blair
57	21	20	P	Paterson
59	24	20	P	Paterson
63	24	23	P	Van Gisbergen
64	24	23		Rees > Dawson
69	24	23		Skivington > Shaw
70	27	23	P	Paterson
71	27	23		Jacobsen > Hewett
73	27	28	T	Sackey
74	27	28		Dawson > Bracken
74	27	28		Webster > Jorgensen
74	27	28		Strokosch > Mustchin
77	27	28		Taylor
78	27	31	P	Van Gisbergen
81	32	31	T	Webster
Full time 32-31				

Scoring Statistics

Edinburgh Gunners

by Situation		by Half	
TC:	7	first:	41%
T:	10	second:	59%
P:	15		

London Wasps

by Situation		by Half	
TC:	14	first:	65%
T:	5	second:	35%
P:	12		

London Wasps 15
Toulouse 15

Heineken Cup

30.10.05

Quote

Ian McGeechan

We know how dangerous Toulouse can be, and there were no gimmes out there today. Both teams were just happy to take what points were on offer against quality opposition.

London Wasps kept their European dream alive with a 15-all draw against Toulouse in a classic Heineken Cup tie, complete with a nerve-shredding climax.

With the French giants leading 15-12 in the dying moments, Wasps were awarded a penalty near the try-line and opted to go for the points, with a Mark Van Gisbergen penalty leveling matters at the death. It was the full back's fifth penalty in a game of Test-match intensity that was a marvelous advert for the premier competition in northern hemisphere rugby.

Wasps took the lead via a Van Gisbergen penalty before Toulouse's Gareth Thomas crossed the whitewash following good work from lock Trevor Brennan. The European champions of 2004 hit back with another two Van Gisbergen penalties to give Wasps a 9-7 half-time advantage over the defending European champions.

In the second half, Wasps continued to employ an expansive brand of rugby, but struggled to execute moves with consistent accuracy in the slippery, rain-soaked conditions. In fact, the home side conceded two kickable penalties, but Jean-Baptiste Elissalde failed to convert the chances.

Toulouse's class shone out nine minutes after the re-start when Vincent Clerc touched down near the corner, although five minutes later Van Gisbergen was again on target to bring Wasps level at 12 points a-piece. The stalemate didn't last long however. Just a minute later, Freddie Michalak potted a drop goal to edge Toulouse ahead. With three points separating the teams and seconds remaining on the clock, the nerveless Van Gisbergen ensured Wasps salvaged a draw with the last kick of the game.

Venue:	Causeway Stadium	Referee:	Alain Rolland
Attendance:	10,000		
Capacity:	10,200		
Occupancy:	98%		

London Wasps
Toulouse

Starting Line-Ups

London Wasps		Toulouse
Van Gisbergen	15	Thomas
Sackey	14	Clerc
Lewsey	13	Jauzion
Abbott	12	Fritz
Voyce	11	Heymans
King	10	Michalak
M Dawson	9	Elissalde
Payne	1	Poux
Ibanez	2	Bru (c)
J Dawson	3	Hasan Jalil
Shaw	4	Pelous
Birkett	5	Brennan
Hart	6	Bouilhou
O'Connor	7	Maka
Dallaglio (c)	8	Maka

Replacements

Hoadley	22	Nyanga
Brooks	21	Poitrenaud
Reddan	20	Dubois
Rees	19	Millo-Chlusky
Skivington	18	Lamboley
Bracken	17	Menkarska
Gotting	16	Lacombe

Match Stats

Tackles	46	91
Missed Tackles	9	7
Ball Carries	89	65
Metres	318	475
Defenders Beaten	8	5
Passes	85	70
Clean Breaks	2	9
Pens Conceded	7	11
Turnovers	14	11
Breakdowns Won	68	37
% Scrums Won	100%	100%
% Line-Outs Won	74%	67%

Heineken Cup Table

Team	P	W	D	L	F	A	BP	Pts
1 Toulouse	2	1	1	0	65	43	1	7
2 Edinburgh Gunners	2	1	0	1	45	46	1	5
3 Llanelli Scarlets	2	1	0	1	43	63	0	4
4 London Wasps	2	0	1	1	46	47	1	3

Event Line

TC Try Converted
T Try
P Penalty
DG Drop Goal

Min	Score Progress		Event	Players
6	3	0	P	Van Gisbergen
12	3	0	⇄	Menkarska > Poux
16	3	7	TC	Thomas / Elissalde
22	3	7	⇄	Poux > Menkarska
35	6	7	P	Van Gisbergen
40	9	7	P	Van Gisbergen
Half time 9-7				
50	9	12	T	Clerc
51	9	12	⇄	Skivington > Shaw
54	9	12	⇄	Poitrenaud > Fritz
54	9	12	⇄	Millo-Chlusky > Pelous
54	12	12	P	Van Gisbergen
56	12	12	⇄	Pelous > Millo-Chlusky
56	12	15	DG	Michalak
61	12	15	⇄	Millo-Chlusky > Brennan
70	12	15	⇄	Bracken > Dawson
70	12	15	⇄	Nyanga > Maka
72	12	15	⇄	Rees > Dallaglio
77	12	15	⇄	Dubois > Elissalde
80	12	15	⇄	Lamboley > Maka
83	12	15	⇄	Brooks > King
88	15	15	P	Van Gisbergen
Full time 15-15				

Scoring Statistics

London Wasps

by Situation: TC: 0, T: 0, P: 15, DG: 0

by Half: first: 60%, second: 40%

Toulouse

by Situation: TC: 7, T: 5, P: 0, DG: 3

by Half: first: 47%, second: 53%

London Wasps 21
Bristol Rugby 16

Guinness Premiership

04.11.05

Premiership Home Record vs Bristol Rugby					
Played	Won	Drawn	Lost	For	Against
6	5	0	1	173	133

Quote

Ian McGeechan

It was very important for us to win tonight. We have some players missing because of the internationals, and having achieved only a draw last week, to get the win was exactly what we needed.

London Wasps created their own brand of fireworks with an explosive display of attacking rugby in a convincing win over Bristol.

Two great tries, from Tom Rees and Tom Voyce, were the highlights of a memorable November night in Buckinghamshire. Voyce's effort was a spectacular 85-metre dash from his own 22 – later voted London Wasps' try of the season – while Rees broke down the narrow side before evading two tackles to touch down. The back rower's performance earned him his second Man of the Match accolade of the season.

Wasps' fly half Alex King scored the rest of the champions' points with his trusty boot, whilst Bristol's points came from a forwards' drive, touched down by Mark Regan, and the boot of fly half Jason Strange. Despite the end result, the opening hour looked decidedly bleak for the home crowd. Strange's kicking game led to Regan's try after seven minutes. Bristol then gained a 10-point lead after two further Strange penalties before Sam Cox was sin-binned by referee David Rose for tripping Paul Sackey. Wasps capitalised on the one-man advantage, with Rees showing genuine quality with a try, but the champions still trailed 13-8 at half-time.

In the second-half Wasps were sharper, with King adding his second penalty before Voyce gave England coach Andy Robinson a reminder of his ability with his pitch-length score. Strange countered with a penalty before Alex King rounded off the scoring with a penalty.

Venue:	Causeway Stadium	Referee:	David Rose - Season 05/06
Attendance:	7,901	Matches:	3
Capacity:	10,200	Yellow Cards:	7
Occupancy:	77%	Red Cards:	0

London Wasps
Bristol Rugby

Starting Line-Ups

London Wasps		Bristol Rugby
Brooks	15	Going
Sackey	14	Stanojevic
Erinle	13	Higgitt
Abbott	12	Cox
Voyce	11	Lemi
King	10	Strange
Reddan	9	Rauluni
Payne	1	Hilton
Ibanez	2	Regan
J Dawson	3	Crompton
Skivington	4	Winters
Birkett	5	Llewellyn
Hart	6	Salter (c)
Rees	7	El Abd
Dallaglio (c)	8	Lewis

Replacements

Staunton	22	Robinson
Hoadley	21	Denney
Honeyben	20	Teague
Chamberlain	19	Martin-Redman
Lock	18	Kohn
Bracken	17	Clark
Gotting	16	Clarke

Match Stats

	London Wasps	Bristol Rugby
Tackles	86	120
Missed Tackles	16	27
Ball Carries	107	89
Metres	419	368
Defenders Beaten	27	16
Passes	105	87
Clean Breaks	9	6
Pens Conceded	4	14
Turnovers	13	13
Breakdowns Won	84	63
% Scrums Won	100%	100%
% Line-Outs Won	64%	75%

Premiership Table

Team	P	W	D	L	F	A	BP	Pts
1 London Wasps	6	4	1	1	164	117	2	20
2 Leicester Tigers	6	3	2	1	156	106	3	19
3 Sale Sharks	5	4	0	1	131	91	3	19

Event Line

TC Try Converted | P Penalty
T Try | DG Drop Goal

Min	Score Progress		Event	Players
10	0	7	TC	El Abd / Strange
22	0	10	P	Strange
24	3	10	P	King
26	3	13	P	Strange
29	3	13		Cox
31	8	13	T	Rees
Half time 8-13				
41	8	13	⇄	Gotting > Ibanez
41	8	13	⇄	Denney > Cox
48	11	13	P	King
49	11	13	⇄	Bracken > Dawson
54	18	13	TC	Voyce / King
62	18	13	⇄	Clarke > Hilton
64	18	16	P	Strange
71	21	16	P	King
73	21	16	⇄	Hoadley > Brooks
Full time 21-16				

Scoring Statistics

London Wasps

by Situation		by Half	
TC:	7	first:	38%
T:	5	second:	62%
P:	9		
DG:	0		

Bristol Rugby

by Situation		by Half	
TC:	7	first:	81%
T:	0	second:	19%
P:	9		
DG:	0		

Northampton Saints 13
London Wasps 21

Guinness Premiership

12.11.05

Premiership Away Record vs Northampton Saints

Played	Won	Drawn	Lost	For	Against
9	4	0	5	184	180

A decisive try in the final 10 minutes earned London Wasps a victory in front of a sell-out Franklin's Gardens crowd.

Quote

Ian McGeechan

Today was a very important win,the sort of win that will definitely count when it comes to the final placing at the end of the season.

Following an enterprising start, Wasps went ahead with two penalties from Alex King, but Saints' fly-half Carlos Spencer was also at his creative best, putting angled kicks, chips and grubbers behind the Wasps back-three. The former New Zealand international then reduced the deficit with an opportunistic drop goal from just outside Wasps 22 to put Northampton back into the game. Northampton's Bruce Reihana slotted a penalty two minutes before half-time to make the scores level at 6-6 at the break.

A scrappy start to the second half saw both sides conceding possession through turnovers. Wasps edged ahead through an Eoin Reddan try, although King was unable to convert. The fly half made amends on 68 minutes when he slotted a penalty from 42 metres out to give Wasps a 14-6 lead.

With three minutes remaining, Saints' Rhodri Davies touched down and Reihana's conversion brought Northampton to 13-14, but from the restart, Rob Hoadley swiftly caught Spencer in possession and proceeded to audaciously strip the ball from the ex-All Black before crossing the try-line to secure maximum points for his team.

Alex King's conversion heightened Ian McGeechan's joy on the genial Scot's first return to the Gardens since leaving Northampton in 1999.

Venue:	Franklins Gardens	Referee:	Rob Debney - Season 05/06
Attendance:	13,585	Matches:	5
Capacity:	13,591	Yellow Cards:	4
Occupancy:	100%	Red Cards:	0

Northampton Saints
London Wasps

Starting Line-Ups

Northampton Saints		London Wasps
Reihana (c)	15	Voyce
Diggin	14	Sackey
Clarke	13	Erinle
Quinlan	12	Abbott
Rudd	11	Hoadley
Spencer	10	King
Robinson	9	Reddan
Budgen	1	Payne
Richmond	2	Ward
Barnard	3	Bracken
Gerard	4	Skivington
Dm Browne	5	Birkett
Fox	6	Hart (c)
Harding	7	Rees
Dn Browne	8	Lock

Replacements

Davies	22	Staunton
Vilk	21	Baxter
Howard	20	Fury
Lewitt	19	Dallaglio
Lord	18	Shaw
Harbut	17	McKenzie
Hartley	16	Gotting

Match Stats

Tackles	74	129
Missed Tackles	14	24
Ball Carries	124	74
Metres	777	495
Defenders Beaten	25	14
Passes	174	81
Clean Breaks	12	12
Pens Conceded	10	9
Turnovers	21	13
Breakdowns Won	90	59
% Scrums Won	100%	94%
% Line-Outs Won	77%	73%

Premiership Table

Team	P	W	D	L	F	A	BP	Pts
1 Sale Sharks	7	6	0	1	172	115	3	27
2 London Wasps	7	5	1	1	185	130	2	24
3 Leicester Tigers	7	4	2	1	181	126	3	23

Event Line

TC Try Converted | P Penalty
T Try | DG Drop Goal

Min	Score Progress		Event	Players
2	0	3	P	King
7	0	6	P	King
24	3	6	DG	Spencer
27	3	6	▪	Hoadley
38	6	6	P	Reihana
Half time 6-6				
41	6	6	⇄	Lord > Gerard
45	6	6	⇄	Vilk > Diggin
46	6	6	⇄	McKenzie > Bracken
46	6	6	⇄	Shaw > Birkett
46	6	6	⇄	Dallaglio > Lock
54	6	11	T	Reddan
56	6	11	⇄	Davies > Rudd
65	6	11	⇄	Gotting > Ward
67	6	11	⇄	Harbut > Budgen
68	6	14	P	King
71	6	14	⇄	Lewitt > Browne
72	6	14	⇄	Hartley > Richmond
72	6	14	⇄	Baxter > Erinle
76	6	14	⇄	Howard > Robinson
77	13	14	TC	Davies / Reihana
78	13	21	TC	Hoadley / King
79	13	21	⇄	Staunton > Abbott
79	13	21	⇄	Fury > Reddan
Full time 13-21				

Scoring Statistics

Northampton Saints

by Situation		by Half	
TC:	7	first:	46%
T:	0	second:	54%
P:	3		
DG:	3		

London Wasps

by Situation		by Half	
TC:	7	first:	29%
T:	5	second:	71%
P:	9		
DG:	0		

London Wasps 28
Bath Rugby 20

Guinness Premiership

20.11.05

Quote

Ian McGeechan

It was obvious Bath were going to play for penalties - there was only one team playing rugby out there,but you've got to be careful not to let them in.

Premiership Home Record vs Bath Rugby

Played	Won	Drawn	Lost	For	Against
9	5	0	4	202	167

Although West Countryman Tom Voyce proved the final undoing of his former employers with his 74th minute match-winning try, it was London Wasps' home debutant, Neil Baxter, who stole the plaudits in a closely-fought contest.

The Mancunian winger's pace enabled him to open the scoring after nine minutes following good support play from Lawrence Dallaglio, though Bath responded promptly through a Chris Malone penalty and a Michael Lipman try. Tempers frayed shortly after, with Bath No8 Zak Feaunati being sin binned and Jeremy Staunton restoring parity with the resultant penalty.

The scoreline was all square at half-time, but Bath went ahead early in the second-half with a third penalty from Malone. Wasps replied with some sustained pressure, and their perseverance paid off with another try from Baxter.

However, despite being short-staffed after Lipman was shown the yellow card, Bath came back with a Malone penalty on the hour followed by a drop goal that put his team ahead. Replacement Alex King converted a penalty for Wasps to nudge the champions ahead by one point, but with less than ten minutes left, Bath were awarded a controversial penalty.

Malone's kick left his side trailing by one point, but Voyce's last-gasp heroics proved decisive and gave Wasps their sixth league win of the season.

Venue:	Causeway Stadium	Referee:	Roy Maybank - Season 05/06
Attendance:	8,656	Matches:	5
Capacity:	10,200	Yellow Cards:	7
Occupancy:	85%	Red Cards:	0

London Wasps
Bath Rugby

Starting Line-Ups

London Wasps		Bath Rugby
Voyce	15	Best
Sackey	14	Maddock
Erinle	13	Cheeseman
Hoadley	12	Crockett
Baxter	11	Bory
Staunton	10	Malone
Reddan	9	Williams
Payne	1	Barnes
Ward	2	Dixon
J Dawson	3	Bell
Shaw	4	Short
Skivington	5	Fidler
Hart	6	Beattie (c)
Rees	7	Lipman
Dallaglio (c)	8	Feau'nati

Replacements

Mbu	22	Stephenson
King	21	Davis
Honeyben	20	Baxter
Lock	19	Scaysbrook
Birkett	18	Delve
Bracken	17	Loader
Gotting	16	Hawkins

Match Stats

	London Wasps	Bath Rugby
Tackles	92	96
Missed Tackles	7	19
Ball Carries	84	70
Metres	356	238
Defenders Beaten	19	8
Passes	103	63
Clean Breaks	5	2
Pens Conceded	9	18
Turnovers	14	7
Breakdowns Won	69	66
% Scrums Won	100%	71%
% Line-Outs Won	71%	70%

Premiership Table

Team	P	W	D	L	F	A	BP	Pts
1 Sale Sharks	8	7	0	1	196	131	3	31
2 London Wasps	8	6	1	1	213	150	2	28
3 London Irish	8	5	0	3	176	150	4	24

Event Line

TC Try Converted
T Try
P Penalty
DG Drop Goal

Min	Score Progress		Event	Players
9	5	0	T	Baxter
12	5	3	P	Malone
16	5	8	T	Lipman
20	5	8		Feau'nati
20	8	8	P	Staunton
30	8	11	P	Malone
39	11	11	P	Staunton
Half time 11-11				
42	11	14	P	Malone
52	18	14	TC	Baxter / Staunton
56	18	14		Lipman
58	18	14	⇄	Hawkins > Dixon
58	18	14	⇄	Stephenson > Maddock
59	18	17	P	Malone
60	18	17	⇄	Birkett > Skivington
60	18	17	⇄	Bracken > Dawson
60	18	20	DG	Malone
62	18	20	⇄	King > Staunton
68	18	20	⇄	Scaysbrook > Lipman
68	21	20	P	King
70	21	20	⇄	Delve > Short
73	21	20	⇄	Davis > Bory
74	28	20	TC	Voyce / King
Full time 28-20				

Scoring Statistics

London Wasps

by Situation		by Half	
TC:	14	first:	39%
T:	5	second:	61%
P:	9		
DG:	0		

Bath Rugby

by Situation		by Half	
TC:	0	first:	55%
T:	5	second:	45%
P:	12		
DG:	3		

Newcastle Falcons 17
London Wasps 15

Guinness Premiership

27.11.05

Quote

Ian McGeechan

I thought we were in a winning position, but Newcastle kept plugging away. You have to hand it to them and Walder was able to nail the kick at the end to win it.

Premiership Away Record vs Newcastle Falcons					
Played	Won	Drawn	Lost	For	Against
9	3	0	6	193	226

London Wasps good run of results in November ground to a halt at Kingston Park as Newcastle grabbed a last-minute win in controversial circumstances.

With less than a minute left on the clock, Wasps were holding a one-point lead when Ian McGeechan's men conceded a questionable penalty. Newcastle's Dave Walder slotted the kick over from 35 metres out to snatch victory and leave Wasps with only a losing bonus point to take on the 290-mile trip back home.

In freezing conditions Newcastle struck first through Mike McCarthy but Wasps replied immediately, Mark Van Gisbergen creating the space to allow Paul Sackey to touch down in the corner. Although Van Gisbergen couldn't convert the score – leaving Wasps 7-5 behind at half time – he made amends with a penalty in front of the posts early in the second half before Jeremy Staunton grabbed Wasps' second try to give the visitors a 15-7 advantage.

Newcastle launched an attack from the restart and Walder put Jamie Noon clean through to score, with Matt Burke adding the extras to bring Falcons within a point.

The final quarter of the game lacked fluency and was punctuated by errors. Then, with 30 seconds remaining, Tom Rees appared to be restrained from rolling away from the ball and, after a moment's hesitation, referee David Rose gave his fateful decision – leading to Walder's decisive kick.

Venue:	Kingston Park	Referee:	David Rose - Season 05/06
Attendance:	7,379	Matches:	5
Capacity:	10,000	Yellow Cards:	10
Occupancy:	74%	Red Cards:	0

Newcastle Falcons
London Wasps

Starting Line-Ups

Newcastle Falcons		London Wasps
Burke (c)	**15**	Van Gisbergen
May	**14**	Sackey
Noon	**13**	Erinle
Mayerhofler	**12**	Abbott
Tait	**11**	Hoadley
Flood	**10**	Staunton
Grindal	**9**	Reddan
Ward	**1**	Payne
Long	**2**	Gotting
Morris	**3**	J Dawson
Perry	**4**	Skivington
Parling	**5**	Birkett
McCarthy	**6**	Hart
Harris	**7**	Rees
Smithson	**8**	Dallaglio (c)

Replacements

Walder	**22**	Baxter
Dickson	**21**	King
Finegan	**20**	Honeyben
Buist	**19**	Chamberlain
Woods	**18**	Lock
Thompson	**17**	McKenzie
Wilson	**16**	Ward

Match Stats

	Newcastle Falcons	London Wasps
Tackles	76	143
Missed Tackles	16	30
Ball Carries	145	95
Metres	510	470
Defenders Beaten	28	14
Passes	123	87
Clean Breaks	10	7
Pens Conceded	10	7
Turnovers	21	17
Breakdowns Won	118	53
% Scrums Won	100%	93%
% Line-Outs Won	80%	67%

Premiership Table

Team	P	W	D	L	F	A	BP	Pts
1 Sale Sharks	9	7	0	2	210	153	3	31
2 London Wasps	9	6	1	2	228	167	3	29
3 Leicester Tigers	9	5	2	2	232	153	4	28

Event Line

TC Try Converted — P Penalty
T Try — DG Drop Goal

Min	Score Progress		Event	Players
8	0	0	⇄	Ward > Gotting
8	7	0	TC	McCarthy / Burke
9	7	5	T	Sackey
Half time 7-5				
41	7	5	⇄	Wilson > Ward
48	7	8	P	Van Gisbergen
49	7	15	TC	Staunton / Van Gisbergen
51	7	15	⇄	Walder > Flood
53	7	15	⇄	Dickson > May
53	7	15	⇄	Woods > Smithson
55	14	15	TC	Noon / Burke
59	14	15	⇄	Thompson > Long
64	14	15	⇄	Finegan > Dickson
67	14	15	⇄	King > Staunton
70	14	15	⇄	Buist > Perry
80	17	15	P	Walder
Full time 17-15				

Scoring Statistics

Newcastle Falcons

by Situation		by Half	
TC:	14	first:	41%
T:	0	second:	59%
P:	3		
DG:	0		

London Wasps

by Situation		by Half	
TC:	7	first:	33%
T:	5	second:	67%
P:	3		
DG:	0		

London Wasps 42
Saracens 8

Powergen Cup

04.12.05

Quote

Ian McGeechan

We're looking forward to playing at the Millennium Stadium, which I think will be a first for the club.

London Wasps booked their place in the Powergen Cup semi-finals with a 42-8 victory over an inexperienced Saracens side, Paul Sackey contributing two tries.

Saracens fielded a young team, with senior players Shane Byrne and Hugh Vyvyan named on the bench. In contrast, Wasps fielded a strong fifteen including Simon Shaw, Josh Lewsey and Tom Voyce – all returning to club duties after their involvement in the autumn internationals. Despite the obvious mis-match, Saracens put up a good fight for an hour, limiting Wasps to a 14-8 lead until fatigue set in for the visitors and floodgates opened – Wasps running in four tries in the last 15 minutes.

Wasps started purposefully with George Skivington diving over the try-line from close range after three minutes. Alex King made amends for missing the conversion by nailing a 35-metre penalty on 10 minutes, but Saracens hit back through a try from Paul Bailey.

With the referee awarding a huge amount of penalties, King was handed two penalty attempts in two minutes – sending one over to make it 11-5 in Wasps favour. After Wasps had edged into a 14-8 lead through a further King penalty, Sackey turned on the style by racing in at the corner.

With 10 minutes remaining, Wasps stepped up a gear and blew Saracens away with Lewsey, Sackey and Eoin Reddan all crossing the whitewash after some enterprising play. The only downside was the withdrawal of flanker Tom Rees – the England Under 21 captain leaving the field with a shoulder injury.

Venue:	Causeway Stadium	Referee:	Ashley Rowden - Season 05/06
Attendance:	6,377		
Capacity:	10,200		
Occupancy:	63%		

London Wasps
Saracens

Starting Line-Ups

London Wasps		Saracens
Lewsey	15	Russell
Sackey	14	Obi
Erinle	13	Bartholomeusz
Abbott	12	Powell
Voyce	11	Bailey
King	10	Little
Reddan	9	Dickens
Payne	1	Liffchak
Barrett	2	Kyriacou
Bracken	3	Broster
Shaw	4	Chesney (c)
Skivington	5	Ryder
Hart	6	Amapakabo
Rees	7	Seymour
Dallaglio (c)	8	Armitage

Replacements

Van Gisbergen	22	O'Driscoll
Hoadley	21	Vaikona
M Dawson	20	Bedford
Lock	19	Skirving
O'Connor	18	Vyvyan
J Dawson	17	Mitchell
Webber	16	Byrne

Match Stats

	London Wasps	Saracens
Tackles	109	99
Missed Tackles	9	9
Ball Carries	88	95
Metres	539	255
Defenders Beaten	9	9
Passes	137	116
Clean Breaks	5	2
Pens Conceded	10	12
Turnovers	10	9
Breakdowns Won	70	81
% Scrums Won	89%	100%
% Line-Outs Won	86%	82%

Powergen Cup Table

Team	P	W	D	L	F	A	BP	Pts
1 London Wasps	3	3	0	0	112	53	2	14
2 Cardiff Blues	3	1	0	2	79	87	2	6
3 Saracens	3	1	0	2	60	92	1	5
4 London Irish	3	1	0	2	66	85	1	5

Event Line

TC Try Converted
T Try
P Penalty
DG Drop Goal

Min	Score Progress		Event	Players
2	5	0	T	Skivington
10	8	0	P	King
11	8	5	T	Bailey
17	11	5	P	King
26	11	5	⇄	O'Connor > Rees
40	11	5	⇄	Dawson > Bracken
40	11	8	DG	Powell
Half time 11-8				
41	11	8	⇄	Lock > Hart
43	14	8	P	King
46	14	8	⇄	Vaikona > Obi
60	14	8	■	Armitage
61	14	8	⇄	Hoadley > Voyce
61	14	8	⇄	O'Driscoll > Bartholomeusz
64	14	8	⇄	Mitchell > Liffchak
67	21	8	TC	Sackey / King
71	21	8	⇄	Webber > O'Connor
72	21	8	⇄	Skirving > Seymour
72	21	8	⇄	Vyvyan > Amapakabo
72	21	8	⇄	Byrne > Kyriacou
72	28	8	TC	Lewsey / King
75	35	8	TC	Sackey / King
76	35	8	⇄	Van Gisbergen > Abbott
77	35	8	⇄	Bedford > Dickens
80	42	8	TC	Reddan / King
Full time 42-8				

Scoring Statistics

London Wasps

by Situation		by Half	
TC:	28	first:	26%
T:	5	second:	74%
P:	9		
DG:	0		

Saracens

by Situation		by Half	
TC:	0	first:	100%
T:	5	second:	0%
P:	0		
DG:	3		

Llanelli Scarlets 21
London Wasps 13

Heineken Cup

11.12.05

Quote

Ian McGeechan

We have probably produced our worst performance of the season so far in European competition. Today we made a lot of errors. There are no excuses – they played better than us.

Llanelli virtually ended London Wasps' 2006 Heineken Cup dream, inflicting an agonising 21-13 defeat on the visitors after playing hard-ball in the Stradey Park mist.

Wasps faced a predictably partisan crowd in wild, west Wales and responded with an uncharacteristically lacklustre performance, littered with unforced errors. It was a performance to forget as Llanelli secured the lion's share of possession and scored mainly courtesy of Wasps' conceded penalties and errors.

Wasps' troubles started as early as the fifth minute, with Scarlets' Gareth Bowen putting Llanelli 3-0 ahead. For the next 10 minutes Llanelli were in the ascendancy, winning good ball and making ground.

The visitors weathered the storm and Alex King leveled the scores with a penalty after 14 minutes. Although King's kicking display kept his side out of trouble, errors meant that Wasps could only add one more penalty before half-time.

As the second half began, the mist descended and had a wholly detrimental affect on Wasps' fortunes. A careless mistake in midfield meant that Llanelli's Dafydd James scored. Scarlett's winger Mark Jones stretched the lead with a try out of nothing in the 64th minute before the game opened up and Tom Rees crossed the whitewash to pull Wasps back to 15-13 in the 67th minute.

However, two further penalties from Bowen denied Wasps even a losing bonus point in a thoroughly unproductive afternoon.

Venue: Stradey Park | Referee: Alain Rolland
Attendance: 7,348
Capacity: 10,800
Occupancy: 68%

Llanelli Scarlets
London Wasps

Starting Line-Ups

Llanelli Scarlets		London Wasps
Byrne	15	Lewsey
Evans	14	Sackey
Watkins	13	Erinle
James	12	Abbott
Jones	11	Voyce
Bowen	10	King
Peel	9	M Dawson
Williams	1	Payne
Rees	2	Ibanez
Davies	3	J Dawson
Louw	4	Shaw
Jones	5	Birkett
Easterby (c)	6	Worsley
Thomas	7	O'Connor
Popham	8	Dallaglio (c)

Replacements

Davies	22	Van Gisbergen
Hercus	21	Hoadley
Stuart-Smith	20	Reddan
Wyatt	19	Rees
Afeaki	18	Skivington
Gravello	17	McKenzie
Davies	16	Barrett

Match Stats

	Llanelli Scarlets	London Wasps
Tackles	93	66
Missed Tackles	11	9
Ball Carries	60	76
Metres	257	389
Defenders Beaten	9	11
Passes	56	111
Clean Breaks	1	4
Pens Conceded	13	13
Turnovers	12	17
Breakdowns Won	49	65
% Scrums Won	77%	100%
% Line-Outs Won	89%	55%

Heineken Cup Table

Team	P	W	D	L	F	A	BP	Pts
1 Toulouse	3	2	1	0	85	56	1	11
2 Llanelli Scarlets	3	2	0	1	64	76	0	8
3 Edinburgh Gunners	3	1	0	2	58	66	2	6
4 London Wasps	3	0	1	2	59	68	1	3

Event Line

TC Try Converted | P Penalty
T Try | DG Drop Goal

Min	Score Progress		Event	Players
4	3	0	P	Bowen
13	3	3	P	King
15	3	3		Popham
40	3	6	P	King
Half time 3-6				
46	10	6	TC	James / Bowen
62	10	6	⇄	Van Gisbergen > Abbott
63	10	6	⇄	Rees > Worsley
65	15	6	T	Jones
67	15	6	⇄	Afeaki > Easterby
68	15	13	TC	Rees / Van Gisbergen
73	15	13	⇄	Barrett > Ibanez
73	18	13	P	Bowen
80	18	13		O'Connor
82	18	13	⇄	Reddan > Dawson
84	21	13	P	Bowen
Full time 21-13				

Scoring Statistics

Llanelli Scarlets

by Situation: TC: 7, T: 5, P: 9, DG: 0
by Half: first: 14%, second: 86%

London Wasps

by Situation: TC: 7, T: 0, P: 6, DG: 0
by Half: first: 46%, second: 54%

London Wasps 48
Llanelli Scarlets 14

Heineken Cup

18.12.05

Quote

Ian McGeechan

We've been pretty hard on ourselves as we were the ones making the mistakes. Today though, we gave ourselves the right base and this was definitely our best game of the season.

After disappointment at Stradey, London Wasps set the record straight with a resounding home win but, as far as the Heineken Cup was concerned, it promised to be too little, too late.

Wasps ran in six tries, including a Tom Voyce hat-trick, against a shell-shocked Scarlets side.

An Alex King penalty sailed over in the fourth minute before the fly-half fed Voyce for his first score four minutes later. Josh Lewsey then got in on the act, powering over the line after an exhibition of both pace and know-how, with King adding the conversion to give Wasps a 17-0 advantage inside the half-hour. King struck another penalty before Llanelli centre Matthew J Watkins capitalised on a wayward pass to give Wasps a sharp shock.

The hosts responded immediately however, with lock George Skivington dotting the ball down over the line following some enterprising build-up play involving Sackey and King.

After the break, Lewsey continued his good work and shrugged off two tackles before offloading to Voyce, who accelerated through to score his second.

Voyce was searching for his third and it arrived when the Cornishman scooped up a loose ball and sprinted over the whitewash.

A frazzled Llanelli replied with a late consolation try from Barry Davies following a break from Garan Evans, Hercus adding the conversion for a final score of 48-14.

Venue: Causeway Stadium
Attendance: 7,157
Capacity: 10,200
Occupancy: 70%

Referee: Alan Lewis

London Wasps
Llanelli Scarlets

Starting Line-Ups

London Wasps		Llanelli Scarlets
Van Gisbergen	15	Byrne
Sackey	14	Jones
Lewsey	13	Watkins
Abbott	12	James
Voyce	11	Evans
King	10	Bowen
Reddan	9	Peel
McKenzie	1	Williams
Ibanez	2	Rees
Payne	3	Davies
Shaw	4	Louw
Skivington	5	Jones
Hart	6	Easterby (c)
O'Connor	7	Thomas
Dallaglio (c)	8	Popham

Replacements

Erinle	22	Davies
Hoadley	21	Hercus
M Dawson	20	Stuart-Smith
Birkett	19	Mills
Lock	18	Afeaki
J Dawson	17	Hawkins
Barrett	16	Madden

Match Stats

	London Wasps	Llanelli Scarlets
Tackles	62	118
Missed Tackles	12	17
Ball Carries	113	67
Metres	631	273
Defenders Beaten	17	12
Passes	114	83
Clean Breaks	11	4
Pens Conceded	9	16
Turnovers	15	14
Breakdowns Won	80	46
% Scrums Won	100%	100%
% Line-Outs Won	93%	83%

Heineken Cup Table

Team	P	W	D	L	F	A	BP	Pts
1 Toulouse	4	3	1	0	120	69	2	16
2 London Wasps	4	1	1	2	107	82	2	8
3 Llanelli Scarlets	4	2	0	2	78	124	0	8
4 Edinburgh Gunners	4	1	0	3	71	101	2	6

Event Line

TC Try Converted
T Try
P Penalty
DG Drop Goal

Min	Score Progress		Event	Players
5	3	0	P	King
7	10	0	TC	Voyce / King
21	10	0	⇄	Mills > Easterby
27	17	0	TC	Lewsey / King
34	17	0	▪	Mills
36	20	0	P	King
37	20	7	TC	Watkins / Bowen
40	27	7	TC	Skivington / King
Half time 27-7				
41	27	7	⇄	Davies > Byrne
50	27	7	▪	McKenzie
52	27	7	⇄	Afeaki > Louw
53	27	7	⇄	Dawson > O'Connor
56	34	7	TC	Voyce / King
63	34	7	⇄	O'Connor > Dawson
63	34	7	⇄	Dawson > Payne
63	41	7	TC	Ibanez / King
64	41	7	⇄	Barrett > Ibanez
64	41	7	⇄	Madden > Davies
64	41	7	⇄	Hercus > Bowen
66	41	7	▪	Jones
68	41	7	⇄	Dawson > Reddan
70	48	7	TC	Voyce / King
71	48	7	⇄	Lock > Dallaglio
72	48	7	⇄	Erinle > Lewsey
75	48	14	TC	Davies / Hercus
76	48	14	⇄	Hoadley > Voyce
77	48	14	⇄	Stuart-Smith > Watkins
Full time 48-14				

Scoring Statistics

London Wasps

by Situation		by Half	
TC:	42	first:	56%
T:	0	second:	44%
P:	6		
DG:	0		

Llanelli Scarlets

by Situation		by Half	
TC:	14	first:	50%
T:	0	second:	50%
P:	0		
DG:	0		

London Wasps 32
Gloucester Rugby 25

Guinness Premiership

26.12.05

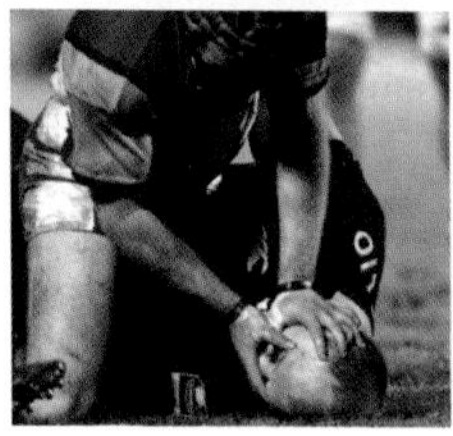

Premiership Home Record vs Gloucester Rugby					
Played	Won	Drawn	Lost	For	Against
9	9	0	0	274	160

Quote

Ian McGeechan

Both teams came out intending to play some rugby and I think it has been a great advert for the Premiership.

London Wasps came out fighting on Boxing Day to secure maximum points against a revitalised Gloucester side, with John Hart producing a Man of the Match winning display.

Hart scored early on as Wasps started in promising fashion, with Alex King adding the conversion before Gloucester's Ludovic Mercier narrowed the gap with a penalty. The game continued at breakneck speed: Paul Sackey scored immediately after the re-start, King added a simple penalty to give Wasps a 15-3 lead with just 15 minutes gone, and the momentum continued with Shaw touching down five minutes later.

Gloucester responded positively, and were rewarded with a try under the posts by Mercier, which he converted. Josh Lewsey then contributed Wasps' bonus point score although Mercier had the last word of the first half with a penalty.

After the turnaround, Gloucester changed their style to blunt the Wasps attack and Tim Payne was sin-binned before the Cherry & Whites struck twice, via a penalty try and a score from James Bailey. However, replacement Mark Van Gisbergen's penalty – sandwiched in between the tries – ensured Gloucester's comeback was unsuccessful and Wasps remained hot on the heels of Sale in the title chase as the New Year beckoned.

Venue:	Causeway Stadium	Referee:	Roy Maybank - Season 05/06
Attendance:	10,000	Matches:	7
Capacity:	10,200	Yellow Cards:	11
Occupancy:	98%	Red Cards:	0

London Wasps
Gloucester Rugby

Starting Line-Ups

London Wasps		Gloucester Rugby
Van Gisbergen	15	Morgan
Sackey	14	Foster
Lewsey	13	Simpson-Daniel
Abbott	12	Tindall
Voyce	11	Bailey
King	10	Mercier
Reddan	9	Richards
McKenzie	1	Collazo
Ibanez	2	Davies
Payne	3	Vickery (c)
Shaw	4	Pendlebury
Skivington	5	Brown
Hart	6	Balding
O'Connor	7	Hazell
Dallaglio (c)	8	Forrester

Replacements

Erinle	22	Davies
Hoadley	21	Fanolua
M Dawson	20	Thomas
Lock	19	Boer
Chamberlain	18	Eustace
J Dawson	17	Sigley
Ward	16	Elloway

Match Stats

Tackles	97	111
Missed Tackles	11	7
Ball Carries	105	88
Metres	371	402
Defenders Beaten	7	10
Passes	108	91
Clean Breaks	5	2
Pens Conceded	10	9
Turnovers	6	16
Breakdowns Won	82	77
% Scrums Won	75%	86%
% Line-Outs Won	94%	82%

Premiership Table

Team	P	W	D	L	F	A	BP	Pts
1 Sale Sharks	10	8	0	2	244	167	3	35
2 London Wasps	10	7	1	2	260	192	4	34
3 Leicester Tigers	9	5	2	2	232	153	4	28

Event Line

TC Try Converted   P Penalty
T Try   DG Drop Goal

Min	Score Progress		Event	Players
5	0	0		Richards
6	7	0	TC	Hart / King
9	7	3	P	Mercier
10	12	3	T	Sackey
14	15	3	P	King
19	22	3	TC	Shaw / King
24	22	10	TC	Mercier / Mercier
38	29	10	TC	Lewsey / King
40	29	13	P	Mercier
Half time 29-13				
41	29	13	⇄	Dawson > Reddan
46	29	13		Payne
47	29	13	⇄	Boer > Balding
49	29	13	⇄	Dawson > O'Connor
55	29	13	⇄	Sigley > Collazo
56	29	13	⇄	Erinle > King
56	29	13	⇄	Ward > Ibanez
57	29	20	TC	Pen Try / Mercier
59	29	20	⇄	O'Connor > Dawson
61	29	20	⇄	Eustace > Forrester
67	32	20	P	Van Gisbergen
69	32	20	⇄	Hoadley > Abbott
74	32	20	⇄	Dawson > McKenzie
74	32	25	T	Bailey
Full time 32-25				

Scoring Statistics

London Wasps

by Situation		by Half	
TC:	21	first:	91%
T:	5	second:	9%
P:	6		
DG:	0		

Gloucester Rugby

by Situation		by Half	
TC:	14	first:	52%
T:	5	second:	48%
P:	6		
DG:	0		

London Irish 19
London Wasps 35

Guinness Premiership

31.12.05

Premiership Away Record vs London Irish					
Played	Won	Drawn	Lost	For	Against
9	5	0	4	240	214

London Wasps finished 2005 on a high note with a richly-deserved win at the Madejski Stadium against an in-form London Irish side.

Quote

Ian McGeechan

We have played two very physical sides in the last week, in Gloucester and London Irish. We knew we would have to front up for a second time in seven days – and we did it well.

The encounter started in pragmatic fashion with two penalties a-piece for both Mark Van Gisbergen and Irish's Ross Laidlaw. However the irrepressible Josh Lewsey then ghosted through the Exiles' defence to touch down and Joe Worsley followed that up with another expert finish, splitting Irish's pack to score a well-taken try.

At that point Wasps were comfortably ahead 20-6 but the home side, spurred on by the vocal Madejski Stadium crowd, produced a buoyant response. A good long-range penalty from Laidlaw put Irish back in contention before half time, and the Exiles started the second half at full pelt, but it was Wasps who struck next through Ibanez.

Irish's Bob Casey then scored before Lawrence Dallaglio was shown a yellow card – putting further pressure on the champions. Van Gisbergen was successful with a third penalty, but more indiscipline from Wasps allowed Laidlaw to respond with three points of his own, keeping his side in the chase.

With six minutes remaining, emerging talent George Skivington ensured victory for Wasps by driving over the whitewash from close range. It brought the year to an end with a pleasing victory that allowed Wasps to celebrate the New Year at the top of the Premiership table.

Venue:	Madejski Stadium	Referee:	Tony Spreadbury - Season 05/06
Attendance:	18,122	Matches:	4
Capacity:	24,104	Yellow Cards:	3
Occupancy:	75%	Red Cards:	2

London Irish
London Wasps

Starting Line-Ups

London Irish		London Wasps
Horak	15	Van Gisbergen
Armitage	14	Sackey
Franze	13	Lewsey
Catt (c)	12	Abbott
Feau'nati	11	Voyce
Laidlaw	10	Staunton
Edwards	9	Reddan
Collins	1	Payne
Flavin	2	Ibanez
Rautenbach	3	Va'a
Strudwick	4	Hart
Kennedy	5	Skivington
Thorpe	6	Worsley
Dawson	7	O'Connor
Murphy	8	Dallaglio (c)

Replacements

Everitt	22	Hoadley
Hodgson	21	Erinle
Leguizamon	20	M Dawson
Casey	19	Rees
Wheatley	18	Purdy
Coetzee	17	McKenzie
Hatley	16	Barrett

Match Stats

	London Irish	London Wasps
Tackles	98	91
Missed Tackles	17	8
Ball Carries	77	89
Metres	278	503
Defenders Beaten	9	16
Passes	101	93
Clean Breaks	0	14
Pens Conceded	10	11
Turnovers	10	12
Breakdowns Won	58	48
% Scrums Won	100%	92%
% Line-Outs Won	91%	65%

Premiership Table

Team	P	W	D	L	F	A	BP	Pts
1 London Wasps	11	8	1	2	295	211	5	39
2 Sale Sharks	10	8	0	2	244	167	3	35
3 Gloucester Rugby	11	6	1	4	253	201	5	31

Event Line

TC Try Converted
T Try
P Penalty
DG Drop Goal

Min	Score Progress		Event	Players
9	0	3	P	Van Gisbergen
13	3	3	P	Laidlaw
16	3	6	P	Van Gisbergen
20	6	6	P	Laidlaw
25	6	13	TC	Lewsey / Van Gisbergen
28	6	20	TC	Worsley / Van Gisbergen
31	9	20	P	Laidlaw
39	9	20	⇄	Hodgson > Feau'nati
Half time 9-20				
41	9	20	⇄	Coetzee > Flavin
41	9	20	⇄	Erinle > Abbott
45	9	20	⇄	Hatley > Collins
47	9	27	TC	Ibanez / Van Gisbergen
48	9	27	⇄	McKenzie > Va'a
48	9	27	⇄	Casey > Strudwick
53	16	27	TC	Casey / Laidlaw
55	16	27	■	Dallaglio
55	16	27	⇄	Leguizamon > Catt
56	16	27	⇄	Barrett > Ibanez
62	16	27	⇄	Purdy > Hart
62	16	30	P	Van Gisbergen
64	19	30	P	Laidlaw
69	19	30	⇄	Dawson > Reddan
70	19	30	⇄	Everitt > Edwards
71	19	30	⇄	Hoadley > Sackey
71	19	30	⇄	Wheatley > Rautenbach
77	19	35	T	Skivington
78	19	35	⇄	Rees > Worsley
Full time 19-35				

Scoring Statistics

London Irish

by Situation		by Half	
TC:	7	first:	47%
T:	0	second:	53%
P:	12		
DG:	0		

London Wasps

by Situation		by Half	
TC:	21	first:	57%
T:	5	second:	43%
P:	9		
DG:	0		

London Wasps 21
Newcastle Falcons 6

Guinness Premiership

08.01.06

Premiership Home Record vs Newcastle Falcons

Played	Won	Drawn	Lost	For	Against
9	7	1	1	252	182

A new year, but the same end-product for London Wasps as the champions registered another home victory – outplaying Newcastle in almost unplayable conditions.

Quote

Ian McGeechan

I was very pleased with the way we played today. These were difficult conditions, and they can become a leveller – leaving the result a lottery – but today it was not so.

Paul Sackey opened the scoring after only three minutes when he latched onto Mark Van Gisbergen's pass to hurtle in at the corner. After defeating Wasps at Kingston Park earlier on in the season, Newcastle wanted to record a famous 'double' over the champions and Matthew Burke opened their account by kicking two penalties to give the Tynesiders a 6-5 lead. Van Gisbergen responded with calm efficiency to give Wasps a two-point advantage as the teams went in at the interval.

Straight after the break it was a case of déjà vu for Wasps with Sackey showing both panache and pace to score the his second of the day, although Van Gisbergen couldn't convert from the touchline. Wasps continued to surge forward though, and minutes later with Jeremy Staunton, who had assumed the kicking duties, successfully sent over his first penalty of the day for the champions.

The only blip for Wasps in a game played in torrential rain was Martin Purdy's ill fortune, as the lock was forced from the pitch with a recurrence of his fractured arm in only his second game back. The gloom lifted in injury time though with a classic try from replacement Matt Dawson. The former England captain combined with Alex King to slide over for a clever try.

Venue:	Causeway Stadium	Referee:	Wayne Barnes - Season 05/06
Attendance:	10,000	Matches:	3
Capacity:	10,200	Yellow Cards:	6
Occupancy:	98%	Red Cards:	1

London Wasps
Newcastle Falcons

Starting Line-Ups

London Wasps		Newcastle Falcons
Van Gisbergen	15	Burke
Sackey	14	Phillips
Lewsey	13	Noon
Abbott	12	Mayerhofler
Voyce	11	Tait
Staunton	10	Flood
Reddan	9	Grindal
McKenzie	1	Ward
Barrett	2	Long
Bracken	3	Morris
Shaw	4	Perry
Skivington	5	Parling
Hart	6	Finegan
Worsley	7	Harris
Dallaglio (c)	8	Charvis (c)

Replacements

Erinle	22	Shaw
King	21	Richardson
M Dawson	20	Woods
Rees	19	McCarthy
Purdy	18	Thompson
Va'a	17	Buist
Ibanez	16	Wilson

Match Stats

	London Wasps	Newcastle Falcons
Tackles	107	117
Missed Tackles	15	27
Ball Carries	141	105
Metres	667	362
Defenders Beaten	25	15
Passes	109	97
Clean Breaks	12	3
Pens Conceded	7	7
Turnovers	21	11
Breakdowns Won	96	88
% Scrums Won	87%	88%
% Line-Outs Won	100%	91%

Premiership Table

Team	P	W	D	L	F	A	BP	Pts
1 London Wasps	12	9	1	2	316	217	5	43
2 Sale Sharks	12	10	0	2	296	205	3	43
3 Leicester Tigers	12	7	2	3	297	220	4	36

Event Line

TC Try Converted
T Try
P Penalty
DG Drop Goal

Min	Score Progress		Event	Players
3	5	0	T	Sackey
11	5	3	P	Burke
32	5	6	P	Burke
37	8	6	P	Van Gisbergen
Half time 8-6				
41	8	6	⇄	Va'a > Bracken
41	8	6	⇄	McCarthy > Finegan
45	13	6	T	Sackey
47	13	6	■	Long
48	16	6	P	Staunton
51	16	6	⇄	Thompson > Harris
59	16	6	⇄	Purdy > Skivington
59	16	6	⇄	Erinle > Abbott
59	16	6	⇄	Thompson > Long
59	16	6	⇄	Woods > Harris
59	16	6	⇄	Harris > Thompson
63	16	6	⇄	Wilson > Morris
66	16	6	⇄	King > Staunton
66	16	6	⇄	Dawson > Reddan
69	16	6	⇄	Rees > Purdy
77	21	6	T	Dawson
79	21	6	⇄	Ibanez > McKenzie
Full time 21-6				

Scoring Statistics

London Wasps

by Situation		by Half	
TC:	0	first:	38%
T:	15	second:	62%
P:	6		
DG:	0		

Newcastle Falcons

by Situation		by Half	
TC:	0	first:	100%
T:	0	second:	0%
P:	6		
DG:	0		

Toulouse 19
London Wasps 13

Heineken Cup

14.01.06

Quote

Lawrence Dallaglio

A lot of teams would have gone 13 down and ended up losing by 30 or 40 points. It is sad then that the damage was done for us in the early stages of the tournament in Edinburgh and Llanelli.

Toulouse brought the curtain down on London Wasps' involvement in the Heineken Cup with a 19-13 victory in front of a 34,000 crowd in the Stade Toulouse.

Going into the game, it was still mathematically possible for Wasps to progress through to the next stage of the competition, but winning at the home of the European champions was always going to be tall order. Despite turning in a creditable performance, Wasps could not contain Toulouse's awesome attacking armoury.

Wasps suffered a horrible start. Scrum half Jean-Baptiste Elissalde converted two early penalties, and Toulouse extended their advantage to 13-0 after 12 minutes, courtesy of a stunning try from Welsh captain Gareth Thomas.

With Toulouse playing expansive rugby, Wasps changed tack to nullify their illustrious opponents and former France captain Raphael Ibanez scored a try to keep Wasps hopes of victory alive.

Hopes of a famous Wasps revival faded when prop Tim Payne was shown the yellow card early in the second half. Despite losing a player, Wasps matched their opponents in the second 40 with Elissalde and Van Gisbergen successfully striking two penalities each. The Frenchmen had already done enough though, clinching victory by 19-13.

Even though Wasps had crashed out of the competition, Wasps captain Lawrence Dallaglio said: "I admire the character my team showed. We often get criticised in the tight five, but I was proud of the pack today."

Venue:	Stade Toulouse	Referee:	Nigel Owens
Attendance:	34,000		
Capacity:	37,000		
Occupancy:	92%		

Toulouse
London Wasps

Starting Line-Ups

Toulouse		London Wasps
Thomas	15	Van Gisbergen
Clerc	14	Sackey
Jauzion	13	Lewsey
Fritz	12	Abbott
Garbajosa	11	Voyce
Michalak	10	Staunton
Elissalde	9	M Dawson
Poux	1	McKenzie
Bru (c)	2	Ibanez
Hasan Jalil	3	Payne
Pelous	4	Shaw
Brennan	5	Skivington
Bouilhou	6	Worsley
Nyanga	7	O'Connor
Maka	8	Dallaglio (c)

Replacements

Montauriol	22	Erinle
Dubois	21	Hoadley
Mermoz	20	Reddan
Maka	19	Hart
Millo-Chlusky	18	Birkett
Human	17	Bracken
Lacombe	16	Barrett

Match Stats

	Toulouse	London Wasps
Tackles	146	53
Missed Tackles	10	5
Ball Carries	57	125
Metres	361	551
Defenders Beaten	5	10
Passes	76	107
Clean Breaks	6	5
Pens Conceded	13	13
Turnovers	4	12
Breakdowns Won	47	101
% Scrums Won	83%	82%
% Line-Outs Won	71%	90%

Heineken Cup Table

Team	P	W	D	L	F	A	BP	Pts
1 Toulouse	5	4	1	0	139	82	2	20
2 Edinburgh Gunners	5	2	0	3	104	133	3	11
3 Llanelli Scarlets	5	2	0	3	110	157	2	10
4 London Wasps	5	1	1	3	120	101	3	9

Event Line

TC Try Converted | P Penalty
T Try | DG Drop Goal

Min	Score Progress		Event	Players
8	3	0	P	Elissalde
11	6	0	P	Elissalde
12	13	0	TC	Thomas / Elissalde
20	13	0	⇄	Reddan > Dawson
31	13	0	⇄	Dawson > Reddan
36	13	0	⇄	Maka > Nyanga
40	13	0	▪	Fritz
40	13	7	TC	Ibanez / Van Gisbergen
Half time 13-7				
41	13	7	⇄	Nyanga > Maka
42	13	7	⇄	Dubois > Thomas
49	13	7	▪	Payne
52	13	7	⇄	Bracken > O'Connor
52	13	7	⇄	Barrett > Ibanez
53	16	7	P	Elissalde
60	16	10	P	Van Gisbergen
61	16	10	⇄	O'Connor > Bracken
64	16	10	⇄	Ibanez > Barrett
67	19	10	P	Elissalde
69	19	10	⇄	Hart > O'Connor
70	19	13	P	Van Gisbergen
71	19	13	⇄	Birkett > Shaw
75	19	13	⇄	Erinle > Sackey
76	19	13	⇄	Human > Hasan Jalil
Full time 19-13				

Scoring Statistics

Toulouse

by Situation		by Half	
TC:	7	first:	68%
T:	0	second:	32%
P:	12		
DG:	0		

London Wasps

by Situation		by Half	
TC:	7	first:	54%
T:	0	second:	46%
P:	6		
DG:	0		

London Wasps 53
Edinburgh Gunners 17

Heineken Cup

21.01.06

Quote

Ian McGeechan

I thought we had managed to ride out their impetus in the game but they played with the ball in the right parts of the field.

There was only pride at stake as London Wasps took care of business against Edinburgh, and the English champions ran in seven tries as they wreaked revenge for the earlier defeat at Murrayfield in October.

Wasps came out of the blocks with purpose and Mark Van Gisbergen sent his first penalty over after just three minutes, but Edinburgh's Hugo Southwell hadn't read the script and grounded his own grubber to give Edinburgh a 3-5 lead and Wasps another sharp shock.

However the English side weren't afflicted by the same lethargy that had plagued them in Edinburgh, and Alex King crossed the whitewash minutes later. Van Gisbergen set up Ali McKenzie who drove over, but Edinburgh hit back through Rob Dewey as he caught Matt Dey's offload to score.

Van Gisbergen made the scoreboard look healthier, adding another penalty, then twisting his way through the Edinburgh defence to touch down before slotting the conversion for good measure. Wasps' next score came from Simon Shaw just before the hour, and Tom Voyce made it try number five – stepping inside from the left wing.

Replacement Fraser Waters made a great impact by hitting an excellent line and giving a long pass to Voyce for the winger's second try. A penalty try awarded in favour of Wasps gave the hosts a handsome victory at the final whistle.

Venue: Causeway Stadium
Attendance: 7,303
Capacity: 10,200
Occupancy: 72%

Referee: Romain Poite

London Wasps
Edinburgh Gunners

Starting Line-Ups

London Wasps		Edinburgh Gunners
Van Gisbergen	15	Southwell
Sackey	14	Dewey
Erinle	13	Leonelli Morey
Hoadley	12	Dey
Voyce	11	Pyke
King	10	Godman
Reddan	9	Lawson
McKenzie	1	Hewett
Barrett	2	Kelly
Payne	3	Smith
Shaw	4	Kellock (c)
Skivington	5	Murray
Haskell	6	Mustchin
O'Connor	7	MacDonald
Hart (c)	8	Taylor

Replacements

Waters	22	Di Rollo
Staunton	21	Hodge
M Dawson	20	Blair
Gotting	19	Cross
Birkett	18	Strokosch
Bracken	17	Dickinson
Ibanez	16	Hall

Match Stats

Tackles	53	161
Missed Tackles	12	35
Ball Carries	181	70
Metres	966	420
Defenders Beaten	34	11
Passes	189	118
Clean Breaks	23	8
Pens Conceded	11	12
Turnovers	17	12
Breakdowns Won	115	38
% Scrums Won	100%	85%
% Line-Outs Won	70%	67%

Heineken Cup Table

Team	P	W	D	L	F	A	BP	Pts
1 Toulouse	6	5	1	0	188	124	3	25
2 London Wasps	6	2	1	3	173	118	4	14
3 Llanelli Scarlets	6	2	0	4	152	206	4	12
4 Edinburgh Gunners	6	2	0	4	121	186	3	11

Event Line

TC Try Converted
T Try
P Penalty
DG Drop Goal

Min	Score Progress		Event	Players
4	3	0	P	Van Gisbergen
14	3	5	T	Southwell
17	10	5	TC	King / Van Gisbergen
31	17	5	TC	McKenzie / Van Gisbergen
32	17	5	⇄	Blair > Lawson
34	17	5	⇄	Dickinson > Smith
35	17	10	T	Dewey
40	17	10	⇄	Lawson > Blair
40	17	10	▪	Mustchin
40	20	10	P	Van Gisbergen
Half time 20-10				
43	27	10	TC	Van Gisbergen / Van Gisbergen
50	32	10	T	Shaw
51	32	10	⇄	Cross > MacDonald
53	32	10	⇄	Hodge > Godman
56	32	10	⇄	Waters > Van Gisbergen
56	32	10	⇄	Birkett > Shaw
56	32	10	⇄	Gotting > Barrett
58	32	10	⇄	Di Rollo > Dey
58	39	10	TC	Voyce / King
61	39	10	⇄	Bracken > Payne
68	39	10	⇄	Blair > Pyke
71	39	10	⇄	Strokosch > Murray
74	46	10	TC	Voyce / King
78	46	17	TC	Lawson / Hodge
84	46	17	▪	Taylor
85	53	17	TC	Pen Try / King
Full time 53-17				

Scoring Statistics

London Wasps

by Situation: TC: 42, T: 5, P: 6, DG: 0

by Half: first: 38%, second: 62%

Edinburgh Gunners

by Situation: TC: 7, T: 10, P: 0, DG: 0

by Half: first: 59%, second: 41%

Bath Rugby 28
London Wasps 16

Guinness Premiership

28.01.06

Premiership Away Record vs Bath Rugby					
Played	Won	Drawn	Lost	For	Against
9	3	1	5	179	221

London Wasps resumed Premiership action by suffering a surprise defeat against a struggling Bath side at The Rec.

Quote

Ian McGeechan

We were second at a lot of things today and we never really got control of the business end of the game

An uncharacteristically poor defensive performance by the champions allowed the home team to outscore them by three tries to one. With the threat of relegation looming over their heads, Bath came out fighting and sheer bloody-minded determination led to a try for prop Duncan Bell after just five minutes.

Wasps just could not get into any sort of rhythm against the brute force of the West Country side's pack. After 12 minutes, fly-half Alex King reduced the deficit with a penalty, but both his kicking game and Wasps' general strategy were off-key on the day. A Chris Malone penalty extended Bath's lead as they squeezed the life out of Wasps.

Bath wing David Bory set up two more tries for Bath in the second half, scored by Eliota Fuimaono-Sapolu and Malone. Ayoola Erinle silenced The Rec crowd with a try from the restart following an 80-yard dash to the whitewash, but Wasps made further mistakes in the final 25 minutes to dim hopes of a recovery.

The visitors then made it mission impossible by conceding two penalties for Bath to gain a 28-13 lead. Jeremy Staunton pulled back three points near the end, but it was too little, too late to change the outcome.

Venue:	Recreation Ground	Referee:	David Rose - Season 05/06
Attendance:	10,600	Matches:	6
Capacity:	10,600	Yellow Cards:	10
Occupancy:	100%	Red Cards:	0

Bath Rugby
London Wasps

Starting Line-Ups

Bath Rugby		London Wasps
Maddock	15	Lewsey
Higgins	14	Sackey
Crockett	13	Erinle
Fuimaono-Sapolu	12	Abbott
Bory	11	Voyce
Malone	10	King
Walshe	9	M Dawson
Stevens	1	McKenzie
Mears	2	Ibanez
Bell	3	Payne
Borthwick (c)	4	Shaw
Grewcock	5	Skivington
Beattie	6	Dallaglio (c)
Lipman	7	Worsley
Feau'nati	8	Hart

Replacements

Stephenson	22	Waters
Dunne	21	Staunton
Williams	20	Reddan
Delve	19	O'Connor
Short	18	Birkett
Flatman	17	Va'a
Dixon	16	Barrett

Match Stats

Tackles	87	124
Missed Tackles	18	25
Ball Carries	127	81
Metres	490	546
Defenders Beaten	25	18
Passes	144	93
Clean Breaks	3	1
Pens Conceded	7	14
Turnovers	13	18
Breakdowns Won	95	63
% Scrums Won	100%	86%
% Line-Outs Won	82%	75%

Premiership Table

Team	P	W	D	L	F	A	BP	Pts
1 Sale Sharks	13	10	1	2	323	232	3	45
2 London Wasps	13	9	1	3	332	245	5	43
3 Leicester Tigers	13	7	3	3	324	247	4	38

Event Line

TC Try Converted — P Penalty
T Try — DG Drop Goal

Min	Score Progress		Event	Players
5	7	0	TC	Bell / Malone
10	7	0	⇄	Delve > Lipman
10	7	0	⇄	Barrett > Ibanez
12	7	3	P	King
16	7	3	■	Crockett
18	7	3	⇄	Ibanez > Barrett
25	10	3	P	Malone
30	10	3	⇄	O'Connor > Hart
37	10	3	■	Higgins
38	10	6	P	King
Half time 10-6				
44	10	6	⇄	Va'a > McKenzie
45	15	6	T	Fuimaono-Sapolu
50	15	6	⇄	Reddan > Dawson
52	15	6	⇄	Birkett > Shaw
53	22	6	TC	Malone / Malone
56	22	13	TC	Erinle / King
58	22	13	⇄	Stephenson > Crockett
61	25	13	P	Malone
63	25	13	⇄	Flatman > Bell
64	25	13	■	O'Connor
68	25	13	⇄	Waters > Erinle
68	28	13	P	Malone
73	28	13	⇄	Staunton > King
74	28	13	■	Feau'nati
74	28	16	P	Staunton
Full time 28-16				

Scoring Statistics

Bath Rugby

by Situation		by Half	
TC:	14	first:	36%
T:	5	second:	64%
P:	9		
DG:	0		

London Wasps

by Situation		by Half	
TC:	7	first:	38%
T:	0	second:	63%
P:	9		
DG:	0		

London Wasps 19
Northampton Saints 19

Guinness Premiership

12.02.06

Premiership Home Record vs Northampton Saints

Played	Won	Drawn	Lost	For	Against
9	6	1	2	236	125

A last-gasp Alex King drop goal preserved London Wasps' unbeaten home record as the champions sluttered to a draw against Northampton.

Quote

Lawrence Dallaglio

I think a draw was a fair result. This is a difficult time of the season for us, we have to regroup, hang in there and get the points where we can.

Despite the exciting climax, the game was far from being a Guinness Premiership classic, with rain-soaked conditions leading to countless handling errors.

Wasps took the lead via an Alex King penalty after seven minutes, but Saints struck back immediately through a Jon Clarke try, with Bruce Reihana converting to give Northampton a 7-3 lead. King pulled his side back with a long range penalty, but Wasps generally found it difficult to execute their moves and a Reihana penalty extended Northampton's lead before half-time.

Two further Reihana penalties saw Saints stretch their lead to ten points, but Wasps kept plugging away. Mark Van Gisbergen narrowed Northampton's lead with a try then sent over a penalty before Reihana responded with another three-pointer to take his side 16-19 ahead.

It was therefore left to King, who was playing on despite a fractured thumb, to save Wasps at the death, his drop goal securing the draw at full time.

Venue:	Causeway Stadium	Referee:	Rob Debney - Season 05/06
Attendance:	8,143	Matches:	8
Capacity:	10,200	Yellow Cards:	9
Occupancy:	80%	Red Cards:	0

London Wasps
Northampton Saints

Starting Line-Ups

London Wasps		Northampton Saints
Van Gisbergen	15	Kydd
Sackey	14	Rudd
Hoadley	13	Clarke
Abbott	12	Quinlan
Erinle	11	Reihana (c)
King	10	Spencer
Reddan	9	Robinson
Payne	1	Smith
Barrett	2	Richmond
Bracken	3	Budgen
Skivington	4	Dm Browne
Birkett	5	Lord
Rees	6	Tupai
O'Connor	7	Lewitt
Dallaglio (c)	8	Dn Browne

Replacements

Laird	22	Pritchard
Staunton	21	Howard
M Dawson	20	Fox
Haskell	19	Harding
Leo	18	Gerard
Va'a	17	Emms
Gotting	16	Hartley

Match Stats

Tackles	81	103
Missed Tackles	16	8
Ball Carries	102	87
Metres	301	349
Defenders Beaten	8	16
Passes	65	48
Clean Breaks	5	3
Pens Conceded	7	15
Turnovers	16	16
Breakdowns Won	84	63
% Scrums Won	100%	94%
% Line-Outs Won	81%	57%

Premiership Table

Team	P	W	D	L	F	A	BP	Pts
1 Sale Sharks	14	11	1	2	371	265	4	50
2 London Wasps	14	9	2	3	351	264	5	45
3 Gloucester Rugby	14	8	1	5	315	239	6	40

Event Line

TC Try Converted — P Penalty
T Try — DG Drop Goal

Min	Score Progress		Event	Players
6	3	0	P	King
7	3	7	TC	Clarke / Reihana
11	6	7	P	King
28	6	10	P	Reihana
Half time 6-10				
42	6	13	P	Reihana
52	6	13	⇄	Gerard > Lord
52	6	16	P	Reihana
54	13	16	TC	Van Gisbergen / King
57	13	16	⇄	Va'a > Payne
57	13	16	⇄	Haskell > Rees
57	13	16	⇄	Fox > Lewitt
63	13	16	⇄	Emms > Smith
63	13	16	⇄	Hartley > Richmond
63	13	16	⇄	Dawson > Reddan
65	13	16	⇄	Payne > Bracken
68	13	16	■	Spencer
69	13	16	⇄	Gotting > Barrett
69	13	16	⇄	Leo > Birkett
69	13	16	⇄	Harding > Tupai
69	16	16	P	Van Gisbergen
74	16	19	P	Reihana
76	19	19	DG	King
Full time 19-19				

Scoring Statistics

London Wasps

by Situation		by Half	
TC:	7	first:	32%
T:	0	second:	68%
P:	9		
DG:	3		

Northampton Saints

by Situation		by Half	
TC:	7	first:	53%
T:	0	second:	47%
P:	12		
DG:	0		

Bristol Rugby 9
London Wasps 9

Guinness Premiership

19.02.06

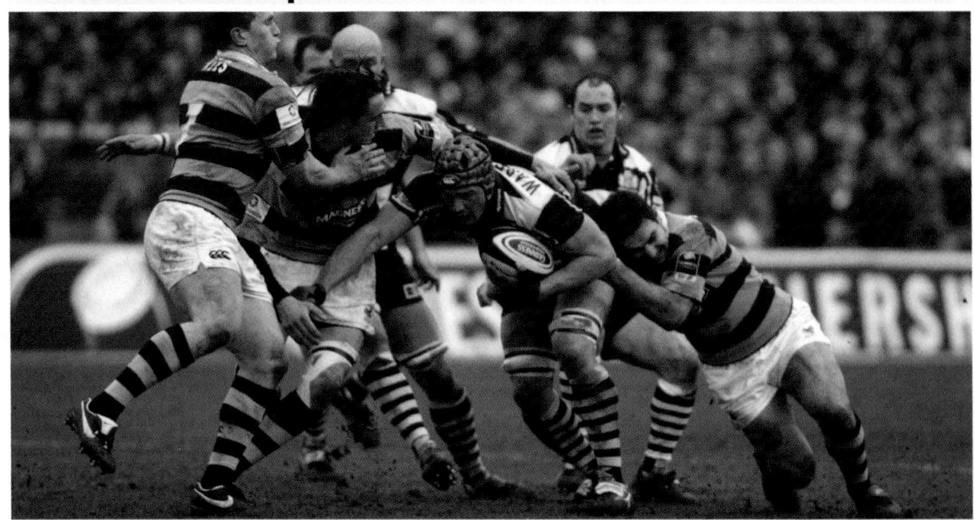

Premiership Away Record vs Bristol Rugby

Played	Won	Drawn	Lost	For	Against
6	3	1	2	140	124

London Wasps recorded their second GUINNESS PREMIERSHIP draw against Bristol in 2005/06 after a gutsy affair at the Memorial Stadium.

Quote

Ian McGeechan

The line-out has been going well, but today wasn't a good day. Bristol are competitive. Probably half the league are still in the (relegation) equation, and a good side will go down.

Bristol's Tommy Hayes opened the scoring but the home team's eagerness at the breakdown quickly led to an equalising penalty from Mark Van Gisbergen. Stuart Abbott then was replaced by Ayoola Erinle after just nine minutes with a calf problem as Wasps reshuffled the backs' department.

Bristol continued to add pressure in the collision zone while Wasps, in contrast, were looking to pick up the pace. Then handling errors meant that continuity was missing from the visitors attack.

A second Hayes penalty nudged his side ahead and Bristol's confidence was clear. Wasps struggled for possession from the line-out, and Hayes missed another penalty attempt that would have put Bristol 9-3 ahead. When Wasps finally put together some phases on the half-hour, but Bristol were able to slow down the ball effectively, thus stifling any danger.

This tactic subsequently back-fired, and the hosts conceded a penalty that allowed Van Gisbergen to re-establish parity with a straightforward kick before Jeremy Staunton added another penalty that put Wasps 9-6 up at the break. Just before the hour, Jason Strange levelled matters and the game was concluded as a gruelling stalemate that did neither side any long-term favours.

Venue:	Memorial Stadium	Referee:	Ashley Rowden - Season 05/06
Attendance:	9,028	Matches:	7
Capacity:	12,000	Yellow Cards:	9
Occupancy:	75%	Red Cards:	0

Bristol Rugby
London Wasps

Starting Line-Ups

Bristol Rugby		London Wasps
Stortoni	15	Van Gisbergen
Robinson	14	Sackey
Higgitt	13	Hoadley
Cox	12	Abbott
Lemi	11	Voyce
Hayes	10	Staunton
Perry	9	M Dawson
Hilton	1	Payne
Regan	2	Barrett
Crompton	3	Bracken
Budgett	4	Shaw
Llewellyn	5	Skivington
Salter (c)	6	Leo
Short	7	Rees
Ward-Smith	8	Dallaglio (c)

Replacements

Going	22	Waters
Strange	21	Erinle
Nicholls	20	Reddan
Lewis	19	O'Connor
Sambucetti	18	Lock
Nelson	17	Va'a
Clarke	16	Gotting

Match Stats

	Bristol Rugby	London Wasps
Tackles	96	72
Missed Tackles	6	11
Ball Carries	62	94
Metres	294	332
Defenders Beaten	11	6
Passes	75	100
Clean Breaks	4	11
Pens Conceded	10	13
Turnovers	12	17
Breakdowns Won	60	79
% Scrums Won	80%	73%
% Line-Outs Won	100%	78%

Premiership Table

Team	P	W	D	L	F	A	BP	Pts
1 Sale Sharks	15	12	1	2	406	289	5	55
2 London Wasps	15	9	3	3	360	273	5	47
3 Gloucester Rugby	15	9	1	5	328	248	6	44

Event Line

TC Try Converted — P Penalty
T Try — DG Drop Goal

Min	Score Progress		Event	Players
4	3	0	P	Hayes
6	3	3	P	Van Gisbergen
10	3	3	⇄	Erinle > Abbott
19	6	3	P	Hayes
32	6	6	P	Van Gisbergen
39	6	9	P	Staunton
Half time 6-9				
47	6	9	⇄	Va'a > Bracken
50	6	9	⇄	Gotting > Barrett
50	6	9	⇄	Strange > Hayes
51	6	9	⇄	O'Connor > Rees
54	6	9	⇄	Waters > Voyce
58	9	9	P	Strange
64	9	9	⇄	Going > Stortoni
64	9	9	⇄	Sambucetti > Budgett
Full time 9-9				

Scoring Statistics

Bristol Rugby

by Situation		by Half	
TC:	0	first:	67%
T:	0	second:	33%
P:	9		
DG:	0		

London Wasps

by Situation		by Half	
TC:	0	first:	100%
T:	0	second:	0%
P:	9		
DG:	0		

London Wasps 26
Sale Sharks 16

Guinness Premiership

26.02.06

Quote

Ian McGeechan

The determination that the players showed in the last few minutes, to deny Sale even a bonus point, reflected their attitude throughout the match.

Premiership Home Record vs Sale Sharks

Played	Won	Drawn	Lost	For	Against
9	5	0	4	273	217

London Wasps stretched their unbeaten home record to 13 months with a deserved triumph over league leaders Sale Sharks.

In the absence of senior scrum-halves Matt Dawson and Eoin Reddan, teenager James Honeyben rose to the occasion on his GUINNESS PREMIERSHIP debut, guiding the champions to victory against the favourites.

But it didn't all go according to plan as Sale's Robert Todd opened the scoring following a defensive error. In actual fact, it wasn't until near the hour mark that Wasps hit back with Man of the Match, Richard Birkett scoring a try to draw level. The response coincided with a treble substitution. Lawrence Dallaglio, Simon Shaw and Tom Voyce – all returning from England duty – taking the field to make an immediate impact.

Shaw's surging run up-field sparked off a move that culminated in a Rob Hoadley try, and Van Gisbergen added his fourth penalty in the dying minutes to seal the victory. On paper, Sale looked the stronger side, with captain Jason Robinson alongside Steve Hanley and Oriol Ripol, but Wasps upset the odds in style.

Venue:	Causeway Stadium	Referee:	Roy Maybank - Season 05/06	London Wasps
Attendance:	10,000	Matches:	12	Sale Sharks
Capacity:	10,200	Yellow Cards:	18	
Occupancy:	98%	Red Cards:	0	

Starting Line-Ups

London Wasps		Sale Sharks
Van Gisbergen	**15**	Robinson (c)
Sackey	**14**	Ripol Fortuny
Erinle	**13**	Taylor
Waters	**12**	Todd
Hoadley	**11**	Hanley
Staunton	**10**	Wigglesworth
Honeyben	**9**	Martens
McKenzie	**1**	Coutts
Ward	**2**	Titterrell
Payne (c)	**3**	Turner
Skivington	**4**	Fernandez Lobbe
Birkett	**5**	Schofield
Leo	**6**	Jones
Rees	**7**	Lund
Lock	**8**	Bonner-Evans

Replacements

Voyce	**22**	Mayor
Brooks	**21**	Wakley
Biljon	**20**	Courrent
Shaw	**19**	Chabal
Dallaglio	**18**	Day
J Dawson	**17**	Stewart
Barrett	**16**	Faure

Match Stats

	London Wasps	Sale Sharks
Tackles	95	116
Missed Tackles	24	16
Ball Carries	133	105
Metres	474	421
Defenders Beaten	16	25
Passes	124	89
Clean Breaks	9	6
Pens Conceded	16	14
Turnovers	8	5
Breakdowns Won	94	83
% Scrums Won	90%	100%
% Line-Outs Won	69%	85%

Premiership Table

Team	P	W	D	L	F	A	BP	Pts
1 Sale Sharks	16	12	1	3	422	315	5	55
2 London Wasps	16	10	3	3	386	289	5	51
3 Gloucester Rugby	16	9	1	6	343	266	7	45

Event Line

TC Try Converted　P Penalty
T Try　DG Drop Goal

Min	Score Progress		Event	Players
8	3	0	P	Van Gisbergen
12	3	7	TC	Todd / Wigglesworth
23	6	7	P	Van Gisbergen
28	6	10	P	Wigglesworth
30	6	10		Fernandez Lobbe
30	6	10	⇄	Dallaglio > Lock
30	9	10	P	Van Gisbergen
32	9	10	⇄	Lock > Dallaglio
33	9	13	P	Wigglesworth
Half time 9-13				
47	9	13	⇄	Chabal > Bonner-Evans
47	9	16	P	Wigglesworth
49	9	16	⇄	Barrett > Ward
56	9	16	⇄	Shaw > Skivington
56	9	16	⇄	Dallaglio > Leo
56	9	16	⇄	Voyce > Sackey
58	16	16	TC	Birkett / Van Gisbergen
60	16	16	⇄	Stewart > Turner
60	16	16	⇄	Faure > Coutts
61	16	16	⇄	Dawson > Payne
64	16	16	⇄	Mayor > Ripol Fortuny
68	23	16	TC	Hoadley / Van Gisbergen
71	23	16	⇄	Day > Schofield
72	23	16		Chabal
75	26	16	P	Van Gisbergen
77	26	16	⇄	Biljon > Honeyben
Full time 26-16				

Scoring Statistics

London Wasps

by Situation		by Half	
TC:	14	first:	35%
T:	0	second:	65%
P:	12		
DG:	0		

Sale Sharks

by Situation		by Half	
TC:	7	first:	81%
T:	0	second:	19%
P:	9		
DG:	0		

London Wasps 22
Leicester Tigers 17

Powergen Cup

04.03.06

Quote

Lawrence Dallaglio

We have played some rubbish rugby in the last few weeks, but I think today you saw the true Wasps. Today's win is the result of a massive effort from everyone.

London Wasps booked a place in the Powergen Cup Final after sweeping aside arch-rivals Leicester at Cardiff's Millennium Stadium.

In front of an expectant crowd, Wasps produced an accomplished performance to dominate the opening hour, and even a late Tigers revival could not take the gloss off the occasion.

Wasps were clinical, showing courage and discipline despite a potentially unsettling last minute change to the starting line-up. Regular place-kicker Mark Van Gisbergen was forced to withdraw minutes from kick-off after suffering a back spasm. As a result, Jeremy Staunton was handed kicking responsibilities and Ayoola Erinle was given a starting berth – both seizing the opportunity to shine with aplomb.

Staunton contributed five penalties and one conversion in an impeccable kicking display and Erinle's second half try, starting from inside his own 22, sealed victory for McGeechan's men.

Leicester attempted a late revival but the score from Leicester's Dan Hipkiss proved to be nothing more than a consolation.

Afterwards, Ian McGeechan looked forward to his first Cup Final outing with the club: "Raphael Ibanez said to me, 'Now I know what it is to be a Wasp,' and I concur. It's a great feeling."

Venue:	Millennium Stadium	Referee:	Nigel Owens
Attendance:	50,811		
Capacity:	74,500		
Occupancy:	68%		

London Wasps
Leicester Tigers

Starting Line-Ups

London Wasps		Leicester Tigers
Erinle	15	Vesty
Lewsey	14	Murphy
Waters	13	Lloyd
Abbott	12	Hipkiss
Voyce	11	Varndell
Staunton	10	Goode
Reddan	9	Healey
McKenzie	1	Rowntree
Ibanez	2	Chuter
Payne	3	White
Shaw	4	Deacon
Birkett	5	Kay
Worsley	6	Corry (c)
O'Connor	7	Moody
Dallaglio (c)	8	Tuilagi

Replacements

London Wasps		Leicester Tigers
Van Gisbergen	22	Tuilagi
Brooks	21	Cornwell
M Dawson	20	Ellis
Haskell	19	Jennings
Skivington	18	Cullen
J Dawson	17	Holford
Barrett	16	Buckland

Match Stats

	London Wasps	Leicester Tigers
Tackles	121	104
Missed Tackles	11	9
Ball Carries	96	103
Metres	592	439
Defenders Beaten	10	10
Passes	125	96
Clean Breaks	4	6
Pens Conceded	7	12
Turnovers	11	14
Breakdowns Won	74	78
% Scrums Won	89%	90%
% Line-Outs Won	92%	77%

Event Line

TC Try Converted
T Try
P Penalty
DG Drop Goal

Min	Score Progress		Event	Players
9	3	0	P	Staunton
11	6	0	P	Staunton
30	9	0	P	Staunton
32	9	0	⇄	Jennings > Tuilagi
33	9	5	T	Varndell
39	12	5	P	Staunton
Half time 12-5				
47	12	10	T	Lloyd
50	12	10	⇄	Dawson > McKenzie
59	15	10	P	Staunton
64	15	10	⇄	Haskell > O'Connor
64	15	10	⇄	Ellis > Healey
65	15	10	⇄	Brooks > Abbott
65	15	10	⇄	Dawson > Reddan
74	22	10	TC	Erinle / Staunton
75	22	10	⇄	Cullen > Kay
78	22	10	⇄	Holford > Rowntree
79	22	10	⇄	McKenzie > Payne
81	22	17	TC	Hipkiss / Goode
Full time 22-17				

Scoring Statistics

London Wasps

by Situation		by Half	
TC:	7	first:	55%
T:	0	second:	45%
P:	15		
DG:	0		

Leicester Tigers

by Situation		by Half	
TC:	7	first:	29%
T:	10	second:	71%
P:	0		
DG:	0		

Worcester Warriors 37
London Wasps 8

Guinness Premiership

10.03.06

Quote

Ian McGeechan

We lost it in the first half really. There were a lot of mistakes and the score could have been quite close, which would have lead to a very different second half.

Premiership Away Record vs Worcester Warriors					
Played	Won	Drawn	Lost	For	Against
2	0	0	2	32	64

An under-strength London Wasps side collapsed at Sixways as Worcester's seasoned pack dominated.

Stripped of nine senior players because of Six Nations duties, an inexperienced Wasps side faced a Worcester front-five packed with brawn and nous – and it led to a one-sided scoreline.

In a first half that was strewn with errors, Worcester capitalised on Wasps' mistakes and raced into a 23-8 half-time lead. As the home side grew in confidence, with Shane Drahm controlling matters in the second-half, the Warriors added a further 14 points to cement a deserved victory, via Phil Murphy and Aisea Havili.

In reply, Wasps managed just one touch down from Tom Rees, who just before the half-hour mark gathered a line-out throw and spun off the defence to drive over. Worcester charged Jeremy Staunton's conversion, which put him off his stride, and consequently the ball rebounded off the post.

Afterwards, Ian McGeechan said: "It was a poor performance from us, by far our worst of the season, which is disappointing as up to this point we had been playing pretty well when our internationals weren't with us."

Venue: Sixways
Attendance: 9,726
Capacity: 9,726
Occupancy: 100%

Referee: Sean Davey - Season 05/06
Matches: 13
Yellow Cards: 14
Red Cards: 0

Worcester Warriors
London Wasps

Starting Line-Ups

Worcester Warriors		London Wasps
Le Roux	15	Van Gisbergen
Havili	14	Sackey
Rasmussen	13	Waters
Lombard	12	Abbott
Tucker	11	Erinle
Drahm	10	Staunton
Gomarsall	9	Honeyben
Windo (c)	1	McKenzie
C Fortey	2	Ward
Taumoepeau	3	J Dawson
Murphy	4	Skivington
Gillies	5	Birkett
Horstmann	6	Leo
Harding	7	Rees
Hickey	8	Lock (c)

Replacements

Delport	22	Hoadley
Whatling	21	Brooks
Powell	20	Laird
Vaili	19	Chamberlain
O'Donoghue	18	Corker
L Fortey	17	Va'a
Hickie	16	Barrett

Match Stats

Tackles	98	73
Missed Tackles	12	7
Ball Carries	75	105
Metres	282	405
Defenders Beaten	7	13
Passes	88	113
Clean Breaks	5	9
Pens Conceded	17	12
Turnovers	12	17
Breakdowns Won	59	77
% Scrums Won	86%	86%
% Line-Outs Won	93%	67%

Premiership Table

Team	P	W	D	L	F	A	BP	Pts
1 Sale Sharks	17	12	1	4	431	330	6	56
2 London Wasps	17	10	3	4	394	326	5	51
3 Leicester Tigers	17	9	3	5	410	350	5	47

Event Line

TC Try Converted
T Try
P Penalty
DG Drop Goal

Min	Score Progress		Event	Players
5	3	0	P	Drahm
8	10	0	TC	Havili / Drahm
12	10	0		Ward
15	10	0	⇄	Barrett > Rees
17	10	3	P	Staunton
22	10	3	⇄	Rees > Barrett
25	13	3	P	Drahm
27	16	3	P	Drahm
30	16	8	T	Rees
40	23	8	TC	Pen Try / Drahm
Half time 23-8				
43	30	8	TC	Murphy / Drahm
54	30	8	⇄	Brooks > Staunton
55	30	8	⇄	Hickie > Fortey
55	30	8	⇄	Hoadley > Waters
56	30	8	⇄	Va'a > McKenzie
62	30	8	⇄	Vaili > Horstmann
63	30	8	⇄	Barrett > Ward
68	30	8		Sackey
69	30	8	⇄	O'Donoghue > Murphy
69	30	8	⇄	Fortey > Taumoepeau
70	30	8	⇄	Corker > Birkett
70	30	8	⇄	Delport > Tucker
73	30	8	⇄	Laird > Erinle
73	30	8	⇄	Chamberlain > Rees
77	37	8	TC	Delport / Drahm
80	37	8	⇄	Powell > Gomarsall
Full time 37-8				

Scoring Statistics

Worcester Warriors

by Situation		by Half	
TC:	28	first:	62%
T:	0	second:	38%
P:	9		
DG:	0		

London Wasps

by Situation		by Half	
TC:	0	first:	100%
T:	5	second:	0%
P:	3		
DG:	0		

London Wasps 28
Leeds Tykes 0

Guinness Premiership

26.03.06

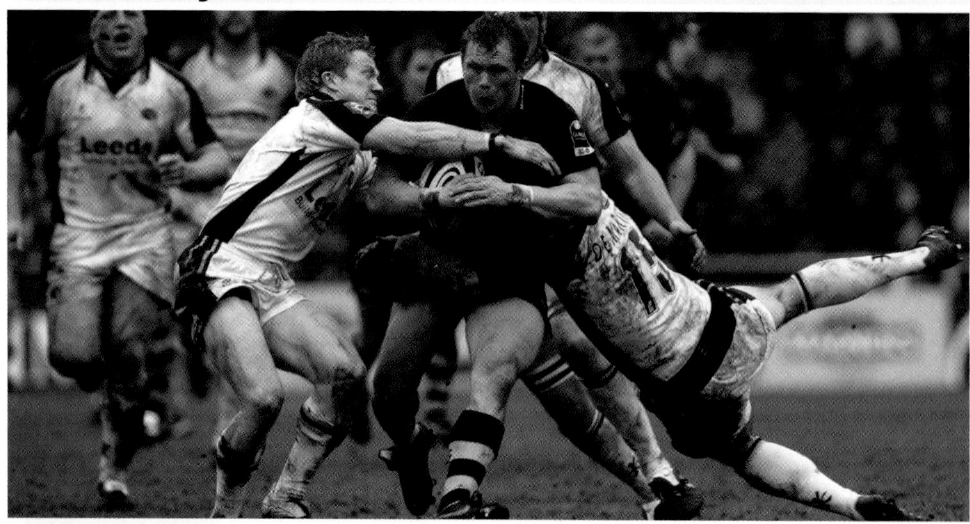

Premiership Home Record vs Leeds Tykes

Played	Won	Drawn	Lost	For	Against
5	4	1	0	182	66

London Wasps returned to winning ways with a four-try demolition of Leeds.

Quote

Ian McGeechan

I think it was the control we had for virtually the whole game that was pleasing.

As well as illustrating that Wasps' hunger for trophies was still intact, this game also showed the phenomenal versatility within the senior squad. Lions full-back Josh Lewsey was outstanding at centre alongside Stuart Abbott, and centre Ayoola Erinle performed well as a replacement for Paul Sackey on the wing.

Raphael Ibanez also had a brief run out on the blind side, replacing Joe Worsley five minutes from the end. England international Tom Voyce racked up two tries, with Mark Van Gisbergen and Sackey also contributing one a-piece as Wasps shut-out the doomed Tykes.

The champions' defence was solid and well-drilled with the front-five dominating up front. There was bad news for Tom Rees though, who had to be helped from the field after just 15 minutes with an ankle injury that ended his season.

After the huge win, Ian McGeechan said: 'I think it was the control we had for virtually the whole game that was pleasing. Our defence was outstanding. A lot of the set piece was good today too, and that gives you the ability to play."

Venue:	Causeway Stadium	Referee:	Ashley Rowden - Season 05/06
Attendance:	8,186	Matches:	9
Capacity:	10,200	Yellow Cards:	10
Occupancy:	80%	Red Cards:	0

London Wasps
Leeds Tykes

Starting Line-Ups

London Wasps		Leeds Tykes
Van Gisbergen	15	De Marigny
Sackey	14	Snyman
Lewsey	13	Bell
Abbott	12	Jones
Voyce	11	Biggs
Staunton	10	Ross
Reddan	9	Marshall
Payne	1	Kerr
Ward	2	Rawlinson
Bracken	3	Gerber
Shaw	4	Hooper (c)
Birkett	5	Palmer
Worsley	6	Hyde
Rees	7	Parks
Dallaglio (c)	8	Thomas

Replacements

Erinle	22	Blackett
Brooks	21	Balshaw
M Dawson	20	McMillan
Haskell	19	Crane
Leo	18	Murphy
McKenzie	17	Bulloch
Ibanez	16	Shelley

Match Stats

Tackles	148	98
Missed Tackles	7	12
Ball Carries	87	131
Metres	515	356
Defenders Beaten	8	7
Passes	115	128
Clean Breaks	12	7
Pens Conceded	16	9
Turnovers	20	21
Breakdowns Won	64	104
% Scrums Won	100%	86%
% Line-Outs Won	100%	100%

Premiership Table

Team	P	W	D	L	F	A	BP	Pts
1 Sale Sharks	18	13	1	4	460	351	6	60
2 London Wasps	18	11	3	4	422	326	6	56
3 Leicester Tigers	18	10	3	5	429	362	5	51

Event Line

TC Try Converted
T Try
P Penalty
DG Drop Goal

Min	Score Progress		Event	Players
4	7	0	TC	Voyce / Van Gisbergen
9	7	0	⇄	Crane > Hyde
13	7	0	⇄	Hyde > Crane
19	7	0	⇄	Leo > Rees
20	14	0	TC	Sackey / Van Gisbergen
22	14	0	⇄	Erinle > Sackey
30	14	0	⇄	Shelley > Gerber
39	14	0	■	Shaw
Half time 14-0				
41	14	0	⇄	Haskell > Birkett
41	14	0	⇄	Balshaw > Ross
41	14	0	⇄	Crane > Hyde
51	14	0	⇄	Bulloch > Rawlinson
55	21	0	TC	Voyce / Van Gisbergen
56	21	0	⇄	Gerber > Kerr
56	21	0	⇄	Dawson > Reddan
63	21	0	⇄	Brooks > Staunton
65	21	0	⇄	McKenzie > Bracken
70	21	0	⇄	Murphy > Palmer
76	21	0	⇄	Ibanez > Worsley
79	21	0	⇄	McMillan > Marshall
79	28	0	TC	Van Gisbergen / Van Gisbergen
80	28	0	■	Parks
80	28	0	■	Parks
Full time 28-0				

Scoring Statistics

London Wasps

by Situation		by Half	
TC:	28	first:	50%
T:	0	second:	50%
P:	0		
DG:	0		

Leeds Tykes

by Situation		by Half	
TC:	0	first:	0%
T:	0	second:	0%
P:	0		
DG:	0		

London Wasps 26
Llanelli Scarlets 10

Powergen Cup Final

09.04.06

London Wasps lifted their sixth trophy in four seasons after an exciting Powergen Cup Final win over Llanelli Scarlets at Twickenham.

In torrential rain, Wasps resurrected their uncanny knack of winning when it matters with a hugely professional performance.

But it wasn't all plain sailing for Wasps – Ireland flanker Jonny O'Connor was stretchered off with a neck injury just seconds into the game. Samoan forward Daniel Leo replaced the unfortunate Galwayman, and Wasps tried to get a grip on a stop-start opening 40 minutes of rugby, albeit with difficulty.

The poor weather seemed to favour Llanelli and the Scarlets' Barry Davies broke through to touch down within the opening 10 minutes. Referee Alan Lewis then handed Llanelli two penalty chances, but Mike Hercus could not convert either.

Mark Van Gisbergen finally put Wasps on the scoreboard with a successful penalty before Hercus extended the Celtic League side's lead early in the second quarter.

Wasps' fans at HQ began to question whether or not their name was on the trophy when the English champions' luck went from bad to worse. Prop Ali McKenzie was sin-binned and Simon Shaw gave away a penalty – though Hercus was again off target.

However, Jeremy Staunton's timely interception brought Wasps back into the game when the Irishman's pass enabled Tom Voyce to dart over the try-line.

In the second half, Stuart Abbott's breathtaking run and offload helped Voyce score his second try before an Alex King drop goal sealed a famous win at Twickenham.

Quote

Ian McGeechan

There's a great atmosphere at the club and it's good to be part of it. Winning this trophy has been very important to all of us.

Venue:	Twickenham	Referee:	Alan Lewis
Attendance:	57,212		
Capacity:	75,000		
Occupancy:	76%		

London Wasps
Llanelli Scarlets

Starting Line-Ups

London Wasps		Llanelli Scarlets
Van Gisbergen	**15**	Davies
Sackey	**14**	Jones
Lewsey	**13**	Watkins
Abbott	**12**	King
Voyce	**11**	James
Staunton	**10**	Hercus
Reddan	**9**	Stuart-Smith
McKenzie	**1**	John
Ibanez	**2**	Rees
Payne	**3**	Davies
Shaw	**4**	Afeaki
Birkett	**5**	Jones
Worsley	**6**	Easterby (c)
O'Connor	**7**	Thomas
Dallaglio (c)	**8**	Popham

Replacements

Erinle	**22**	Evans
King	**21**	Bowen
M Dawson	**20**	Davies
Haskell	**19**	Jones
Leo	**18**	Cooper
Bracken	**17**	Gravelle
Ward	**16**	Madden

Event Line

TC Try Converted — P Penalty
T Try — DG Drop Goal

Min	Score Progress		Event	Players
1	0	0	⇄	Leo > O'Connor
10	0	7	TC	Davies / Hercus
23	3	7	P	Van Gisbergen
24	3	10	P	Hercus
28	3	10	⇄	Jones > Easterby
29	3	10	■	McKenzie
31	3	10	⇄	Bracken > Leo
37	10	10	TC	Voyce / Van Gisbergen
39	10	10	⇄	Leo > Bracken
Half time 10-10				
53	17	10	TC	Voyce / Van Gisbergen
54	17	10	⇄	King > Staunton
54	17	10	⇄	Bracken > McKenzie
54	17	10	⇄	Dawson > Reddan
61	17	10	⇄	Ward > Ibanez
64	17	10	⇄	Madden > Davies
67	17	10	⇄	Cooper > Afeaki
69	20	10	P	Van Gisbergen
73	20	10	⇄	Gravelle > Rees
77	23	10	DG	King
79	23	10	⇄	Haskell > Worsley
80	26	10	P	Van Gisbergen
Full time 26-10				

Scoring Statistics

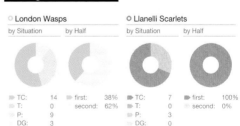

London Wasps

by Situation		by Half	
TC:	14	first:	38%
T:	0	second:	62%
P:	9		
DG:	3		

Llanelli Scarlets

by Situation		by Half	
TC:	7	first:	100%
T:	0	second:	0%
P:	3		
DG:	0		

Saracens 13
London Wasps 12

Guinness Premiership

16.04.06

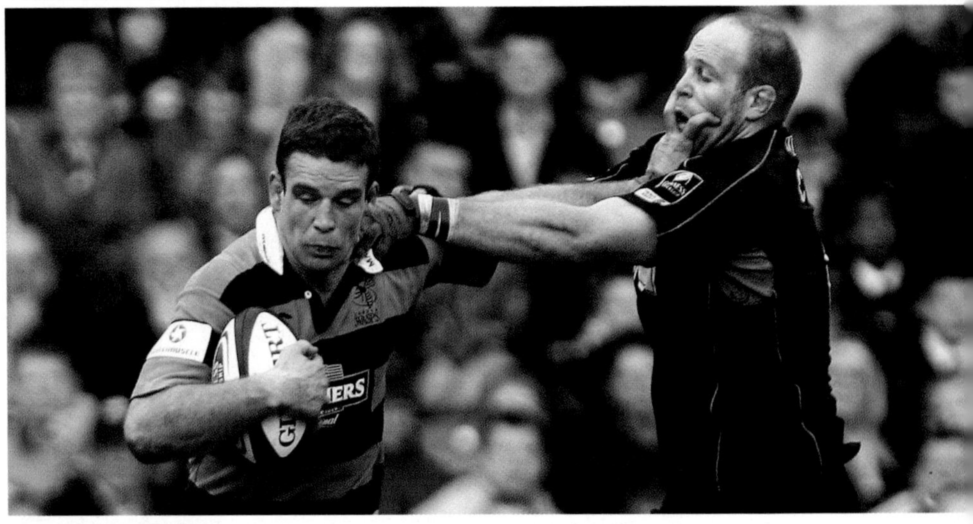

Premiership Away Record vs Saracens					
Played	Won	Drawn	Lost	For	Against
9	5	0	4	241	175

London Wasps fell victim to a Saracens' renaissance, spearheaded by French international Thomas Castaignede, as the visitors lost by a point at Vicarage Road.

Quote

Ian McGeechan

I'm disappointed that we weren't clinical enough and that we didn't score tries when we had the chances.

The major talking point for Wasps' supporters, however, was the ankle injury sustained by scrum-half Matt Dawson after he was hit late by Taine Randall. The 33-year-old had only just announced his forthcoming retirement at the end of the season.

With former Australia coach Eddie Jones revamping Sarries' general approach to good effect, the home side looked like a team with a point to prove and racked up an important win for them at the expense of travelsick Wasps.

Despite struggling to retain the ball from the outset, Wasps took the lead with a penalty from Mark Van Gisbergen. A second penalty followed minutes later, the Wasps full back again making no mistake from just inside his own half, but Saracens fly half Glen Jackson countered with three points of his own to put pressure on the visitors.

Van Gisbergen added a further three points before Thomas Castaignede scored the only try of the match. The decisive try from the mercurial Frenchman came after he danced his way through the Wasps' defence early in the second half. Wasps pulled back to within a point after Van Gisbergen slotted his fourth penalty of the day on the hour, but the home side hung on for a slender victory at full time.

Venue: Vicarage Road	Referee: Martin Fox - Season 05/06		Saracens
Attendance: 10,391	Matches: 9		London Wasps
Capacity: 20,000	Yellow Cards: 10		
Occupancy: 52%	Red Cards: 0		

Starting Line-Ups

Saracens		London Wasps
Bartholomeusz	15	Van Gisbergen
Castaignede	14	Sackey
Johnston	13	Lewsey
Sorrell	12	Abbott
Vaikona	11	Voyce
Jackson	10	King
Bracken	9	M Dawson
Yates	1	Payne
Byrne	2	Ward
Visagie	3	Bracken
Raiwalui	4	Leo
Ryder	5	Birkett
Chesney	6	Haskell
Randell	7	Worsley
Vyvyan (c)	8	Dallaglio (c)

Replacements

Scarbrough	22	Erinle
Harris	21	Staunton
Rauluni	20	Reddan
Russell	19	Corker
Broster	18	Lock
Lloyd	17	McKenzie
Cairns	16	Ibanez

Match Stats

	Saracens	London Wasps
Tackles	107	93
Missed Tackles	8	15
Ball Carries	95	104
Metres	525	465
Defenders Beaten	14	9
Passes	130	133
Clean Breaks	15	7
Pens Conceded	11	8
Turnovers	14	15
Breakdowns Won	84	86
% Scrums Won	100%	100%
% Line-Outs Won	80%	76%

Premiership Table

Team	P	W	D	L	F	A	BP	Pts
1 Sale Sharks	20	14	1	5	499	398	6	64
2 London Wasps	19	11	3	5	434	339	7	57
3 London Irish	20	12	0	8	407	399	8	56

Event Line

TC Try Converted — P Penalty
T Try — DG Drop Goal

Min	Score Progress		Event	Players
5	0	3	P	Van Gisbergen
13	0	6	P	Van Gisbergen
17	3	6	P	Jackson
26	3	9	P	Van Gisbergen
30	3	9	⇄	Reddan > Dawson
34	6	9	P	Jackson
Half time 6-9				
48	13	9	TC	Castaignede / Jackson
49	13	9	⇄	Rauluni > Bracken
49	13	9	⇄	Harris > Johnston
60	13	12	P	Van Gisbergen
65	13	12	⇄	McKenzie > Bracken
67	13	12	⇄	Erinle > Lewsey
67	13	12	⇄	Staunton > King
68	13	12	⇄	Cairns > Byrne
70	13	12	⇄	Ibanez > Ward
Full time 13-12				

Scoring Statistics

Saracens

by Situation		by Half	
TC:	7	first:	46%
T:	0	second:	54%
P:	6		
DG:	0		

London Wasps

by Situation		by Half	
TC:	0	first:	75%
T:	0	second:	25%
P:	12		
DG:	0		

Leicester Tigers 20
London Wasps 19

Guinness Premiership

22.04.06

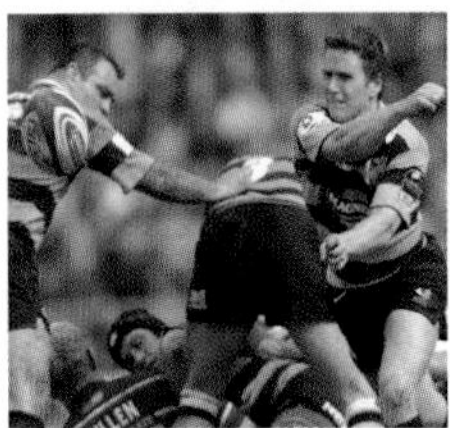

Premiership Away Record vs Leicester Tigers

Played	Won	Drawn	Lost	For	Against
9	0	0	9	121	268

London Wasps lost their second game by a one-point margin in as many weeks at Leicester.

Quote

Ian McGeechan

Our fate is still in our own hands. We've now got two wins to go for, and I believe we'll be there at the death.

Lapses in concentration by Wasps proved costly, with Tigers' wing Tom Varndell exploiting Wasps' mistakes with ruthless precision. The visitors began the match without the services of Joe Worsley, who was a last minute withdrawal through injury, and the team looked unsettled. After sensing a lack of cohesion in their opponents, Leicester came flying out of the blocks, and chalked up a lead within two minutes through Varndell, Andy Goode's conversion giving Leicester an early seven-point advantage.

Despite the stuttering start, Wasps managed to regroup and hit back through a Jeremy Staunton drop goal and a Mark Van Gisbergen penalty. But a penalty from Goode gave his team a four point cushion before lightning quick Varndell swept over the line again. Wasps managed to stay within touching distance – Van Gisbergen's second penalty pulling the visitors back into the game – but it was short-lived because, from the restart, Tigers' Shane Jennings capitalised on some generous defending to set-up Varndell for his hat-trick. A penalty chance for the visitors followed soon after though, Van Gisbergen bringing the score to 20-12 at half time.

After the break Wasps chased the game with genuine hunger. Van Gisbergen set up Paul Sackey to score and notched the conversion, making it 20-19 to Leicester. In the closing stages, Staunton saw his penalty attempt cannon off the posts in agonising fashion meaning that Wasps came away empty-handed.

Venue:	Welford Road	Referee:	Dave Pearson - Season 05/06
Attendance:	16,815	Matches:	14
Capacity:	16,815	Yellow Cards:	29
Occupancy:	100%	Red Cards:	2

Leicester Tigers
London Wasps

Starting Line-Ups

Leicester Tigers		London Wasps
Goode	15	Van Gisbergen
Tuilagi	14	Sackey
Smith	13	Erinle
Vesty	12	Hoadley
Varndell	11	Evans
Healey	10	Staunton
Bemand	9	Reddan
Holford	1	Payne
Buckland	2	Ibanez
White	3	Bracken
Cullen	4	Shaw
Kay	5	Birkett
Deacon	6	Leo
Jennings	7	Lock
Corry (c)	8	Dallaglio (c)

Replacements

Gibson	22	Abbott
Cornwell	21	King
Lloyd	20	Honeyben
Skinner	19	Barrett
Hamilton	18	Haskell
Young	17	Va'a
Chuter	16	Ward

Match Stats

	Leicester Tigers	London Wasps
Tackles	79	68
Missed Tackles	8	11
Ball Carries	68	85
Metres	371	487
Defenders Beaten	11	8
Passes	108	99
Clean Breaks	8	3
Pens Conceded	11	10
Turnovers	9	10
Breakdowns Won	65	61
% Scrums Won	100%	75%
% Line-Outs Won	89%	68%

Premiership Table

Team	P	W	D	L	F	A	BP	Pts
2 Leicester Tigers	20	12	3	5	473	400	5	59
3 London Wasps	20	11	3	6	453	359	8	58
4 London Irish	20	12	0	8	407	399	8	56

Event Line

TC Try Converted · P Penalty · T Try · DG Drop Goal

Min	Score Progress		Event	Players
2	7	0	TC	Varndell / Goode
6	7	3	DG	Staunton
15	7	6	P	Van Gisbergen
22	10	6	P	Goode
25	15	6	T	Varndell
32	15	9	P	Van Gisbergen
33	20	9	T	Varndell
40	20	12	P	Van Gisbergen
Half time 20-12				
49	20	12	⇄	Chuter > Buckland
49	20	12	⇄	Lloyd > Tuilagi
52	20	12	⇄	Gibson > Healey
53	20	19	TC	Sackey / Van Gisbergen
54	20	19	⇄	Abbott > Evans
55	20	19	⇄	Ward > Ibanez
59	20	19	⇄	Va'a > Bracken
64	20	19	⇄	Cornwell > Smith
64	20	19	⇄	Hamilton > Cullen
69	20	19	⇄	Bracken > Payne
72	20	19	⇄	Skinner > Jennings
Full time 20-19				

Scoring Statistics

Leicester Tigers

by Situation		by Half	
TC:	7	first:	100%
T:	10	second:	0%
P:	3		
DG:	0		

London Wasps

by Situation		by Half	
TC:	7	first:	63%
T:	0	second:	37%
P:	9		
DG:	3		

London Wasps 37
London Irish 56

Guinness Premiership

30.04.06

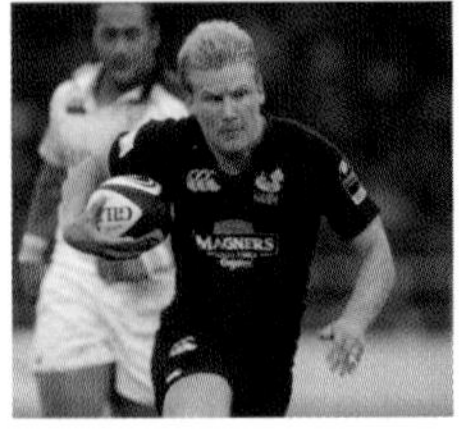

Quote

Ian McGeechan

It was a bizarre game but we didn't respect the ball enough. We've put ourselves in a position where we've got it all to do next week.

Premiership Home Record vs London Irish

Played	Won	Drawn	Lost	For	Against
9	6	0	3	273	229

London Wasps' unbeaten home record – stretching back 20 games – was finally overturned in bizarre fashion as London Irish ran in an unprecedented nine tries at High Wycombe.

Wasps' leading try scorer, Tom Voyce, recorded a hat-trick, but despite his 15 points he still ended up on the losing side. In a thrillingly open game, eight tries were scored within the opening half-hour as both teams threw caution to the wind and put the emphasis firmly on all-out attack.

Irish scored after 35 seconds through Dominic Feau'nati, but Wasps responded with Ayoola Erinle, Tom Voyce and Jeremy Staunton all getting on the score-sheet and Mark Van Gisbergen converting twice.

But Irish's response visibly shocked Wasps and ultimately determined the outcome of the match. Topsy Ojo, Riki Flutey, Sailosi Tagicakibau and Bob Casey all crossed the whitewash for the Exiles as the visitors clocked up a 29-19 lead.

An interception try from Voyce brought the sides level on the stroke of half-time and, moments after the interval, another score from the Cornishman put Wasps back in front. But rather than kill Irish off, the try seemed to spark them into life as Mike Catt and Delon Armitage both crossed the line. With Wasps surging forward in search of points, Irish exposed the gaps and secured victory with further tries from Ojo and Flutey.

Venue:	Causeway Stadium	Referee:	Tony Spreadbury - Season 05/06
Attendance:	10,000	Matches:	12
Capacity:	10,200	Yellow Cards:	10
Occupancy:	98%	Red Cards:	2

London Wasps
London Irish

Starting Line-Ups

London Wasps		London Irish
Van Gisbergen	15	Armitage
Sackey	14	Ojo
Erinle	13	Catt (c)
Abbott	12	Feau'nati
Voyce	11	Tagicakibau
Staunton	10	Flutey
Reddan	9	Hodgson
Payne	1	Hatley
Ibanez	2	Paice
Bracken	3	Skuse
Shaw	4	Casey
Birkett	5	Roche
Leo	6	Danaher
Lock	7	Magne
Dallaglio (c)	8	Leguizamon

Replacements

Lewsey	22	Geraghty
Waters	21	Willis
Honeyben	20	Tiesi
Worsley	19	Murphy
Haskell	18	Kennedy
Va'a	17	Russell
Ward	16	Collins

Match Stats

	London Wasps	London Irish
Tackles	75	109
Missed Tackles	10	24
Ball Carries	96	84
Metres	625	566
Defenders Beaten	23	10
Passes	124	85
Clean Breaks	13	7
Pens Conceded	7	8
Turnovers	19	10
Breakdowns Won	75	58
% Scrums Won	100%	100%
% Line-Outs Won	92%	91%

Premiership Table

Team	P	W	D	L	F	A	BP	Pts
3 London Irish	21	13	0	8	463	436	9	61
4 London Wasps	21	11	3	7	490	415	9	59
5 Gloucester Rugby	21	11	1	9	451	348	11	57

Event Line

Min	Score Progress		Event	Players
1	0	5	T	Feau'nati
3	5	5	T	Erinle
7	12	5	TC	Voyce / Van Gisbergen
9	12	10	T	Ojo
13	19	10	TC	Staunton / Van Gisbergen
17	19	17	TC	Flutey / Catt
20	19	22	T	Tagicakibau
26	19	29	TC	Casey / Catt
34	19	29		Paice
34	22	29	P	Van Gisbergen
37	22	29	⇄	Russell > Magne
40	29	29	TC	Voyce / Van Gisbergen
Half time 29-29				
41	29	29	⇄	Ward > Ibanez
41	34	29	T	Voyce
42	34	29	⇄	Collins > Hatley
43	34	29	⇄	Magne > Russell
43	34	36	TC	Catt / Catt
48	34	36	⇄	Lewsey > Sackey
48	34	36	⇄	Worsley > Lock
50	34	36	⇄	Russell > Paice
51	34	36	⇄	Va'a > Bracken
51	34	43	TC	Armitage / Catt
53	34	43	⇄	Kennedy > Casey
56	34	43	⇄	Bracken > Va'a
59	34	43	⇄	Willis > Hodgson
60	37	43	P	Van Gisbergen
62	37	43	⇄	Tiesi > Feau'nati
62	37	43	⇄	Murphy > Leguizamon
63	37	43	⇄	Haskell > Leo
73	37	43	⇄	Paice > Skuse
74	37	43	⇄	Waters > Abbott
76	37	46	P	Flutey
78	37	51	T	Ojo
80	37	51	⇄	Geraghty > Catt
80	37	56	T	Flutey
Full time 37-56				

Scoring Statistics

London Wasps

by Situation

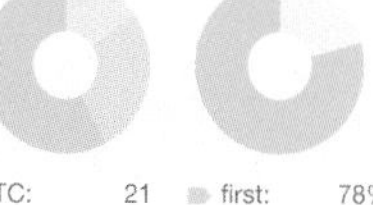

TC:	21
T:	10
P:	6
DG:	0

by Half

first:	78%
second:	22%

London Irish

by Situation

TC:	28
T:	25
P:	3
DG:	0

by Half

first:	52%
second:	48%

Gloucester Rugby 32
London Wasps 37

Guinness Premiership

06.05.06

Quote

Lawrence Dallaglio

You don't become champions three times running without having fighting spirit. We showed a lot of courage and heart to come here and get the result.

Premiership Away Record vs Gloucester Rugby

Played	Won	Drawn	Lost	For	Against
9	4	0	5	187	207

London Wasps produced a magnificent performance to seal a place in the play-offs at Gloucester's expense in one of the games of the season at Kingsholm.

The Cherry & Whites were favourites to win but Wasps had clearly not read the script as they staged a remarkable late comeback.

Backed by a vocal Kingsholm crowd, Gloucester took the lead on nine minutes when Anthony Allen cut through the midfield to score. However, Man of the Match Lamb missed the conversion, and two penalties from Mark Van Gisbergen put Wasps in front before Joe Worsley extended the visitors lead with a try. Van Gisbergen continued with an inspired sortie upfield that culminated in a well-taken try and conversion, but before the break, Lamb nailed a penalty to narrow Wasps' advantage to 20-8 at half time.

Gloucester came out after the interval with all guns blazing and conjured up three stunning tries to set up a tense climax. Allen, Lamb and James Bailey all swept over the line to suggest that Wasps were in danger of crashing out of the play-offs, but the unshakeable self-belief synonymous with the Wasps team of the last few seasons came to the fore, with a Van Gisbergen penalty and Paul Sackey try narrowing Gloucester's lead to two points. Then, with five minutes left, Worsley was perfectly placed to collect Tom Voyce's off-load and finish with expertise to book a place for his team in the last four of the GUINNESS PREMIERSHIP.

Venue:	Kingsholm	Referee:	Tony Spreadbury - Season 05/06
Attendance:	12,500	Matches:	13
Capacity:	13,000	Yellow Cards:	11
Occupancy:	96%	Red Cards:	2

Gloucester Rugby
London Wasps

Starting Line-Ups

Gloucester Rugby		London Wasps
Morgan	15	Van Gisbergen
Simpson-Daniel	14	Sackey
Tindall	13	Lewsey
Allen	12	Abbott
Foster	11	Voyce
Lamb	10	Staunton
Richards	9	Reddan
Collazo	1	Payne
Davies	2	Ward
Forster	3	Bracken
Pendlebury	4	Shaw
Brown	5	Birkett
Buxton (c)	6	Leo
Hazell	7	Worsley
Forrester	8	Dallaglio (c)

Replacements

Bailey	22	Waters
Mercier	21	King
Thomas	20	Honeyben
Narraway	19	Haskell
Eustace	18	Lock
Sigley	17	Va'a
Azam	16	Barrett

Match Stats

	Gloucester Rugby	London Wasps
Tackles	110	75
Missed Tackles	18	17
Ball Carries	68	104
Metres	596	524
Defenders Beaten	14	15
Passes	81	134
Clean Breaks	11	9
Pens Conceded	6	9
Turnovers	15	15
Breakdowns Won	47	76
% Scrums Won	100%	60%
% Line-Outs Won	94%	100%

Premiership Table

Team	P	W	D	L	F	A	BP	Pts
3 London Irish	22	14	0	8	493	454	10	66
4 London Wasps	22	12	3	7	527	447	10	64
5 Gloucester Rugby	22	11	1	10	483	385	13	59

Event Line

TC Try Converted · T Try · P Penalty · DG Drop Goal

Min	Score Progress		Event	Players
9	5	0	T	Allen
16	5	3	P	Van Gisbergen
16	5	6	P	Van Gisbergen
24	5	13	TC	Worsley / Van Gisbergen
32	5	20	TC	Van Gisbergen / Van Gisbergen
37	8	20	P	Lamb
Half time 8-20				
41	8	20	⇄	Bailey > Tindall
41	8	20	⇄	Thomas > Richards
42	15	20	TC	Allen / Lamb
44	22	20	TC	Lamb / Lamb
48	22	20	▮	Worsley
49	25	20	P	Lamb
59	32	20	TC	Bailey / Lamb
63	32	23	P	Van Gisbergen
64	32	23	⇄	Narraway > Forrester
68	32	30	TC	Sackey / Van Gisbergen
69	32	30	⇄	Mercier > Lamb
69	32	30	⇄	Eustace > Pendlebury
69	32	30	⇄	Azam > Davies
73	32	30	⇄	Waters > Abbott
73	32	30	⇄	Sigley > Collazo
74	32	30	⇄	Va'a > Bracken
75	32	37	TC	Worsley / Van Gisbergen
78	32	37	⇄	Honeyben > Reddan
Full time 32-37				

Scoring Statistics

Gloucester Rugby

by Situation		by Half	
TC:	21	first:	25%
T:	5	second:	75%
P:	6		
DG:	0		

London Wasps

by Situation		by Half	
TC:	28	first:	54%
T:	0	second:	46%
P:	9		
DG:	0		

Sale Sharks 22
London Wasps 12

Guinness Premiership Semi-Final

14.05.06

Premiership Away Record vs Sale Sharks

Played	Won	Drawn	Lost	For	Against
9	5	1	3	234	198

London Wasps surrendered their GUINNESS PREMIERSHIP crown at Edgeley Park as eventual Champions Sale won 22-12 to progress to the Premiership Final.

Quote

Ian McGeechan

We gave it everything today and obviously we are very disappointed not to have won. Good luck to Sale ... I hope they do well in the final.

Sale had finished the regular season in top spot, and showed why with a convincing performance. The defining moments were an early hamstring injury to Tom Voyce, quickly followed by a sparkling try from Sale captain Jason Robinson.

In front of a vocal home crowd, the Sharks took an early lead through a Charlie Hodgson penalty. In fact, Hodgson kicked accurately throughout – even though a huge hit from Simon Shaw left the England stand-off nursing a painful rib injury. Wasps struggled to generate any momentum against a Sale side who persistently turned the ball over and dominated the line-out. The champions restored parity via a Mark Van Gisbergen penalty, although two further penalties from Hodgson's boot brought the partisan crowd back to life before Robinson crossed the line.

After the half-time interval, another Van Gisbergen penalty reduced the home team's lead to ten points, and Wasps gradually steadied the ship as another two Van Gisbergen kicks reduced the margin on the scoreboard even further. But it proved something of a false dawn. Despite the introduction of replacements Raphael Ibanez and Matt Dawson, Wasps could not find a way past the impenetrable blue wall of Sale's defence. The final nail in the coffin was a late penalty from Hodgson that signalled Wasps three year reign as Champions was over.

Venue:	Edgeley Park	Referee:	Chris White - Season 05/06
Attendance:	10,641	Matches:	12
Capacity:	10,641	Yellow Cards:	4
Occupancy:	100%	Red Cards:	1

Sale Sharks
London Wasps

Starting Line-Ups

Sale Sharks		London Wasps
Robinson (c)	15	Van Gisbergen
Cueto	14	Sackey
Taylor	13	Lewsey
Seveali'i	12	Abbott
Ripol Fortuny	11	Voyce
Hodgson	10	Staunton
Martens	9	Reddan
Faure	1	Payne
Titterrell	2	Ward
Turner	3	Bracken
Fernandez Lobbe	4	Shaw
Jones	5	Birkett
White	6	Leo
Lund	7	Worsley
Chabal	8	Dallaglio (c)

Replacements

Mayor	22	Waters
Courrent	21	King
Foden	20	M Dawson
Day	19	Haskell
Schofield	18	Lock
Stewart	17	Va'a
Bruno	16	Ibanez

Match Stats

	Sale Sharks	London Wasps
Tackles	121	96
Missed Tackles	15	24
Ball Carries	124	132
Metres	453	517
Defenders Beaten	25	16
Passes	82	116
Clean Breaks	12	9
Pens Conceded	15	9
Turnovers	10	16
Breakdowns Won	84	93
% Scrums Won	100%	89%
% Line-Outs Won	79%	63%

Premiership Table

Team	P	W	D	L	F	A	BP	Pts
2 Sale Sharks	1	1	0	0	22	12	0	4
3 London Wasps	1	0	0	1	12	22	0	0
4 London Irish	1	0	0	1	8	40	0	0

Event Line

TC Try Converted
T Try
P Penalty
DG Drop Goal

Min	Score Progress		Event	Players
1	3	0	P	Hodgson
5	3	3	P	Van Gisbergen
16	6	3	P	Hodgson
18	6	3	⇄	Waters > Voyce
18	6	3	⇄	Haskell > Leo
20	9	3	P	Hodgson
24	9	3	⇄	Leo > Haskell
31	16	3	TC	Robinson / Hodgson
Half time 16-3				
43	16	6	P	Van Gisbergen
45	19	6	P	Hodgson
49	19	6	⇄	Haskell > Birkett
51	19	6	⇄	Bruno > Titterrell
51	19	9	P	Van Gisbergen
55	19	9	⇄	Dawson > Reddan
55	19	9	⇄	Ibanez > Ward
55	19	9	⇄	Stewart > Turner
59	19	9	⇄	Foden > Martens
59	19	9	⇄	King > Staunton
61	19	9	⇄	Schofield > Fernandez Lobbe
61	19	9	⇄	Mayor > Seveali'i
65	19	12	P	Van Gisbergen
72	19	12	⇄	Va'a > Payne
73	19	12	⇄	Day > Lund
73	19	12	⇄	Lock > Leo
78	22	12	P	Hodgson
79	22	12	⇄	Turner > Faure
79	22	12	⇄	Lund > Day
Full time 22-12				

Scoring Statistics

Sale Sharks

by Situation		by Half	
TC:	7	first:	73%
T:	0	second:	27%
P:	15		
DG:	0		

London Wasps

by Situation		by Half	
TC:	0	first:	25%
T:	0	second:	75%
P:	12		
DG:	0		

Player Profiles

adidas

DAWSON
9
HASKELL
6
ABBOT ALE

Stuart Abbott
Centre

Date of Birth:	03.06.1978
Place of Birth:	Cape Town
Qualified for:	England
Height:	6'
Weight:	14st 2lb

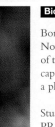

Biography

Born in South Africa, Stuart moved to Wasps in November 2001. He quickly established himself as one of the best centres in the English game, earning his first cap for England against Wales in August 2003 and later a place in England's World Cup winning squad.

Stuart made a welcome comeback to the GUINNESS PREMIERSHIP in 2005-6, having missed large chunks of the previous season with a series of injuries, his form winning him back his place in the Six Nations squad and selection for the summer tour of Australia.

Player Performance 05/06

Premiership Performance

Percentage of total possible time player was on pitch — position in league table at end of month

Month:	Sep	Oct	Nov	Dec	Jan	Feb	Mar	Apr	May	Total
% on pitch	100%	100%	75%	68%	87%	38%	100%	75%	96%	80%
League position	2	3	2	1	2	2	2	4	4	
League Pts:	16/20	0/5	13/20	10/10	4/10	8/15	5/10	3/15	5/10	64/115
Points F:	133	10	85	67	37	54	36	68	49	539
Points A:	83	18	66	44	34	44	37	89	54	469
Try Bonus:	2	0	0	2	0	0	1	1	1	7
Lose Bonus:	0	0	1	0	0	0	0	2	0	3
Total mins:	319	80	239	109	139	90	160	180	153	1,469
Starts (sub):	4	1	3	2	2	2	2	2 (1)	2	20 (1)
Points:	0	0	0	0	0	0	0	0	0	0
Tries:	0	0	0	0	0	0	0	0	0	0
Ball Carries:	26	4	11	8	11	4	15	16	12	107
Metres:	138	11	56	38	87	4	62	103	50	549
Tackles:	20	2	26	5	6	5	12	16	11	103

Prem. Performance Totals

Tries

Abbott:	0
Team-mates:	53
Total:	**53**

Points

Abbott:	0
Team-mates:	539
Total:	**539**

Cards

Abbott:	0
Team-mates:	9
Total:	**9**

Cup Games

	Apps	Pts
Heineken Cup	5	0
Powergen Cup	4	0
Total	**9**	**0**

Prem. Career History

Premiership Career Milestones

Club Debut:

vs Newcastle (H), L, 30-33

11.11.01

First Try Scored for the Club:

vs Leeds (H), W, 64-14

18.11.01

Time Spent at the Club:

5 Seasons

Full International:

England

Premiership Totals

97–06

Appearances	69
Points	50
Tries	10
Yellow Cards	1
Red Cards	0

Clubs

Year	Club	Apps	Pts
01-06	London Wasps	67	50
99-00	Leicester Tigers	2	0

Off the Pitch

Age:

- Abbott: 27 years, 11 months
- Team: 26 years, 2 months
- League: 26 years, 10 months

Height:

- Abbott: 6'
- Team: 6'1"
- League: 6'1"

Weight:

- Abbott: 14st 2lb
- Team: 16st
- League: 15st 10lb

Jonny Barrett
Hooker

Date of Birth:	20.12.1979
Place of Birth:	London
Nationality:	English
Height:	5'10"
Weight:	16st 4lb

Biography

Jonny Barrett is a talented young hooker and in 2005-6 enjoyed his best season with Wasps to date, showing good form to clock up 13 1XV appearances. He showed his flexibility, playing in the back row as well as at hooker for the A team.

Jonny was spotted by Wasps whilst at Millfield School and during his time at the club he has also captained the U21s and played for England Students. He has a BSc in Human Biology and is a qualified personal trainer.

Player Performance 05/06

Premiership Performance

Percentage of total possible time player was on pitch — position in league table at end of month

Month:	Sep	Oct	Nov	Dec	Jan	Feb	Mar	Apr	May	Total
League position	2	3	2	1	2	2	2	4	4	
% time on pitch	0%	0%	0%	15%	55%	63%	15%	0%	0%	16%
League Pts:	16/20	0/5	13/20	10/10	4/10	8/15	5/10	3/15	5/10	64/115
Points F:	133	10	85	67	37	54	36	68	49	539
Points A:	83	18	66	44	34	44	37	89	54	469
Try Bonus:	2	0	0	2	0	0	1	1	1	7
Lose Bonus:	0	0	1	0	0	0	0	2	0	3
Total mins:	0	0	0	24	88	150	24	0	0	286
Starts (sub):	0	0	0	0 (1)	1 (1)	2 (1)	0 (1)	0	0	3 (4)
Points:	0	0	0	0	0	0	0	0	0	0
Tries:	0	0	0	0	0	0	0	0	0	0
Ball Carries:	0	0	0	1	4	6	2	1	0	14
Metres:	0	0	0	9	19	21	4	0	0	53
Tackles:	0	0	0	6	10	11	0	3	0	30

Prem. Performance Totals

Tries

Barrett:	0
Team-mates:	53
Total:	**53**

Points

Barrett:	0
Team-mates:	539
Total:	**539**

Cards

Barrett:	0
Team-mates:	9
Total:	**9**

Cup Games

	Apps	Pts
Heineken Cup	4	0
Powergen Cup	2	0
Total	**6**	**0**

Prem. Career History

Premiership Career Milestones

Club Debut:

vs Sale (H), L, 21-40

16.09.01

First Try Scored for the Club:

–

–

Time Spent at the Club:

5 Seasons

Full International:

–

Premiership Totals

97–06

Appearances	14
Points	0
Tries	0
Yellow Cards	1
Red Cards	0

Clubs

Year	Club	Apps	Pts
01-06	London Wasps	14	0

Off the Pitch

Age:

Barrett: 26 years, 5 months
Team: 26 years, 2 months
League: 26 years, 10 months

Height:

Barrett: 5'10"
Team: 6'1"
League: 6'1"

Weight:

Barrett: 16st 4lb
Team: 16st
League: 15st 10lb

Richard Birkett
Lock

Date of Birth:	01.10.1979
Place of Birth:	Roehampton
Nationality:	English
Height:	6'3"
Weight:	17st 4lb

Biography

A product of the London Wasps Academy, Richard forced his way into the starting line up during the second half 2001-2 and has not looked back since, developing a powerful partnership with fellow lock Simon Shaw and running Wasps line out.

As a result he is now firmly entrenched in Wasps engine room, taking part in many of the club's most famous victories and also winning a place in England's Churchill Cup Squad in 2004.

Player Performance 05/06

Premiership Performance

Percentage of total possible time player was on pitch — position in league table at end of month

Month:	Sep	Oct	Nov	Dec	Jan	Feb	Mar	Apr	May	Total
% time on pitch	100%	100%	71%	0%	18%	62%	69%	100%	81%	70%
League position	2	3	2	1	2	2	2	4	4	
League Pts:	16/20	0/5	13/20	10/10	4/10	8/15	5/10	3/15	5/10	64/115
Points F:	133	10	85	67	37	54	36	68	49	539
Points A:	83	18	66	44	34	44	37	89	54	469
Try Bonus:	2	0	0	2	0	0	1	1	1	7
Lose Bonus:	0	0	1	0	0	0	0	2	0	3
Total mins:	320	80	226	0	28	149	110	240	129	1,282
Starts (sub):	4	1	3 (1)	0	0 (1)	2	2	3	2	17 (2)
Points:	0	0	0	0	0	5	0	0	0	5
Tries:	0	0	0	0	0	1	0	0	0	1
Ball Carries:	15	2	19	0	0	16	7	12	9	80
Metres:	34	6	34	0	0	31	9	20	28	162
Tackles:	30	0	28	0	2	17	15	21	9	122

Prem. Performance Totals

Tries

Birkett:	1
Team-mates:	52
Total:	**53**

Points

Birkett:	5
Team-mates:	534
Total:	**539**

Cards

Birkett:	0
Team-mates:	9
Total:	**9**

Cup Games

	Apps	Pts
Heineken Cup	5	0
Powergen Cup	4	0
Total	**9**	**0**

Prem. Career History

Premiership Career Milestones

Club Debut:

vs Bristol (A), L, 13-20

01.10.99

Time Spent at the Club:

7 Seasons

First Try Scored for the Club:

vs L Irish (A), W, 34-19

27.12.03

Full International:

–

Premiership Totals

97–06

Appearances	103
Points	20
Tries	4
Yellow Cards	0
Red Cards	0

Clubs

Year	Club	Apps	Pts
99-06	London Wasps	103	20

Off the Pitch

Age:

- Birkett: 26 years, 7 months
- Team: 26 years, 2 months
- League: 26 years, 10 months

Height:

- Birkett: 6'3"
- Team: 6'1"
- League: 6'1"

Weight:

- Birkett: 17st 4lb
- Team: 16st
- League: 15st 10lb

Peter Bracken
Prop

Date of Birth:	01.12.1977
Place of Birth:	Tullamore, Offaly, Ireland
Nationality:	Irish
Height:	6'2"
Weight:	18st 7lb

Biography

Prop Peter Bracken's move to Wasps from Connacht at the start of 2005-6 has led to recognition from both club and country for his skill and strength on the tight head side of the scrum, despite a disrupted season due to injury.

Fifteen starts included the Powergen Cup Final, and the end of the season brought a first Barbarians appearance and call up to the Ireland squad for their summer tour.

Player Performance 05/06

Premiership Performance

Percentage of total possible time player was on pitch — position in league table at end of month

Month:	Sep	Oct	Nov	Dec	Jan	Feb	Mar	Apr	May	Total
% on pitch	40%	33%	30%	0%	25%	47%	41%	88%	96%	45%
League position	2	3	2	1	2	2	2	4	4	
League Pts:	16/20	0/5	13/20	10/10	4/10	8/15	5/10	3/15	5/10	64/115
Points F:	133	10	85	67	37	54	36	68	49	539
Points A:	83	18	66	44	34	44	37	89	54	469
Try Bonus:	2	0	0	2	0	0	1	1	1	7
Lose Bonus:	0	0	1	0	0	0	0	2	0	3
Total mins:	128	26	97	0	40	112	65	210	154	832
Starts (sub):	1 (3)	0 (1)	1 (2)	0	1	2	1	3	2	11 (6)
Points:	0	0	0	0	0	0	0	0	0	0
Tries:	0	0	0	0	0	0	0	0	0	0
Ball Carries:	12	0	11	0	4	15	2	13	9	66
Metres:	22	0	18	0	23	43	14	26	10	156
Tackles:	4	1	6	0	2	4	8	13	11	49

Prem. Performance Totals

Tries

Bracken:	0
Team-mates:	53
Total:	**53**

Points

Bracken:	0
Team-mates:	539
Total:	**539**

Cards

Bracken:	0
Team-mates:	9
Total:	**9**

Cup Games

	Apps	Pts
Heineken Cup	4	0
Powergen Cup	4	0
Total	**8**	**0**

Prem. Career History

Premiership Career Milestones

Club Debut:

vs Saracens (H), W, 23-11

03.09.05

Time Spent at the Club:

1 Season

First Try Scored for the Club:

–

–

Full International:

–

Premiership Totals

97–06

Appearances	17
Points	0
Tries	0
Yellow Cards	0
Red Cards	0

Clubs

Year	Club	Apps	Pts
05-06	London Wasps	17	0

Off the Pitch

Age:

- Bracken: 28 years, 5 months
- Team: 26 years, 2 months
- League: 26 years, 10 months

Height:

- Bracken: 6'2"
- Team: 6'1"
- League: 6'1"

Weight:

- Bracken: 18st 7lb
- Team: 16st
- League: 15st 10lb

James Brooks
Fly Half

Date of Birth:	06.04.1980
Place of Birth:	Henley
Nationality:	English
Height:	5'9"
Weight:	13st 9lb

Biography

James Brooks arrived at Wasps in the summer of 2004 and immediately proved himself a strong challenger for Alex King's No10 shirt. He is a very versatile player, with rugby league experience and an expert sevens player.

James withdrew from the Sevens circuit in 2005-6, after having been a regular fixture in the squad for the previous two seasons, but was plagued with injuries, making just two 1XV starts throughout the season. James will be hoping for better health and an opportunity to challenge King and Jeremy Staunton for the No10 shirt in 2006-7.

Player Performance 05/06

Premiership Performance

Percentage of total possible time player was on pitch

position in league table at end of month

Month:	Sep	Oct	Nov	Dec	Jan	Feb	Mar	Apr	May	Total
League position	2	3	2	1	2	2	2	4	4	
% time on pitch	7%	4%	23%	0%	0%	0%	27%	0%	0%	8%
League Pts:	16/20	0/5	13/20	10/10	4/10	8/15	5/10	3/15	5/10	64/115
Points F:	133	10	85	67	37	54	36	68	49	539
Points A:	83	18	66	44	34	44	37	89	54	469
Try Bonus:	2	0	0	2	0	0	1	1	1	7
Lose Bonus:	0	0	1	0	0	0	0	2	0	3
Total mins:	22	3	73	0	0	0	43	0	0	141
Starts (sub):	0 (3)	0 (1)	1	0	0	0	0 (2)	0	0	1 (6)
Points:	0	0	0	0	0	0	0	0	0	0
Tries:	0	0	0	0	0	0	0	0	0	0
Ball Carries:	5	0	13	0	0	0	5	0	0	23
Metres:	68	0	25	0	0	0	11	0	0	104
Tackles:	1	0	1	0	0	0	5	0	0	7

Prem. Performance Totals

Tries

Brooks:	0
Team-mates:	53
Total:	53

Points

Brooks:	0
Team-mates:	539
Total:	539

Cards

Brooks:	0
Team-mates:	9
Total:	9

Cup Games

	Apps	Pts
Heineken Cup	1	0
Powergen Cup	3	7
Total	4	7

Prem. Career History

Premiership Career Milestones

Club Debut:

vs Saracens (A), L, 11-13

04.09.04

Time Spent at the Club:

2 Seasons

First Try Scored for the Club:

–

–

Full International:

–

Premiership Totals

97–06

Appearances	69
Points	41
Tries	6
Yellow Cards	0
Red Cards	0

Clubs

Year	Club	Apps	Pts
04-06	London Wasps	28	8
00-04	Northampton	41	33

Off the Pitch

Age:

Brooks: 26 years, 1 month
Team: 26 years, 2 months
League: 26 years, 10 months

Height:

Brooks: 5'9"
Team: 6'1"
League: 6'1"

Weight:

Brooks: 13st 9lb
Team: 16st
League: 15st 10lb

Lawrence Dallaglio
No8

Date of Birth: 10.08.1972
Place of Birth: Shepherd's Bush
Nationality: English
Height: 6'3"
Weight: 17st 8lb

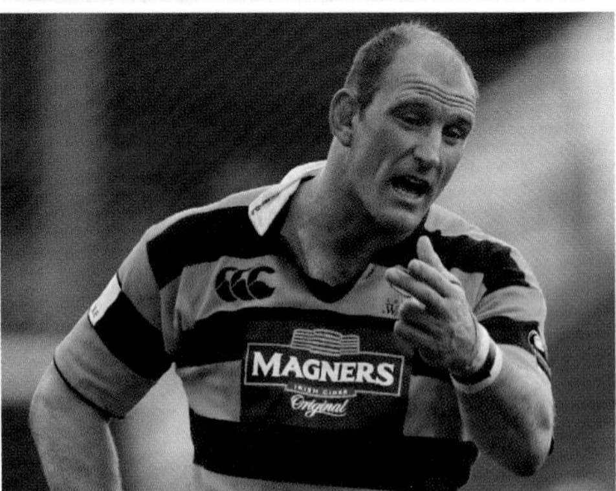

Biography

Joining Wasps as a colt, Lawrence Dallaglio has captained his only club since 1995.

He went on to captain England and has been capped at all levels and in all three positions in the back row. As well as winning the World Cup with England in 2003, Lawrence also won the World Sevens title with England in 1993 and has raised more silverware then any other Wasps captain.

He is the jewel in the Wasps crown

Player Performance 05/06

Premiership Performance

Percentage of total possible time player was on pitch — position in league table at end of month

Month:	Sep	Oct	Nov	Dec	Jan	Feb	Mar	Apr	May	Total
% on pitch	0%	100%	86%	93%	100%	78%	50%	100%	100%	72%
League position	2	3	2	1	2	2	2	4	4	
League Pts:	16/20	0/5	13/20	10/10	4/10	8/15	5/10	3/15	5/10	64/115
Points F:	133	10	85	67	37	54	36	68	49	539
Points A:	83	18	66	44	34	44	37	89	54	469
Try Bonus:	2	0	0	2	0	0	1	1	1	7
Lose Bonus:	0	0	1	0	0	0	0	2	0	3
Total mins:	0	80	274	148	160	186	80	240	160	1,328
Starts (sub):	0	1	3 (1)	2	2	2 (1)	1	3	2	16 (2)
Points:	0	0	0	0	0	0	0	0	0	0
Tries:	0	0	0	0	0	0	0	0	0	0
Ball Carries:	0	2	48	20	23	28	7	17	13	158
Metres:	0	6	142	38	47	43	18	30	20	344
Tackles:	0	4	20	13	24	15	12	16	14	118

Prem. Performance Totals

Tries

Dallaglio:	0
Team-mates:	53
Total:	**53**

Points

Dallaglio:	0
Team-mates:	539
Total:	**539**

Cards

Dallaglio:	1
Team-mates:	8
Total:	**9**

Cup Games

	Apps	Pts
Heineken Cup	5	0
Powergen Cup	4	0
Total	**9**	**0**

Prem. Career History

Premiership Career Milestones

Club Debut:
vs Bristol (A), W, 38-21
30.08.97

First Try Scored for the Club:
vs Saints (H), W, 31-15
26.04.98

Time Spent at the Club:
9 Seasons

Full International:
England

Premiership Totals

97–06

Appearances	151
Points	98
Tries	19
Yellow Cards	8
Red Cards	0

Clubs

Year	Club	Apps	Pts
97-06	London Wasps	151	98

Off the Pitch

Age:
Dallaglio: 33 years, 9 months
Team: 26 years, 2 months
League: 26 years, 10 months

Height:
Dallaglio: 6'3"
Team: 6'1"
League: 6'1"

Weight:
Dallaglio: 17st 8lb
Team: 16st
League: 15st 10lb

Jon Dawson
Prop

Date of Birth:	12.04.1980
Place of Birth:	Hammersmith
Nationality:	English
Height:	5'10"
Weight:	18st 7lb

Biography

Jon joined Wasps in the summer of 2005, and is a product of Dulwich College, whose props production line includes Jon's schoolmates Andrew Sheridan of Sale Sharks and David Flatman of Bath.

He enjoyed a good start to the season, but strong competition from in form Peter Bracken and Ali McKenzie limited his opportunities after Christmas.

Player Performance 05/06

Premiership Performance

Percentage of total possible time player was on pitch

⊖ position in league table at end of month

Month:	Sep	Oct	Nov	Dec	Jan	Feb	Mar	Apr	May	Total
% time on pitch	87%	68%	59%	10%	0%	8%	50%	0%	0%	35%
League position	2	3	2	1	2	2	2	4	4	
League Pts:	16/20	0/5	13/20	10/10	4/10	8/15	5/10	3/15	5/10	64/115
Points F:	133	10	85	67	37	54	36	68	49	539
Points A:	83	18	66	44	34	44	37	89	54	469
Try Bonus:	2	0	0	2	0	0	1	1	1	7
Lose Bonus:	0	0	1	0	0	0	0	2	0	3
Total mins:	277	54	189	16	0	19	80	0	0	635
Starts (sub):	3 (1)	1	3	0 (1)	0	0 (1)	1	0	0	8 (3)
Points:	0	0	0	0	0	0	0	0	0	0
Tries:	0	0	0	0	0	0	0	0	0	0
Ball Carries:	8	2	4	0	0	2	0	0	0	16
Metres:	9	4	2	0	0	0	0	0	0	15
Tackles:	19	3	23	1	0	2	2	0	0	50

Prem. Performance Totals

Tries

Dawson:	0
Team-mates:	53
Total:	**53**

Points

Dawson:	0
Team-mates:	539
Total:	**539**

Cards

Dawson:	0
Team-mates:	9
Total:	**9**

Cup Games

	Apps	Pts
Heineken Cup	4	0
Powergen Cup	4	0
Total	**8**	**0**

Prem. Career History

Premiership Career Milestones

Club Debut:

vs Saracens (H), W, 23-11

03.09.05

Time Spent at the Club:

1 Season

First Try Scored for the Club:

–

–

Full International:

–

Premiership Totals

97–06

Appearances	82
Points	5
Tries	1
Yellow Cards	1
Red Cards	0

Clubs

Year	Club	Apps	Pts
05-06	London Wasps	11	0
00-05	Harlequins	68	5
99-00	Saracens	3	0

Off the Pitch

Age:

Dawson: 26 years, 1 month
Team: 26 years, 2 months
League: 26 years, 10 months

Height:

Dawson: 5'10"
Team: 6'1"
League: 6'1"

Weight:

Dawson: 18st 7lb
Team: 16st
League: 15st 10lb

Matt Dawson
Scrum Half

Date of Birth:	31.10.1972
Place of Birth:	Birkenhead
Nationality:	English
Height:	5'10"
Weight:	14st 2lb

Biography

Joining Wasps from Northampton Saints, Matt was the big Premiership signing of summer, 2004. A World Cup winner at fifteens and sevens, alongside Lawrence Dallaglio on both occasions, Matt gained his first England cap in 1995, and also captained his country to a Grand Slam in 2003.

He is England's most capped scrumhalf and has also taken part in three successive Lions tours. Successive domestic trophies with Wasps in the Premiership and Powergen Cup filled the gaps in Matt's trophy cabinet, and he retired from rugby at the end of 2005-6.

Player Performance 05/06

Premiership Performance

Percentage of total possible time player was on pitch — position in league table at end of month

Month:	Sep	Oct	Nov	Dec	Jan	Feb	Mar	Apr	May	Total
% time on pitch	64%	100%	0%	32%	40%	40%	15%	13%	16%	31%
League position	2	3	2	1	2	2	2	4	4	
League Pts:	16/20	0/5	13/20	10/10	4/10	8/15	5/10	3/15	5/10	64/115
Points F:	133	10	85	67	37	54	36	68	49	539
Points A:	83	18	66	44	34	44	37	89	54	469
Try Bonus:	2	0	0	2	0	0	1	1	1	7
Lose Bonus:	0	0	1	0	0	0	0	2	0	3
Total mins:	204	80	0	51	64	97	24	30	25	575
Starts (sub):	2 (2)	1	0	0 (2)	1 (1)	1 (1)	0 (1)	1	0 (1)	6 (8)
Points:	0	0	0	0	5	0	0	0	0	5
Tries:	0	0	0	0	1	0	0	0	0	1
Ball Carries:	14	8	0	5	8	6	3	2	7	53
Metres:	85	24	0	17	75	46	22	38	15	322
Tackles:	13	5	0	3	4	7	3	0	5	40

Prem. Performance Totals

Tries

Dawson:	1
Team-mates:	52
Total:	**53**

Points

Dawson:	5
Team-mates:	534
Total:	**539**

Cards

Dawson:	0
Team-mates:	9
Total:	**9**

Cup Games

	Apps	Pts
Heineken Cup	5	0
Powergen Cup	4	0
Total	**9**	**0**

Prem. Career History

Premiership Career Milestones

Club Debut:

vs Saracens (A), L, 11-13

04.09.04

First Try Scored for the Club:

vs Sale (H), L, 30-33

11.09.04

Time Spent at the Club:

2 Seasons

Full International:

England

Premiership Totals

97–06

Appearances	126
Points	368
Tries	23
Yellow Cards	0
Red Cards	0

Clubs

Year	Club	Apps	Pts
04-06	London Wasps	32	30
97-04	Northampton	94	338

Off the Pitch

Age:

Dawson: 33 years, 7 months
Team: 26 years, 2 months
League: 26 years, 10 months

Height:

Dawson: 5'10"
Team: 6'1"
League: 6'1"

Weight:

Dawson: 14st 2lb
Team: 16st
League: 15st 10lb

Ayoola Erinle
Centre

Date of Birth:	20.02.1980
Place of Birth:	Lagos, Nigeria
Nationality:	English
Height:	6'3"
Weight:	17st 4lb

Biography

Big, strong and a powerful runner, Ayoola is probably one of the biggest centres in the Guinness Premiership. Having represented England at sevens, he burst onto the fifteens scene in a big way in 2004-5, scoring some electric tries and challenging closely for club top try scorer before his exploits were recognised with selection for the England squad who travelled to the Churchill Cup.

Ayoola has maintained his form in 2005-6 and was tipped for a trip to Australia, but instead gained selection for his second Churchill Cup tournament.

Player Performance 05/06

Premiership Performance

Percentage of total possible time player was on pitch

position in league table at end of month

Month:	Sep	Oct	Nov	Dec	Jan	Feb	Mar	Apr	May	Total
% time on pitch	53%	0%	98%	40%	56%	96%	82%	72%	0%	63%
League position	2	3	2	1	2	2	2	4	4	
League Pts:	16/20	0/5	13/20	10/10	4/10	8/15	5/10	3/15	5/10	64/115
Points F:	133	10	85	67	37	54	36	68	49	539
Points A:	83	18	66	44	34	44	37	89	54	469
Try Bonus:	2	0	0	2	0	0	1	1	1	7
Lose Bonus:	0	0	1	0	0	0	0	2	0	3
Total mins:	169	0	312	64	89	230	131	173	0	1,168
Starts (sub):	2 (1)	0	4	0 (2)	1 (1)	2 (1)	1 (1)	2 (1)	0	12 (7)
Points:	0	0	0	0	5	0	0	5	0	10
Tries:	0	0	0	0	1	0	0	1	0	2
Ball Carries:	25	0	23	7	4	25	9	17	0	110
Metres:	108	0	134	20	89	93	47	157	0	648
Tackles:	7	0	15	6	6	7	5	5	0	51

Prem. Performance Totals

Tries

Erinle:	2
Team-mates:	51
Total:	53

Points

Erinle:	10
Team-mates:	529
Total:	539

Cards

Erinle:	0
Team-mates:	9
Total:	9

Cup Games

	Apps	Pts
Heineken Cup	4	0
Powergen Cup	3	5
Total	**7**	**5**

Prem. Career History

Premiership Career Milestones

Club Debut:

vs Gloucester (H), W, 23-16

26.10.02

First Try Scored for the Club:

vs Bristol (A), W, 34-19

20.04.03

Time Spent at the Club:

4 Seasons

Full International:

–

Premiership Totals

97–06

Appearances	65
Points	90
Tries	18
Yellow Cards	0
Red Cards	0

Clubs

Year	Club	Apps	Pts
02-06	London Wasps	65	90

Off the Pitch

Age:

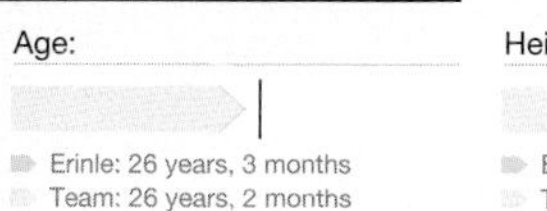

Erinle: 26 years, 3 months
Team: 26 years, 2 months
League: 26 years, 10 months

Height:

Erinle: 6'3"
Team: 6'1"
League: 6'1"

Weight:

Erinle: 17st 4lb
Team: 16st
League: 15st 10lb

Ben Gotting
Hooker

Date of Birth:	15.02.1981
Place of Birth:	Dubai
Nationality:	English
Height:	6'
Weight:	16st 7lb

Biography

Ben Gotting is a hard running, technically sound hooker, and one of the nicest guys in the squad! He made his breakthrough into the 1XV in 2004-5, following his greatest moment with Wasps, when he came on during the Zurich Premiership Final of 2004 to help the team to a second Zurich Premiership title.

After a massive summer's training, Ben looked to have a promising season ahead, but a combination of injury and strong competition from incoming hookers Raphael Ibanez and Joe Ward limited Ben's appearances in 2005-6.

Player Performance 05/06

Premiership Performance

Percentage of total possible time player was on pitch

position in league table at end of month

Month:	Sep	Oct	Nov	Dec	Jan	Feb	Mar	Apr	May	Total
League position	2	3	2	1	2	2	2	4	4	
% time on pitch	50%	21%	20%	0%	0%	17%	0%	0%	0%	15%
League Pts:	16/20	0/5	13/20	10/10	4/10	8/15	5/10	3/15	5/10	64/115
Points F:	133	10	85	67	37	54	36	68	49	539
Points A:	83	18	66	44	34	44	37	89	54	469
Try Bonus:	2	0	0	2	0	0	1	1	1	7
Lose Bonus:	0	0	1	0	0	0	0	2	0	3
Total mins:	159	17	63	0	0	41	0	0	0	280
Starts (sub):	1 (3)	0 (1)	1 (2)	0	0	0 (2)	0	0	0	2 (8)
Points:	0	0	0	0	0	0	0	0	0	0
Tries:	0	0	0	0	0	0	0	0	0	0
Ball Carries:	8	0	1	0	0	2	0	0	0	11
Metres:	30	0	4	0	0	5	0	0	0	39
Tackles:	8	0	7	0	0	2	0	0	0	17

Prem. Performance Totals

Tries

Gotting:	0
Team-mates:	53
Total:	**53**

Points

Gotting:	0
Team-mates:	539
Total:	**539**

Cards

Gotting:	0
Team-mates:	9
Total:	**9**

Cup Games

	Apps	Pts
Heineken Cup	1	0
Powergen Cup	2	5
Total	**3**	**5**

Prem. Career History

Premiership Career Milestones

Club Debut:

vs Newcastle (A), L, 17-24

01.09.02

Time Spent at the Club:

4 Seasons

First Try Scored for the Club:

–

–

Full International:

–

Premiership Totals

97–06

Appearances	36
Points	0
Tries	0
Yellow Cards	0
Red Cards	0

Clubs

Year	Club	Apps	Pts
02-06	London Wasps	36	0

Off the Pitch

Age:

Gotting: 25 years, 3 months
Team: 26 years, 2 months
League: 26 years, 10 months

Height:

Gotting: 6'
Team: 6'1"
League: 6'1"

Weight:

Gotting: 16st 7lb
Team: 16st
League: 15st 10lb

John Hart
Back Row

Date of Birth: 20.03.1982
Place of Birth: Wimbledon
Nationality: English
Height: 6'4"
Weight: 17st 10lb

Biography

Tipped by many to succeed Lawrence Dallaglio as the next captain of Wasps, Hart showed why he commands the respect of his team-mates with an outstanding performance in the back row at Twickenham last May that helped Wasps to their third successive Premiership title.

The No6 began 2005-6 with the captain's armband in the absence of the injured Dallaglio, but his season was cut short after he dislocated his shoulder against Bath in January. Not often in the headlines, John is a back row grafter and a hidden gem in the Wasps squad.

Player Performance 05/06

Premiership Performance

Percentage of total possible time player was on pitch — position in league table at end of month

Month:	Sep	Oct	Nov	Dec	Jan	Feb	Mar	Apr	May	Total
% on pitch	85%	70%	100%	89%	69%	0%	0%	0%	0%	49%
League position	2	3	2	1	2	2	2	4	4	
League Pts:	16/20	0/5	13/20	10/10	4/10	8/15	5/10	3/15	5/10	64/115
Points F:	133	10	85	67	37	54	36	68	49	539
Points A:	83	18	66	44	34	44	37	89	54	469
Try Bonus:	2	0	0	2	0	0	1	1	1	7
Lose Bonus:	0	0	1	0	0	0	0	2	0	3
Total mins:	272	56	320	142	110	0	0	0	0	900
Starts (sub):	3 (1)	0 (1)	4	2	2	0	0	0	0	11 (2)
Points:	5	0	0	5	0	0	0	0	0	10
Tries:	1	0	0	1	0	0	0	0	0	2
Ball Carries:	16	1	13	14	8	0	0	0	0	52
Metres:	34	1	65	17	20	0	0	0	0	137
Tackles:	19	0	32	16	11	0	0	0	0	78

Prem. Performance Totals

Tries

Hart:	2
Team-mates:	51
Total:	**53**

Points

Hart:	10
Team-mates:	529
Total:	**539**

Cards

Hart:	0
Team-mates:	9
Total:	**9**

Cup Games

	Apps	Pts
Heineken Cup	5	0
Powergen Cup	3	0
Total	**8**	**0**

Prem. Career History

Premiership Career Milestones

Club Debut:
vs Sale (H), L, 25-32
24.11.02

First Try Scored for the Club:
vs Leeds (A), W, 47-23
18.09.05

Time Spent at the Club:
4 Seasons

Full International:
–

Premiership Totals

97–06

Appearances	41
Points	10
Tries	2
Yellow Cards	1
Red Cards	0

Clubs

Year	Club	Apps	Pts
02-06	London Wasps	41	10

Off the Pitch

Age:
Hart: 24 years, 2 months
Team: 26 years, 2 months
League: 26 years, 10 months

Height:
Hart: 6'4"
Team: 6'1"
League: 6'1"

Weight:
Hart: 17st 10lb
Team: 16st
League: 15st 10lb

James Haskell
Back Row

Date of Birth: 02.04.1985
Place of Birth: Windsor
Nationality: English
Height: 6'3"
Weight: 17st 6lb

Biography

James Haskell became one of the youngest players to appear in the Premiership when he ran out for the 1XV against Harlequins in September 2003. Aged just 18, James broke Joe Worsley's Wasps' age record by 154 days.

Graduating from the Academy at the start of 2005-6, Haskell has enjoyed a successful season, making eight appearances for the 1XV and winning a Grand Slam with England U21despite missing the first half of the season with a fractured wrist.

Player Performance 05/06

Premiership Performance

Percentage of total possible time player was on pitch

position in league table at end of month

Month:	Sep	Oct	Nov	Dec	Jan	Feb	Mar	Apr	May	Total
Position	2	3	2	1	2	2	2	4	4	
% time on pitch	0%	0%	0%	0%	0%	10%	25%	40%	23%	11%
League Pts:	16/20	0/5	13/20	10/10	4/10	8/15	5/10	3/15	5/10	64/115
Points F:	133	10	85	67	37	54	36	68	49	539
Points A:	83	18	66	44	34	44	37	89	54	469
Try Bonus:	2	0	0	2	0	0	1	1	1	7
Lose Bonus:	0	0	1	0	0	0	0	2	0	3
Total mins:	0	0	0	0	0	23	40	97	37	197
Starts (sub):	0	0	0	0	0	0 (1)	0 (1)	1 (1)	0 (1)	1 (4)
Points:	0	0	0	0	0	0	0	0	0	0
Tries:	0	0	0	0	0	0	0	0	0	0
Ball Carries:	0	0	0	0	0	4	2	6	6	18
Metres:	0	0	0	0	0	18	3	26	25	72
Tackles:	0	0	0	0	0	0	5	7	5	17

Prem. Performance Totals

Tries

Haskell:	0
Team-mates:	53
Total:	**53**

Points

Haskell:	0
Team-mates:	539
Total:	**539**

Cards

Haskell:	0
Team-mates:	9
Total:	**9**

Cup Games

	Apps	Pts
Heineken Cup	1	0
Powergen Cup	2	0
Total	**3**	**0**

Prem. Career History

Premiership Career Milestones

Club Debut:

vs Harlequins (A), L, 27-33

13.09.03

Time Spent at the Club:

3 Seasons

First Try Scored for the Club:

–

–

Full International:

–

Premiership Totals

97–06

Appearances	12
Points	0
Tries	0
Yellow Cards	0
Red Cards	0

Clubs

Year	Club	Apps	Pts
03-06	London Wasps	12	0

Off the Pitch

Age:

Haskell: 21 years, 1 month
Team: 26 years, 2 months
League: 26 years, 10 months

Height:

Haskell: 6'3"
Team: 6'1"
League: 6'1"

Weight:

Haskell: 17st 6lb
Team: 16st
League: 15st 10lb

Rob Hoadley
Centre

Date of Birth:	28.03.1980
Place of Birth:	Hammersmith
Qualified for:	Ireland
Height:	6'
Weight:	14st 2lb

Biography

Rob joined Wasps at the start of 2004-5 from London Irish, were he rose through the ranks from minis to 1XV. He is a strong, well-built centre who offers strength in both attack and defence.

Rob put the icing on the cake in last year's Premiership Final at Twickenham, making a fantastic pick up off his bootlaces to score Wasp final try in the dying minutes. Playing equally well at 12 or 13, Rob is a versatile asset to the squad.

Player Performance 05/06

Premiership Performance

Percentage of total possible time player was on pitch

position in league table at end of month

Month:	Sep	Oct	Nov	Dec	Jan	Feb	Mar	Apr	May	Total
% on pitch	0%	0%	74%	13%	0%	100%	16%	33%	0%	33%
League position	2	3	2	1	2	2	2	4	4	
League Pts:	16/20	0/5	13/20	10/10	4/10	8/15	5/10	3/15	5/10	64/115
Points F:	133	10	85	67	37	54	36	68	49	539
Points A:	83	18	66	44	34	44	37	89	54	469
Try Bonus:	2	0	0	2	0	0	1	1	1	7
Lose Bonus:	0	0	1	0	0	0	0	2	0	3
Total mins:	1	0	237	20	0	240	25	80	0	603
Starts (sub):	0 (1)	0	3 (1)	0 (2)	0	3	0 (1)	1	0	7 (5)
Points:	0	0	5	0	0	5	0	0	0	10
Tries:	0	0	1	0	0	1	0	0	0	2
Ball Carries:	0	0	25	1	0	24	5	8	0	63
Metres:	0	0	181	13	0	100	6	31	0	331
Tackles:	0	0	11	5	0	13	2	12	0	43

Prem. Performance Totals

Tries

Hoadley:	2
Team-mates:	51
Total:	53

Points

Hoadley:	10
Team-mates:	529
Total:	539

Cards

Hoadley:	1
Team-mates:	8
Total:	9

Cup Games

	Apps	Pts
Heineken Cup	2	0
Powergen Cup	1	0
Total	**3**	**0**

Prem. Career History

Premiership Career Milestones

Club Debut:

vs Sale (H), L, 30-33

11.09.04

First Try Scored for the Club:

vs L Irish (A), W, 33-19

27.02.05

Time Spent at the Club:

2 Seasons

Full International:

–

Premiership Totals

97–06

Appearances	60
Points	30
Tries	6
Yellow Cards	6
Red Cards	0

Clubs

Year	Club	Apps	Pts
04-06	London Wasps	25	20
99-04	London Irish	35	10

Off the Pitch

Age:

Hoadley: 26 years, 2 months
Team: 26 years, 2 months
League: 26 years, 10 months

Height:

Hoadley: 6'
Team: 6'1"
League: 6'1"

Weight:

Hoadley: 14st 2lb
Team: 16st
League: 15st 10lb

Raphael Ibanez
Hooker

Date of Birth:	17.02.1973
Place of Birth:	Dax, France
Nationality:	French
Height:	5'10"
Weight:	16st

Biography

Wasps most high profile signing of the summer of 2005, former French Captain Ibanez arrived at Wasps with a fine a pedigree of 72 caps, including two Grand Slams and a World Cup runners-up medal as French captain.

The hooker enjoyed a spectacular renaissance in his first season in black and gold, his fine form earning him a further eight caps for his country as they won the 2006 Six Nations title, and his first club silverware in the shape of the Powergen Cup.

Player Performance 05/06

Premiership Performance

Percentage of total possible time player was on pitch

position in league table at end of month

Month:	Sep	Oct	Nov	Dec	Jan	Feb	Mar	Apr	May	Total
% on pitch	50%	79%	13%	70%	46%	0%	3%	44%	16%	32%
League position	2	3	2	1	2	2	2	4	4	
League Pts:	16/20	0/5	13/20	10/10	4/10	8/15	5/10	3/15	5/10	64/115
Points F:	133	10	85	67	37	54	36	68	49	539
Points A:	83	18	66	44	34	44	37	89	54	469
Try Bonus:	2	0	0	2	0	0	1	1	1	7
Lose Bonus:	0	0	1	0	0	0	0	2	0	3
Total mins:	161	63	40	112	73	0	4	105	25	583
Starts (sub):	3 (1)	1	1	2	1 (1)	0	0 (1)	2 (1)	0 (1)	10 (5)
Points:	15	0	0	5	0	0	0	0	0	20
Tries:	3	0	0	1	0	0	0	0	0	4
Ball Carries:	15	3	2	6	5	0	0	11	1	43
Metres:	62	9	1	13	19	0	0	32	14	150
Tackles:	17	0	0	4	8	0	3	4	3	39

Prem. Performance Totals

Tries

Ibanez:	4
Team-mates:	49
Total:	**53**

Points

Ibanez:	20
Team-mates:	519
Total:	**539**

Cards

Ibanez:	0
Team-mates:	9
Total:	**9**

Cup Games

	Apps	Pts
Heineken Cup	5	10
Powergen Cup	3	0
Total	**8**	**10**

Prem. Career History

Premiership Career Milestones

Club Debut:

vs Saracens (H), W, 23-11

03.09.05

First Try Scored for the Club:

vs LEED (A), W, 47-23

18.09.05

Time Spent at the Club:

1 Season

Full International:

France

Premiership Totals

97–06

Appearances	38
Points	30
Tries	6
Yellow Cards	2
Red Cards	0

Clubs

Year	Club	Apps	Pts
05-06	London Wasps	15	20
03-05	Saracens	23	10

Off the Pitch

Age:

Ibanez: 33 years, 3 months
Team: 26 years, 2 months
League: 26 years, 10 months

Height:

Ibanez: 5'10"
Team: 6'1"
League: 6'1"

Weight:

Ibanez: 16st
Team: 16st
League: 15st 10lb

Alex King
Fly Half

Date of Birth:	17.01.1975
Place of Birth:	Brighton
Nationality:	English
Height:	6'
Weight:	14st 6lb

Biography

Having joined Wasps in 1996, Alex King celebrated his tenth season at Wasps with a benefit year in 2005-6. Alex has been Wasps' most consistent fly half throughout all those years, and at the heart of the clubs' success in the past three seasons.

This season Alex saw off the early challenge for the No10 shirt from new recruit Jeremy Staunton, but bad luck with injury – that undoubtedly prevented him from enjoying a successful international career – also saw him miss a crucial part of 2005-6 and finish the season partnering Matt Dawson on a quality bench!

Player Performance 05/06

Premiership Performance

Percentage of total possible time player was on pitch

position in league table at end of month

Month:	Sep	Oct	Nov	Dec	Jan	Feb	Mar	Apr	May	Total
% on pitch	93%	96%	60%	35%	54%	33%	0%	28%	13%	48%
League position	2	3	2	1	2	2	2	4	4	
League Pts:	16/20	0/5	13/20	10/10	4/10	8/15	5/10	3/15	5/10	64/115
Points F:	133	10	85	67	37	54	36	68	49	539
Points A:	83	18	66	44	34	44	37	89	54	469
Try Bonus:	2	0	0	2	0	0	1	1	1	7
Lose Bonus:	0	0	1	0	0	0	0	2	0	3
Total mins:	298	77	191	56	87	80	0	67	21	877
Starts (sub):	4	1	2 (2)	1	1 (1)	1	0	1	0 (1)	11 (4)
Points:	0	0	27	9	8	11	0	0	0	55
Tries:	0	0	0	0	0	0	0	0	0	0
Ball Carries:	21	3	9	3	3	7	0	1	1	48
Metres:	35	0	9	0	33	14	0	2	8	101
Tackles:	24	6	27	5	15	6	0	7	1	91

Prem. Performance Totals

Tries

King:	0
Team-mates:	53
Total:	**53**

Points

King:	55
Team-mates:	484
Total:	**539**

Cards

King:	0
Team-mates:	9
Total:	**9**

Cup Games

	Apps	Pts
Heineken Cup	5	35
Powergen Cup	4	35
Total	**9**	**70**

Prem. Career History

Premiership Career Milestones

Club Debut:

vs Bristol (A), W, 38-21

30.08.97

First Try Scored for the Club:

vs Newcastle (A), L, 13-20

07.04.98

Time Spent at the Club:

9 Seasons

Full International:

England

Premiership Totals

97–06

Appearances	156
Points	937
Tries	14
Yellow Cards	0
Red Cards	0

Clubs

Year	Club	Apps	Pts
97-06	London Wasps	156	937

Off the Pitch

Age:

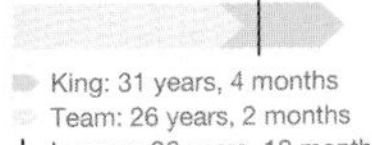

King: 31 years, 4 months
Team: 26 years, 2 months
League: 26 years, 10 months

Height:

King: 6'
Team: 6'1"
League: 6'1"

Weight:

King: 14st 6lb
Team: 16st
League: 15st 10lb

Daniel Leo
Lock/Back Row

Date of Birth:	02.10.1982
Place of Birth:	Palmerston North, NZ
Nationality:	Samoan
Height:	6'6"
Weight:	17st 8lb

Biography

Versatile flanker/lock Daniel Leo joined Wasps in February 2006 following a successful Autumn tour of Britain with Samoa. The former Queensland Red made an immediate impact, scoring a try on his A team debut, and went on to make eight 1XV starts.

His biggest performance was in the Powergen Cup Final, when he came on in the 1st minute to replace Jonny O'Connor and assist Wasps to the 2006 Anglo Welsh title.

Player Performance 05/06

Premiership Performance

Percentage of total possible time player was on pitch

position in league table at end of month

Month:	Sep	Oct	Nov	Dec	Jan	Feb	Mar	Apr	May	Total
League position	2	3	2	1	2	2	2	4	4	
% time on pitch	0%	0%	0%	0%	0%	61%	88%	93%	92%	36%
League Pts:	16/20	0/5	13/20	10/10	4/10	8/15	5/10	3/15	5/10	64/115
Points F:	133	10	85	67	37	54	36	68	49	539
Points A:	83	18	66	44	34	44	37	89	54	469
Try Bonus:	2	0	0	2	0	0	1	1	1	7
Lose Bonus:	0	0	1	0	0	0	0	2	0	3
Total mins:	0	0	0	0	0	147	141	223	147	658
Starts (sub):	0	0	0	0	0	2 (1)	1 (1)	3	2	8 (2)
Points:	0	0	0	0	0	0	0	0	0	0
Tries:	0	0	0	0	0	0	0	0	0	0
Ball Carries:	0	0	0	0	0	12	17	23	14	66
Metres:	0	0	0	0	0	42	69	67	25	203
Tackles:	0	0	0	0	0	13	12	16	9	50

Prem. Performance Totals

Tries

Leo:	0
Team-mates:	53
Total:	53

Points

Leo:	0
Team-mates:	539
Total:	539

Cards

Leo:	0
Team-mates:	9
Total:	9

Cup Games

	Apps	Pts
Heineken Cup	0	0
Powergen Cup	1	0
Total	1	0

Prem. Career History

Premiership Career Milestones

Club Debut:

vs Saints (H), D, 19-19

12.02.06

Time Spent at the Club:

1 Season

First Try Scored for the Club:

–

–

Full International:

W Samoa

Premiership Totals

97–06

Appearances	10
Points	0
Tries	0
Yellow Cards	0
Red Cards	0

Clubs

Year	Club	Apps	Pts
05-06	London Wasps	10	0

Off the Pitch

Age:

Leo: 23 years, 7 months
Team: 26 years, 2 months
League: 26 years, 10 months

Height:

Leo: 6'6"
Team: 6'1"
League: 6'1"

Weight:

Leo: 17st 8lb
Team: 16st
League: 15st 10lb

Josh Lewsey
Wing

Date of Birth:	30.11.1976
Place of Birth:	Bromley
Nationality:	English
Height:	5'10"
Weight:	13st 9lb

Biography

As far as talent, power, speed and dedication are concerned, they don't come better than OJ Lewsey. With his outstanding performances for club and country, Josh has built a reputation as a world-class player. Joining Wasps in 1998, Josh made his England debut the same year, at the age of 21, and his Six Nations debut with some stunning performances in 2002.

A World Cup winner in 2003, he won all the plaudits with outstanding performances for the 2005 Lions. His 2005-6 was disrupted by injury, but also showcased his versatility as he took the field as centre, wing and full back.

Player Performance 05/06

Premiership Performance

Percentage of total possible time player was on pitch

position in league table at end of month

Month:	Sep	Oct	Nov	Dec	Jan	Feb	Mar	Apr	May	Total
% time on pitch	0%	100%	0%	100%	100%	0%	50%	41%	100%	40%
League position	2	3	2	1	2	2	2	4	4	
League Pts:	16/20	0/5	13/20	10/10	4/10	8/15	5/10	3/15	5/10	64/115
Points F:	133	10	85	67	37	54	36	68	49	539
Points A:	83	18	66	44	34	44	37	89	54	469
Try Bonus:	2	0	0	2	0	0	1	1	1	7
Lose Bonus:	0	0	1	0	0	0	0	2	0	3
Total mins:	0	80	0	160	160	0	80	99	160	739
Starts (sub):	0	1	0	2	2	0	1	1 (1)	2	9 (1)
Points:	0	5	0	10	0	0	0	0	0	15
Tries:	0	1	0	2	0	0	0	0	0	3
Ball Carries:	0	8	0	16	14	0	10	13	21	82
Metres:	0	54	0	125	98	0	107	66	109	559
Tackles:	0	5	0	6	11	0	13	9	7	51

Prem. Performance Totals

Tries

Lewsey:	3
Team-mates:	50
Total:	**53**

Points

Lewsey:	15
Team-mates:	524
Total:	**539**

Cards

Lewsey:	0
Team-mates:	9
Total:	**9**

Cup Games

	Apps	Pts
Heineken Cup	5	10
Powergen Cup	5	10
Total	**10**	**20**

Prem. Career History

Premiership Career Milestones

Club Debut:

vs Bath (A), L, 27-36

05.09.98

First Try Scored for the Club:

vs Saracens (A), W, 31-17

25.10.98

Time Spent at the Club:

8 Seasons

Full International:

England

Premiership Totals

97–06

Appearances	146
Points	241
Tries	46
Yellow Cards	0
Red Cards	0

Clubs

Year	Club	Apps	Pts
98-06	London Wasps	129	205
97-98	Bristol Rugby	17	36

Off the Pitch

Age:

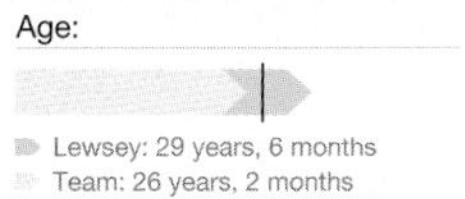

Lewsey: 29 years, 6 months
Team: 26 years, 2 months
League: 26 years, 10 months

Height:

Lewsey: 5'10"
Team: 6'1"
League: 6'1"

Weight:

Lewsey: 13st 9lb
Team: 16st
League: 15st 10lb

Mark Lock
Back Row

Date of Birth: 22.09.1979
Place of Birth: Chichester
Nationality: English
Height: 6'2"
Weight: 16st 2lb

Biography

Mark joined Wasps as an U19 from Eastbourne College, and quickly made his was into the 1XV squad. A fast and explosive back row player, Mark is a big tackler who is willing to put his body on the line to win ball.

A lynchpin in the A Team, and possessing tremendous leadership skills, Mark has consistently faced tough competition for a back row spot and made relatively few first team starts for a player of his calibre.

Player Performance 05/06

Premiership Performance

Percentage of total possible time player was on pitch — position in league table at end of month

Month:	Sep	Oct	Nov	Dec	Jan	Feb	Mar	Apr	May	Total
League position	2	3	2	1	2	2	2	4	4	
% time on pitch	22%	0%	14%	0%	0%	33%	50%	53%	4%	22%
League Pts:	16/20	0/5	13/20	10/10	4/10	8/15	5/10	3/15	5/10	64/115
Points F:	133	10	85	67	37	54	36	68	49	539
Points A:	83	18	66	44	34	44	37	89	54	469
Try Bonus:	2	0	0	2	0	0	1	1	1	7
Lose Bonus:	0	0	1	0	0	0	0	2	0	3
Total mins:	70	0	46	0	0	78	80	128	7	409
Starts (sub):	1 (3)	0	1	0	0	1	1	2	0 (1)	6 (4)
Points:	0	0	0	0	0	0	0	0	0	0
Tries:	0	0	0	0	0	0	0	0	0	0
Ball Carries:	5	0	8	0	0	15	10	3	0	41
Metres:	13	0	22	0	0	60	24	7	0	126
Tackles:	8	0	7	0	0	14	4	2	1	36

Prem. Performance Totals

Tries

Lock:	0
Team-mates:	53
Total:	**53**

Points

Lock:	0
Team-mates:	539
Total:	**539**

Cards

Lock:	0
Team-mates:	9
Total:	**9**

Cup Games

	Apps	Pts
Heineken Cup	1	0
Powergen Cup	3	0
Total	**4**	**0**

Prem. Career History

Premiership Career Milestones

Club Debut:
vs Sale (A), L, 8-16
11.09.99

First Try Scored for the Club:
vs Leeds (A), W, 28-18
30.12.01

Time Spent at the Club:
7 Seasons

Full International:
–

Premiership Totals

97–06

Appearances	70
Points	10
Tries	2
Yellow Cards	0
Red Cards	0

Clubs

Year	Club	Apps	Pts
99-06	London Wasps	70	10

Off the Pitch

Age:
Lock: 26 years, 8 months
Team: 26 years, 2 months
League: 26 years, 10 months

Height:
Lock: 6'2"
Team: 6'1"
League: 6'1"

Weight:
Lock: 16st 2lb
Team: 16st
League: 15st 10lb

Ali McKenzie
Prop

Date of Birth:	05.10.1981
Place of Birth:	Croydon
Nationality:	English
Height:	6'3"
Weight:	18st 12lb

Biography

Ali is a powerful prop whose presence in the loose and as a ball carrier really caught the eye as he enjoyed his best season to date in 2005-6. He was one of the top try scorers in the A Team campaign of 2004-5, that saw them reach the Premiership A League final. Ali built on this with 10 starts for the 1XV in 2005-6 – his most in a season for the club – and his reputation as a destructive runner grew with his confidence.

Ali also became a father for the first time in 2005 – a condition he is enjoying just as much as his achievements on the pitch!

Player Performance 05/06

Premiership Performance

Percentage of total possible time player was on pitch

position in league table at end of month

Month:	Sep	Oct	Nov	Dec	Jan	Feb	Mar	Apr	May	Total
League position	2	3	2	1	2	2	2	4	4	
% time on pitch	0%	0%	11%	66%	77%	33%	44%	6%	0%	23%
League Pts:	16/20	0/5	13/20	10/10	4/10	8/15	5/10	3/15	5/10	64/115
Points F:	133	10	85	67	37	54	36	68	49	539
Points A:	83	18	66	44	34	44	37	89	54	469
Try Bonus:	2	0	0	2	0	0	1	1	1	7
Lose Bonus:	0	0	1	0	0	0	0	2	0	3
Total mins:	0	0	34	106	123	80	71	15	0	429
Starts (sub):	0	0	0 (1)	1 (1)	2	1	1 (1)	0 (1)	0	5 (4)
Points:	0	0	0	0	0	0	0	0	0	0
Tries:	0	0	0	0	0	0	0	0	0	0
Ball Carries:	0	0	0	11	9	9	8	0	0	37
Metres:	0	0	0	21	27	42	17	0	0	107
Tackles:	0	0	6	11	10	10	6	2	0	45

Prem. Performance Totals

Tries

McKenzie:	0
Team-mates:	53
Total:	**53**

Points

McKenzie:	0
Team-mates:	539
Total:	**539**

Cards

McKenzie:	0
Team-mates:	9
Total:	**9**

Cup Games

	Apps	Pts
Heineken Cup	3	5
Powergen Cup	2	0
Total	**5**	**5**

Prem. Career History

Premiership Career Milestones

Club Debut:

vs Newcastle (H), L, 30-33

11.11.01

Time Spent at the Club:

5 Seasons

First Try Scored for the Club:

–

–

Full International:

–

Premiership Totals

97–06

Appearances	34
Points	0
Tries	0
Yellow Cards	0
Red Cards	0

Clubs

Year	Club	Apps	Pts
01-06	London Wasps	34	0

Off the Pitch

Age:

McKenzie: 24 years, 7 months
Team: 26 years, 2 months
League: 26 years, 10 months

Height:

McKenzie: 6'3"
Team: 6'1"
League: 6'1"

Weight:

McKenzie: 18st 12lb
Team: 16st
League: 15st 10lb

Jonny O'Connor
Flanker

Date of Birth:	09.02.1980
Place of Birth:	Galway, Ireland
Nationality:	Irish
Height:	5'10"
Weight:	15st 10lb

Biography

An out and out, body-on-the-line No7, Jonny O'Connor burst onto the Wasps radar in 2003-4, and made the No7 shirt his own after a battle royal that season with Paul Volley. However, appallingly timed injuries have meant that he has missed the final stages of all three of Wasps' historically successful seasons since he joined the club. He blasted into the international arena in 2004-5, and quickly racked up 12 appearances for his country.

2005-6 began well for the Irishman, but disaster struck in the Powergen Cup Final, when he was injured after just 1 minute, meaning another premature end to his season.

Player Performance 05/06

Premiership Performance

Percentage of total possible time player was on pitch — position in league table at end of month

Month:	Sep	Oct	Nov	Dec	Jan	Feb	Mar	Apr	May	Total
% time on pitch	81%	100%	0%	94%	25%	45%	0%	0%	0%	35%
League position	2	3	2	1	2	2	2	4	4	
League Pts:	16/20	0/5	13/20	10/10	4/10	8/15	5/10	3/15	5/10	64/115
Points F:	133	10	85	67	37	54	36	68	49	539
Points A:	83	18	66	44	34	44	37	89	54	469
Try Bonus:	2	0	0	2	0	0	1	1	1	7
Lose Bonus:	0	0	1	0	0	0	0	2	0	3
Total mins:	259	80	0	150	40	109	0	0	0	638
Starts (sub):	3 (1)	1	0	2	0 (1)	1 (1)	0	0	0	7 (3)
Points:	0	0	0	0	0	0	0	0	0	0
Tries:	0	0	0	0	0	0	0	0	0	0
Ball Carries:	16	4	0	15	5	12	0	0	0	52
Metres:	57	9	0	47	11	35	0	0	0	159
Tackles:	30	11	0	20	8	16	0	0	0	85

Prem. Performance Totals

Tries

O'Connor:	0
Team-mates:	53
Total:	**53**

Points

O'Connor:	0
Team-mates:	539
Total:	**539**

Cards

O'Connor:	1
Team-mates:	8
Total:	**9**

Cup Games

	Apps	Pts
Heineken Cup	3	5
Powergen Cup	2	0
Total	**5**	**5**

Prem. Career History

Premiership Career Milestones

Club Debut:
vs Harlequins (A), L, 27-33
13.09.03

First Try Scored for the Club:
vs Saints (A), L, 17-27
27.09.03

Time Spent at the Club:
3 Seasons

Full International:
Ireland

Premiership Totals

97–06

Appearances	38
Points	15
Tries	3
Yellow Cards	2
Red Cards	0

Clubs

Year	Club	Apps	Pts
03-06	London Wasps	38	15

Off the Pitch

Age:
O'Connor: 26 years, 3 months
Team: 26 years, 2 months
League: 26 years, 10 months

Height:
O'Connor: 5'10"
Team: 6'1"
League: 6'1"

Weight:
O'Connor: 15st 10lb
Team: 16st
League: 15st 10lb

Tim Payne
Prop

Date of Birth:	29.04.1979
Place of Birth:	Swindon
Nationality:	English
Height:	6'
Weight:	18st 7lb

Biography

Prop Tim Payne has been a regular fixture in the 1XV over the past two seasons, and became Wasps most experienced prop in 2005-6, following the departure of Will Green and retirement of Craig Dowd.

Payne credits Dowd, now Wasps Forwards Coach, for being the greatest influence in his career, and he continues to reap the benefits of his tutelage under the former All Blacks star, being selected for the England squad that toured Australia in the summer of 2006.

Player Performance 05/06

Premiership Performance

Percentage of total possible time player was on pitch; position in league table at end of month

Month:	Sep	Oct	Nov	Dec	Jan	Feb	Mar	Apr	May	Total
% on pitch	97%	100%	100%	92%	50%	89%	50%	95%	95%	88%
League position	2	3	2	1	2	2	2	4	4	
League Pts:	16/20	0/5	13/20	10/10	4/10	8/15	5/10	3/15	5/10	64/115
Points F:	133	10	85	67	37	54	36	68	49	539
Points A:	83	18	66	44	34	44	37	89	54	469
Try Bonus:	2	0	0	2	0	0	1	1	1	7
Lose Bonus:	0	0	1	0	0	0	0	2	0	3
Total mins:	311	80	320	147	80	213	80	229	152	1,612
Starts (sub):	4	1	4	2	1	3	1	3	2	21
Points:	5	0	0	0	0	0	0	0	0	5
Tries:	1	0	0	0	0	0	0	0	0	1
Ball Carries:	20	2	12	3	3	10	3	11	6	70
Metres:	28	5	33	28	5	13	0	58	8	178
Tackles:	17	2	24	12	8	16	10	6	10	105

Prem. Performance Totals

Tries

Payne:	1
Team-mates:	52
Total:	53

Points

Payne:	5
Team-mates:	534
Total:	539

Cards

Payne:	1
Team-mates:	8
Total:	9

Cup Games

	Apps	Pts
Heineken Cup	6	0
Powergen Cup	4	0
Total	**10**	**0**

Prem. Career History

Premiership Career Milestones

Club Debut:
vs Harlequins (A), L, 27-33
13.09.03

First Try Scored for the Club:
vs ROTH (A), W, 27-20
14.02.04

Time Spent at the Club:
3 Seasons

Full International:
England

Premiership Totals

97–06

Appearances	67
Points	20
Tries	4
Yellow Cards	2
Red Cards	0

Clubs

Year	Club	Apps	Pts
03-06	London Wasps	63	20
01-02	Bristol Rugby	4	0

Off the Pitch

Age:
Payne: 27 years, 1 month
Team: 26 years, 2 months
League: 26 years, 10 months

Height:
Payne: 6'
Team: 6'1"
League: 6'1"

Weight:
Payne: 18st 7lb
Team: 16st
League: 15st 10lb

Martin Purdy
Lock

Date of Birth:	29.10.1981
Place of Birth:	Crawley
Nationality:	English
Height:	6'6"
Weight:	17st 10lb

Biography

Martin debuted with Wasps in early 2003, since when he has figured regularly in Wasps A team and made a number a appearances for the 1XV, including a substitute appearance during the 2005 Zurich Premiership Final victory over Leicester. Although Purdy missed much of 2004-5 with a dislocated shoulder, a strong finish to the season promised to get the former England U21 captain back on track.

However, cruel luck meant the popular lock was restricted to only 5 appearances in 2005-6, another season blighted by injury.

Player Performance 05/06

Premiership Performance

Percentage of total possible time player was on pitch

position in league table at end of month

Month:	Sep	Oct	Nov	Dec	Jan	Feb	Mar	Apr	May	Total
League position	2	3	2	1	2	2	2	4	4	
% time on pitch	49%	0%	0%	11%	6%	0%	0%	0%	0%	10%
League Pts:	16/20	0/5	13/20	10/10	4/10	8/15	5/10	3/15	5/10	64/115
Points F:	133	10	85	67	37	54	36	68	49	539
Points A:	83	18	66	44	34	44	37	89	54	469
Try Bonus:	2	0	0	2	0	0	1	1	1	7
Lose Bonus:	0	0	1	0	0	0	0	2	0	3
Total mins:	157	0	0	18	10	0	0	0	0	185
Starts (sub):	3	0	0	0 (1)	0 (1)	0	0	0	0	3 (2)
Points:	0	0	0	0	0	0	0	0	0	0
Tries:	0	0	0	0	0	0	0	0	0	0
Ball Carries:	7	0	0	1	3	0	0	0	0	11
Metres:	9	0	0	3	9	0	0	0	0	21
Tackles:	8	0	0	4	1	0	0	0	0	13

Prem. Performance Totals

Tries

Purdy:	0
Team-mates:	53
Total:	**53**

Points

Purdy:	0
Team-mates:	539
Total:	**539**

Cards

Purdy:	0
Team-mates:	9
Total:	**9**

Cup Games

	Apps	Pts
Heineken Cup	0	0
Powergen Cup	0	0
Total	**0**	**0**

Prem. Career History

Premiership Career Milestones

Club Debut:

vs Harlequins (A), L, 27-33

13.09.03

Time Spent at the Club:

3 Seasons

First Try Scored for the Club:

–

–

Full International:

–

Premiership Totals

97–06

Appearances	31
Points	0
Tries	0
Yellow Cards	0
Red Cards	0

Clubs

Year	Club	Apps	Pts
03-06	London Wasps	31	0

Off the Pitch

Age:

Purdy: 24 years, 7 months
Team: 26 years, 2 months
League: 26 years, 10 months

Height:

Purdy: 6'6"
Team: 6'1"
League: 6'1"

Weight:

Purdy: 17st 10lb
Team: 16st
League: 15st 10lb

Eoin Reddan
Scrum Half

Date of Birth:	20.11.1980
Place of Birth:	Limerick
Nationality:	Irish
Height:	5'7"
Weight:	12st 8lb

Biography

Eoin joined Wasps from Munster at the start of 2005-6, and has enjoyed a fantastic debut season that saw him displace World Cup winner Matt Dawson as Wasps first choice scrum half.

Young, fast and blessed with a lightning pass, Eoin also caught the eye of the international selectors, winning his first cap in the 2006 Six Nations campaign.

Player Performance 05/06

Premiership Performance

Percentage of total possible time player was on pitch

position in league table at end of month

Month:	Sep	Oct	Nov	Dec	Jan	Feb	Mar	Apr	May	Total
% on pitch	36%	0%	100%	88%	60%	26%	35%	88%	83%	60%
League position	2	3	2	1	2	2	2	4	4	
League Pts:	16/20	0/5	13/20	10/10	4/10	8/15	5/10	3/15	5/10	64/115
Points F:	133	10	85	67	37	54	36	68	49	539
Points A:	83	18	66	44	34	44	37	89	54	469
Try Bonus:	2	0	0	2	0	0	1	1	1	7
Lose Bonus:	0	0	1	0	0	0	0	2	0	3
Total mins:	116	0	319	109	96	63	56	210	133	1,102
Starts (sub):	2 (1)	0	4	2	1 (1)	1	1	2 (1)	2	15 (3)
Points:	0	0	5	0	0	0	0	0	0	5
Tries:	0	0	1	0	0	0	0	0	0	1
Ball Carries:	9	0	15	3	10	4	2	8	8	59
Metres:	64	0	84	8	51	0	9	63	60	339
Tackles:	4	0	30	6	1	7	2	9	4	63

Prem. Performance Totals

Tries

Reddan:	1
Team-mates:	52
Total:	53

Points

Reddan:	5
Team-mates:	534
Total:	539

Cards

Reddan:	0
Team-mates:	9
Total:	9

Cup Games

	Apps	Pts
Heineken Cup	4	0
Powergen Cup	5	10
Total	**9**	**10**

Prem. Career History

Premiership Career Milestones

Club Debut:

vs Saracens (H), W, 23-11

03.09.05

First Try Scored for the Club:

vs Saints (A), W, 21-13

12.11.05

Time Spent at the Club:

1 Season

Full International:

Ireland

Premiership Totals

97–06

Appearances	18
Points	5
Tries	1
Yellow Cards	0
Red Cards	0

Clubs

Year	Club	Apps	Pts
05-06	London Wasps	18	5

Off the Pitch

Age:

Reddan: 25 years, 6 months
Team: 26 years, 2 months
League: 26 years, 10 months

Height:

Reddan: 5'7"
Team: 6'1"
League: 6'1"

Weight:

Reddan: 12st 8lb
Team: 16st
League: 15st 10lb

Tom Rees
Flanker

Date of Birth:	11.09.1984
Place of Birth:	London
Nationality:	English
Height:	5'11"
Weight:	15st 12lb

Biography

Tom Rees burst onto the Premiership scene in 2004-5, and for his efforts won promotion from Academy player to first team squad at the end of the season. Tom then made a spectacular start to 2005-6 that saw him nominated Man of the Match in Wasps home opener, and repeat the feat when returning from injury two months later.

However, despite being tipped as England's next No7, Tom has been dogged by injuries that have prevented him from taking a consistent part in the last two seasons. He will be hoping for better luck in 2006-7.

Player Performance 05/06

Premiership Performance

Percentage of total possible time player was on pitch

position in league table at end of month

Month:	Sep	Oct	Nov	Dec	Jan	Feb	Mar	Apr	May	Total
% time on pitch	34%	0%	100%	1%	7%	78%	53%	0%	0%	39%
League position	2	3	2	1	2	2	2	4	4	
League Pts:	16/20	0/5	13/20	10/10	4/10	8/15	5/10	3/15	5/10	64/115
Points F:	133	10	85	67	37	54	36	68	49	539
Points A:	83	18	66	44	34	44	37	89	54	469
Try Bonus:	2	0	0	2	0	0	1	1	1	7
Lose Bonus:	0	0	1	0	0	0	0	2	0	3
Total mins:	108	0	320	2	11	188	85	0	0	714
Starts (sub):	1 (1)	0	4	0 (1)	0 (1)	3	2	0	0	10 (3)
Points:	10	0	5	0	0	0	5	0	0	20
Tries:	2	0	1	0	0	0	1	0	0	4
Ball Carries:	13	0	25	0	0	11	6	0	0	55
Metres:	105	0	128	0	0	32	16	0	0	281
Tackles:	4	0	47	0	1	10	11	0	0	73

Prem. Performance Totals

Tries

Rees:	4
Team-mates:	49
Total:	**53**

Points

Rees:	20
Team-mates:	519
Total:	**539**

Cards

Rees:	0
Team-mates:	9
Total:	**9**

Cup Games

	Apps	Pts
Heineken Cup	3	5
Powergen Cup	1	0
Total	**4**	**5**

Prem. Career History

Premiership Career Milestones

Club Debut:

vs Harlequins (H), W, 22-21

22.02.04

First Try Scored for the Club:

vs LEED (H), W, 30-15

13.03.05

Time Spent at the Club:

3 Seasons

Full International:

–

Premiership Totals

97–06

Appearances	26
Points	30
Tries	6
Yellow Cards	0
Red Cards	0

Clubs

Year	Club	Apps	Pts
03-06	London Wasps	26	30

Off the Pitch

Age:

Rees: 21 years, 8 months
Team: 26 years, 2 months
League: 26 years, 10 months

Height:

Rees: 5'11"
Team: 6'1"
League: 6'1"

Weight:

Rees: 15st 12lb
Team: 16st
League: 15st 10lb

Paul Sackey
Wing

Date of Birth:	08.11.1979
Place of Birth:	London
Nationality:	English
Height:	6'1"
Weight:	14st 4lb

Biography

Paul returned to Wasps from London Irish in March of 2005, having begun his professional career as a member of the London Wasps Academy. He made an immediate impact, entertaining the crowd with his elusive running and maintaining sparkling form and winning selection for last summer's England squad that travelled to the Churchill Cup in Canada.

A consistent 2005-6 earned Paul the chance of another trip to Canada in summer 2006, though he was forced to withdraw on the eve of the tour, through injury.

Player Performance 05/06

Premiership Performance

Percentage of total possible time player was on pitch — position in league table at end of month

Month:	Sep	Oct	Nov	Dec	Jan	Feb	Mar	Apr	May	Total
% time on pitch	100%	100%	100%	94%	100%	90%	58%	87%	100%	93%
League position	2	3	2	1	2	2	2	4	4	
League Pts:	16/20	0/5	13/20	10/10	4/10	8/15	5/10	3/15	5/10	64/115
Points F:	133	10	85	67	37	54	36	68	49	539
Points A:	83	18	66	44	34	44	37	89	54	469
Try Bonus:	2	0	0	2	0	0	1	1	1	7
Lose Bonus:	0	0	1	0	0	0	0	2	0	3
Total mins:	320	80	320	151	160	216	92	208	160	1,707
Starts (sub):	4	1	4	2	2	3	2	3	2	23
Points:	5	0	5	5	10	0	5	5	5	40
Tries:	1	0	1	1	2	0	1	1	1	8
Ball Carries:	34	9	27	10	13	14	13	22	19	161
Metres:	323	65	225	131	116	60	88	163	112	1283
Tackles:	21	4	22	8	10	13	4	5	8	95

Prem. Performance Totals

Tries

Sackey:	8
Team-mates:	45
Total:	53

Points

Sackey:	40
Team-mates:	499
Total:	539

Cards

Sackey:	1
Team-mates:	8
Total:	9

Cup Games

	Apps	Pts
Heineken Cup	6	5
Powergen Cup	4	15
Total	**10**	**20**

Prem. Career History

Premiership Career Milestones

Club Debut:

vs Saints (H), W, 39-9

20.02.05

First Try Scored for the Club:

vs Saracens (H), W, 45-24

10.04.05

Time Spent at the Club:

2 Seasons

Full International:

–

Premiership Totals

97–06

Appearances	135
Points	245
Tries	49
Yellow Cards	2
Red Cards	0

Clubs

Year	Club	Apps	Pts
04-06	London Wasps	31	55
00-05	London Irish	88	150
99-00	Bedford Blues	16	40

Off the Pitch

Age:

Sackey: 26 years, 6 months
Team: 26 years, 2 months
League: 26 years, 10 months

Height:

Sackey: 6'1"
Team: 6'1"
League: 6'1"

Weight:

Sackey: 14st 4lb
Team: 16st
League: 15st 10lb

Simon Shaw
Lock

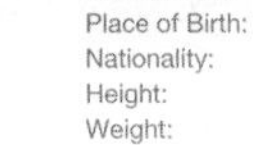

Date of Birth:	01.09.1973
Place of Birth:	Nairobi, Kenya
Nationality:	English
Height:	6'7"
Weight:	19st

Biography

Having joined the club in 1997, Simon Shaw has been a consistent performer throughout his Wasps career. Despite his unjustifiably small number of England caps, Simon returned from Australia in 2003 with a World Cup medal.

He was called out to New Zealand in the summer of 2005 for his second Lions tour, and justified his selection with some barnstorming performances for the unbeaten midweek squad under Ian McGeechan. The mobile lock retained his England squad place in 2005-6 and is looking forward to his testimonial year in 2006-7.

Player Performance 05/06

Premiership Performance — Percentage of total possible time player was on pitch — position in league table at end of month

Month:	Sep	Oct	Nov	Dec	Jan	Feb	Mar	Apr	May	Total
% on pitch	30%	88%	36%	50%	83%	43%	44%	67%	100%	54%
League position	2	3	2	1	2	2	2	4	4	
League Pts:	16/20	0/5	13/20	10/10	4/10	8/15	5/10	3/15	5/10	64/115
Points F:	133	10	85	67	37	54	36	68	49	539
Points A:	83	18	66	44	34	44	37	89	54	469
Try Bonus:	2	0	0	2	0	0	1	1	1	7
Lose Bonus:	0	0	1	0	0	0	0	2	0	3
Total mins:	95	70	114	80	132	104	70	160	160	985
Starts (sub):	1 (1)	1	1 (1)	1	2	1 (1)	1	2	2	12 (3)
Points:	0	0	0	5	0	0	0	0	0	5
Tries:	0	0	0	1	0	0	0	0	0	1
Ball Carries:	2	5	8	5	12	9	3	9	14	67
Metres:	2	12	8	7	23	41	22	34	46	195
Tackles:	4	4	11	8	18	7	11	12	18	93

Prem. Performance Totals

Tries		Points		Cards	
Shaw:	1	Shaw:	5	Shaw:	2
Team-mates:	52	Team-mates:	534	Team-mates:	7
Total:	53	**Total:**	539	**Total:**	9

Cup Games

	Apps	Pts
Heineken Cup	6	5
Powergen Cup	3	0
Total	**9**	**5**

Prem. Career History

Premiership Career Milestones

Club Debut:
vs L Irish (A), L, 17-22
26.10.97

First Try Scored for the Club:
vs L Irish (H), L, 19-38
15.03.98

Time Spent at the Club:
9 Seasons

Full International:
England

Premiership Totals

97–06	
Appearances	171
Points	88
Tries	17
Yellow Cards	6
Red Cards	0

Clubs

Year	Club	Apps	Pts
97-06	London Wasps	171	88

Off the Pitch

Age:
Shaw: 32 years, 8 months
Team: 26 years, 2 months
League: 26 years, 10 months

Height:
Shaw: 6'7"
Team: 6'1"
League: 6'1"

Weight:
Shaw: 19st
Team: 16st
League: 15st 10lb

George Skivington
Lock

Date of Birth:	03.12.1982
Place of Birth:	Warrington
Nationality:	English
Height:	6'6"
Weight:	18st 11lb

Biography

Injury allowed George his best run in the 1XV to date in 2005-6, and he grasped the opportunity with both hands, scoring three tries and showcasing his skill and athleticism around the park to boot.

This came on the back of a promising 2004-5 with Wasps very successful A side, whom he captained on several occasions. However, having promised so much, the end of the season was marred for George by injury that forced him out of contention for the Powergen Cup Final and the play offs.

Player Performance 05/06

Premiership Performance

Percentage of total possible time player was on pitch — position in league table at end of month

Month:	Sep	Oct	Nov	Dec	Jan	Feb	Mar	Apr	May	Total
% time on pitch	0%	0%	94%	100%	87%	90%	50%	0%	0%	49%
League position	2	3	2	1	2	2	2	4	4	
League Pts:	16/20	0/5	13/20	10/10	4/10	8/15	5/10	3/15	5/10	64/115
Points F:	133	10	85	67	37	54	36	68	49	539
Points A:	83	18	66	44	34	44	37	89	54	469
Try Bonus:	2	0	0	2	0	0	1	1	1	7
Lose Bonus:	0	0	1	0	0	0	0	2	0	3
Total mins:	0	0	300	160	139	216	80	0	0	895
Starts (sub):	0	0	4	2	2	3	1	0	0	12
Points:	0	0	0	5	0	0	0	0	0	5
Tries:	0	0	0	1	0	0	0	0	0	1
Ball Carries:	0	0	9	10	9	8	6	0	0	42
Metres:	0	0	36	74	24	15	15	0	0	164
Tackles:	0	2	52	17	16	13	1	0	0	101

Prem. Performance Totals

Tries

Skivington:	1
Team-mates:	52
Total:	**53**

Points

Skivington:	5
Team-mates:	534
Total:	**539**

Cards

Skivington:	0
Team-mates:	9
Total:	**9**

Cup Games

	Apps	Pts
Heineken Cup	5	5
Powergen Cup	2	5
Total	**7**	**10**

Prem. Career History

Premiership Career Milestones

Club Debut:

vs Saints (A), L, 17-27

27.09.03

Time Spent at the Club:

3 Seasons

First Try Scored for the Club:

vs Harlequins (H), W, 22-21

22.02.04

Full International:

–

Premiership Totals

97–06

Appearances	27
Points	10
Tries	2
Yellow Cards	0
Red Cards	0

Clubs

Year	Club	Apps	Pts
03-06	London Wasps	27	10

Off the Pitch

Age:

Skivington: 23 years, 5 months
Team: 26 years, 2 months
League: 26 years, 10 months

Height:

Skivington: 6'6"
Team: 6'1"
League: 6'1"

Weight:

Skivington: 18st 11lb
Team: 16st
League: 15st 10lb

Jeremy Staunton
Fly Half

Date of Birth: 07.05.1980
Place of Birth: Limerick, Ireland
Nationality: Irish
Height: 6'
Weight: 15st 1lb

Biography

One of Wasps high profile signings in the summer of 2005, fly half Staunton proved a powerful contender for the No10 shirt in his first season at Wasps. He did not shirk the challenge, nor the pressure, proving himself on the big game stage and steering Wasps to Powergen Cup victory in the absence of the injured Alex King.

Having toured Japan with Ireland last summer, Jeremy was again selected for the Ireland squad to tour Australia in the summer of 2006.

Player Performance 05/06

Premiership Performance

Percentage of total possible time player was on pitch — position in league table at end of month

Month:	Sep	Oct	Nov	Dec	Jan	Feb	Mar	Apr	May	Total
% time on pitch	0%	0%	41%	50%	46%	67%	73%	72%	87%	47%
League position	2	3	2	1	2	2	2	4	4	
League Pts:	16/20	0/5	13/20	10/10	4/10	8/15	5/10	3/15	5/10	64/115
Points F:	133	10	85	67	37	54	36	68	49	539
Points A:	83	18	66	44	34	44	37	89	54	469
Try Bonus:	2	0	0	2	0	0	1	1	1	7
Lose Bonus:	0	0	1	0	0	0	0	2	0	3
Total mins:	0	0	130	80	73	160	117	173	139	872
Starts (sub):	0	0	2 (1)	1	1 (1)	2	2	2 (1)	2	12 (3)
Points:	0	0	13	0	6	3	3	8	0	33
Tries:	0	0	1	0	0	0	0	1	0	2
Ball Carries:	0	0	13	11	10	23	5	16	17	95
Metres:	0	0	42	23	58	88	20	82	81	394
Tackles:	0	0	18	6	10	18	24	24	10	110

Prem. Performance Totals

Tries		Points		Cards	
Staunton:	2	Staunton:	33	Staunton:	0
Team-mates:	51	Team-mates:	506	Team-mates:	9
Total:	**53**	**Total:**	**539**	**Total:**	**9**

Cup Games

	Apps	Pts
Heineken Cup	1	0
Powergen Cup	2	17
Total	**3**	**17**

Prem. Career History

Premiership Career Milestones

Club Debut:
vs Bristol (H), W, 21-16
04.11.05

First Try Scored for the Club:
vs Newcastle (A), L, 15-17
27.11.05

Time Spent at the Club:
1 Season

Full International:
Ireland

Premiership Totals

97–06

Appearances	35
Points	219
Tries	4
Yellow Cards	1
Red Cards	0

Clubs

Year	Club	Apps	Pts
05-06	London Wasps	15	33
04-05	Harlequins	20	186

Off the Pitch

Age:
- Staunton: 26 years
- Team: 26 years, 2 months
- League: 26 years, 10 months

Height:
- Staunton: 6'
- Team: 6'1"
- League: 6'1"

Weight:
- Staunton: 15st 1lb
- Team: 16st
- League: 15st 10lb

Justin Va'a
Prop

Date of Birth:	26.07.1978
Place of Birth:	Wellington, NZ
Nationality:	Samoan
Height:	6'
Weight:	19st 6lb

Biography

Powerful scrummager Justin had played all his rugby in New Zealand before making the move to Wasps in December 2005 after a successful autumn tour playing for Samoa. Having played rugby league until he was 18, Justin had no problem making the switch to the scrummaging of rugby union, coming up through the ranks at Wellington, NZ before moving to Wasps.

Justin enjoys outdoor sports and going to the pictures, and describes himself as a laid back, relaxed sort of guy!

Player Performance 05/06

Premiership Performance

Percentage of total possible time player was on pitch

position in league table at end of month

Month:	Sep	Oct	Nov	Dec	Jan	Feb	Mar	Apr	May	Total
League position	2	3	2	1	2	2	2	4	4	
% time on pitch	0%	0%	0%	30%	48%	23%	15%	11%	9%	13%
League Pts:	16/20	0/5	13/20	10/10	4/10	8/15	5/10	3/15	5/10	64/115
Points F:	133	10	85	67	37	54	36	68	49	539
Points A:	83	18	66	44	34	44	37	89	54	469
Try Bonus:	2	0	0	2	0	0	1	1	1	7
Lose Bonus:	0	0	1	0	0	0	0	2	0	3
Total mins:	0	0	0	48	76	56	24	26	14	244
Starts (sub):	0	0	0	1	0 (2)	0 (2)	0 (1)	0 (2)	0 (2)	1 (9)
Points:	0	0	0	0	0	0	0	0	0	0
Tries:	0	0	0	0	0	0	0	0	0	0
Ball Carries:	0	0	0	1	8	5	4	1	1	20
Metres:	0	0	0	2	16	10	14	0	0	42
Tackles:	0	0	0	5	15	2	0	1	4	27

Prem. Performance Totals

Tries

Va'a:	0
Team-mates:	53
Total:	**53**

Points

Va'a:	0
Team-mates:	539
Total:	**539**

Cards

Va'a:	0
Team-mates:	9
Total:	**9**

Cup Games

	Apps	Pts
Heineken Cup	0	0
Powergen Cup	0	0
Total	**0**	**0**

Prem. Career History

Premiership Career Milestones

Club Debut:

vs L Irish (A), W, 35-19

31.12.05

Time Spent at the Club:

1 Season

First Try Scored for the Club:

–

–

Full International:

W Samoa

Premiership Totals

97–06

Appearances	10
Points	0
Tries	0
Yellow Cards	0
Red Cards	0

Clubs

Year	Club	Apps	Pts
05-06	London Wasps	10	0

Off the Pitch

Age:

Va'a: 27 years, 10 months
Team: 26 years, 2 months
League: 26 years, 10 months

Height:

Va'a: 6'
Team: 6'1"
League: 6'1"

Weight:

Va'a: 19st 6lb
Team: 16st
League: 15st 10lb

Mark Van Gisbergen
Full Back

Date of Birth:	30.06.1977
Place of Birth:	Hamilton, NZ
Qualified for:	England
Height:	5'10"
Weight:	13st 13lb

Biography

Mark Van Gisbergen's fourth season at Wasps was probably his most difficult. Expectation surrounded the kiwi born full-back's qualification for England, but after winning selection and his first cap in autumn 2005, Mark struggled for form either side of Christmas.

However, supporters know that the little man with the big heart is an unsung hero of the team, and his accurate placekicking has made him the team's top points scorer for the past two seasons. A recovery of form in the latter half of the season and selection for England's tour to Australia ensured Mark a happier end to 2005-6.

Player Performance 05/06

Premiership Performance

Percentage of total possible time player was on pitch — position in league table at end of month

Month:	Sep	Oct	Nov	Dec	Jan	Feb	Mar	Apr	May	Total
% time on pitch	100%	100%	25%	100%	50%	100%	100%	100%	100%	83%
League position	2	3	2	1	2	2	2	4	4	
League Pts:	16/20	0/5	13/20	10/10	4/10	8/15	5/10	3/15	5/10	64/115
Points F:	133	10	85	67	37	54	36	68	49	539
Points A:	83	18	66	44	34	44	37	89	54	469
Try Bonus:	2	0	0	2	0	0	1	1	1	7
Lose Bonus:	0	0	1	0	0	0	0	2	0	3
Total mins:	320	80	80	160	80	240	160	240	160	1,520
Starts (sub):	4	1	1	2	1	3	2	3	2	19
Points:	68	5	5	18	3	30	13	35	34	211
Tries:	0	0	0	0	0	1	1	0	1	3
Ball Carries:	23	12	15	8	15	26	13	29	33	174
Metres:	190	131	136	53	120	105	84	246	209	1274
Tackles:	11	2	5	7	3	2	3	6	1	40

Prem. Performance Totals

Tries

Van Gisbergen:	3
Team-mates:	50
Total:	53

Points

Van Gisbergen:	211
Team-mates:	328
Total:	539

Cards

Van Gisbergen:	0
Team-mates:	9
Total:	9

Cup Games

	Apps	Pts
Heineken Cup	6	58
Powergen Cup	4	36
Total	**10**	**94**

Prem. Career History

Premiership Career Milestones

Club Debut:
vs Saracens (H), W, 51-23
22.09.02

First Try Scored for the Club:
vs Gloucester (H), W, 23-16
26.10.02

Time Spent at the Club:
4 Seasons

Full International:
England

Premiership Totals

97–06

Appearances	85
Points	704
Tries	16
Yellow Cards	0
Red Cards	0

Clubs

Year	Club	Apps	Pts
02-06	London Wasps	85	704

Off the Pitch

Age:
Van Gisbergen: 28 years, 11 month
Team: 26 years, 2 months
League: 26 years, 10 months

Height:
Van Gisbergen: 5'10"
Team: 6'1"
League: 6'1"

Weight:
Van Gisbergen: 13st 13lb
Team: 16st
League: 15st 10lb

Tom Voyce
Wing

Date of Birth:	05.01.1981
Place of Birth:	Truro
Nationality:	English
Height:	6'
Weight:	14st 13lb

Biography

The Wasps' flyer was the Premiership's top try scorer in 2004-5, and it is Tom's proud boast that he has been top try scorer for his club in every full season that he has played professional rugby – 2005-6 being no exception.

A member of the England A side last season, Tom's try scoring form was rewarded with full international recognition this season in the form of a Six Nations start and selection for England's summer tour of Australia.

Player Performance 05/06

Premiership Performance

Percentage of total possible time player was on pitch — position in league table at end of month

Month:	Sep	Oct	Nov	Dec	Jan	Feb	Mar	Apr	May	Total
% on pitch	97%	100%	75%	100%	100%	33%	50%	67%	61%	74%
League position	2	3	2	1	2	2	2	4	4	
League Pts:	16/20	0/5	13/20	10/10	4/10	8/15	5/10	3/15	5/10	64/115
Points F:	133	10	85	67	37	54	36	68	49	539
Points A:	83	18	66	44	34	44	37	89	54	469
Try Bonus:	2	0	0	2	0	0	1	1	1	7
Lose Bonus:	0	0	1	0	0	0	0	2	0	3
Total mins:	310	80	240	160	160	78	80	160	98	1,366
Starts (sub):	4	1	3	2	2	1 (1)	1	2	2	18 (1)
Points:	15	0	10	0	0	0	10	15	0	50
Tries:	3	0	2	0	0	0	2	3	0	10
Ball Carries:	31	11	28	25	28	11	11	22	14	181
Metres:	305	96	243	146	202	84	135	201	89	1501
Tackles:	14	1	3	5	3	3	3	7	4	43

Prem. Performance Totals

Tries

Voyce:	10
Team-mates:	43
Total:	**53**

Points

Voyce:	50
Team-mates:	489
Total:	**539**

Cards

Voyce:	0
Team-mates:	9
Total:	**9**

Cup Games

	Apps	Pts
Heineken Cup	6	25
Powergen Cup	5	10
Total	**11**	**35**

Prem. Career History

Premiership Career Milestones

Club Debut:
vs Harlequins (A), L, 27-33
13.09.03

First Try Scored for the Club:
vs Harlequins (A), L, 27-33
13.09.03

Time Spent at the Club:
3 Seasons

Full International:
England

Premiership Totals

97–06

Appearances	122
Points	230
Tries	46
Yellow Cards	1
Red Cards	0

Clubs

Year	Club	Apps	Pts
03-06	London Wasps	67	155
99-03	Bath Rugby	55	75

Off the Pitch

Age:
- Voyce: 25 years, 4 months
- Team: 26 years, 2 months
- League: 26 years, 10 months

Height:
- Voyce: 6'
- Team: 6'1"
- League: 6'1"

Weight:
- Voyce: 14st 13lb
- Team: 16st
- League: 15st 10lb

Fraser Waters
Centre

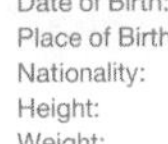

Date of Birth:	31.03.1976
Place of Birth:	Cape Town, SA
Nationality:	English
Height:	6'
Weight:	14st 10lb

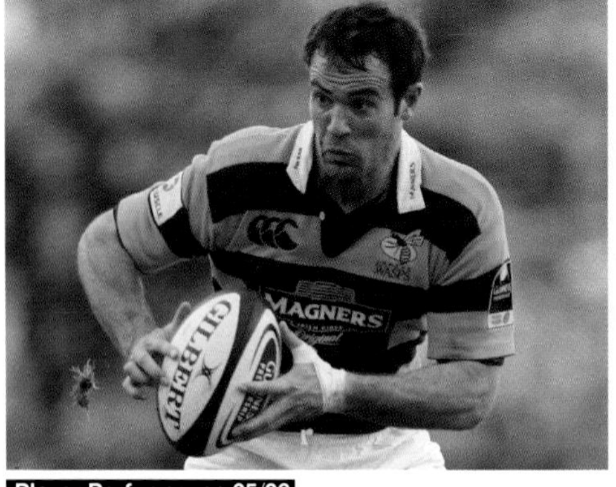

Biography

Fraser Waters is easily one of the top centres in the Premiership and is unlucky not to have more England caps. His classy line breaks, mixed with devastating tackles and toughness have made him one of the most respected players in the Premiership.

However, Fraser missed all of 2004-5 with an ankle injury, and faced strong competition to win his place back from the likes of Josh Lewsey and Ayoola Erinle in 2005-6.

Player Performance 05/06

Premiership Performance

Percentage of total possible time player was on pitch — position in league table at end of month

Month:	Sep	Oct	Nov	Dec	Jan	Feb	Mar	Apr	May	Total
League position	2	3	2	1	2	2	2	4	4	
% time on pitch	50%	0%	0%	0%	8%	44%	34%	3%	43%	22%
League Pts:	16/20	0/5	13/20	10/10	4/10	8/15	5/10	3/15	5/10	64/115
Points F:	133	10	85	67	37	54	36	68	49	539
Points A:	83	18	66	44	34	44	37	89	54	469
Try Bonus:	2	0	0	2	0	0	1	1	1	7
Lose Bonus:	0	0	1	0	0	0	0	2	0	3
Total mins:	161	0	0	0	12	106	55	6	69	409
Starts (sub):	2 (2)	0	0	0	0 (1)	1 (1)	1	0 (1)	0 (2)	4 (7)
Points:	5	0	0	0	0	0	0	0	0	5
Tries:	1	0	0	0	0	0	0	0	0	1
Ball Carries:	11	0	0	0	1	7	3	0	6	28
Metres:	73	0	0	0	0	33	36	0	9	151
Tackles:	10	0	0	0	1	7	3	0	9	30

Prem. Performance Totals

Tries

Waters:	1
Team-mates:	52
Total:	**53**

Points

Waters:	5
Team-mates:	534
Total:	**539**

Cards

Waters:	0
Team-mates:	9
Total:	**9**

Cup Games

	Apps	Pts
Heineken Cup	1	0
Powergen Cup	3	0
Total	**4**	**0**

Prem. Career History

Premiership Career Milestones

Club Debut:

vs Bath (H), W, 35-0

07.02.99

First Try Scored for the Club:

vs LSC (H), W, 45-22

02.05.99

Time Spent at the Club:

8 Seasons

Full International:

England

Premiership Totals

97–06

Appearances	118
Points	109
Tries	21
Yellow Cards	1
Red Cards	0

Clubs

Year	Club	Apps	Pts
98-06	London Wasps	116	109
97-98	Bristol Rugby	2	0

Off the Pitch

Age:

Waters: 30 years, 2 months
Team: 26 years, 2 months
League: 26 years, 10 months

Height:

Waters: 6'
Team: 6'1"
League: 6'1"

Weight:

Waters: 14st 10lb
Team: 16st
League: 15st 10lb

Joe Ward
Hooker

Date of Birth:	03.06.1980
Place of Birth:	Dannevirke, NZ
Nationality:	New Zealand
Height:	6'
Weight:	16st 13lb

Biography

Joe is a promising young talent who joined Wasps in October 2005.

An ambitious player, he met with the approval of All Black hooking legend Sean Fitzpatrick, who selected him to captain the New Zealand U21 side in 2001.

Joe played for the Hurricanes for the past three years, helping them reach the Super 12 semi finals in May 2005 before coming to Wasps. His no-nonsense, physical approach has helped give the Wasps pack real bite.

Player Performance 05/06

Premiership Performance

Percentage of total possible time player was on pitch

position in league table at end of month

Month:	Sep	Oct	Nov	Dec	Jan	Feb	Mar	Apr	May	Total
% time on pitch	0%	0%	68%	15%	0%	20%	91%	56%	84%	38%
League position	2	3	2	1	2	2	2	4	4	
League Pts:	16/20	0/5	13/20	10/10	4/10	8/15	5/10	3/15	5/10	64/115
Points F:	133	10	85	67	37	54	36	68	49	539
Points A:	83	18	66	44	34	44	37	89	54	469
Try Bonus:	2	0	0	2	0	0	1	1	1	7
Lose Bonus:	0	0	1	0	0	0	0	2	0	3
Total mins:	0	0	217	24	0	49	145	135	135	705
Starts (sub):	0	0	2 (1)	0 (1)	0	1	2	1 (2)	2	8 (4)
Points:	0	0	0	0	0	0	0	0	0	0
Tries:	0	0	0	0	0	0	0	0	0	0
Ball Carries:	0	0	14	2	0	6	9	6	16	53
Metres:	0	0	22	1	0	15	13	18	57	126
Tackles:	0	0	24	3	0	4	14	8	7	60

Prem. Performance Totals

Tries

Ward:	0
Team-mates:	53
Total:	**53**

Points

Ward:	0
Team-mates:	539
Total:	**539**

Cards

Ward:	1
Team-mates:	8
Total:	**9**

Cup Games

	Apps	Pts
Heineken Cup	0	0
Powergen Cup	1	0
Total	**1**	**0**

Prem. Career History

Premiership Career Milestones

Club Debut:

vs Saints (A), W, 21-13

12.11.05

First Try Scored for the Club:

–

–

Time Spent at the Club:

1 Season

Full International:

–

Premiership Totals

97–06

Appearances	12
Points	0
Tries	0
Yellow Cards	1
Red Cards	0

Clubs

Year	Club	Apps	Pts
05-06	London Wasps	12	0

Off the Pitch

Age:

Ward: 25 years, 11 months
Team: 26 years, 2 months
League: 26 years, 10 months

Height:

Ward: 6'
Team: 6'1"
League: 6'1"

Weight:

Ward: 16st 13lb
Team: 16st
League: 15st 10lb

Joe Worsley
Flanker

Date of Birth:	14.06.1977
Place of Birth:	London
Nationality:	English
Height:	6'5"
Weight:	17st 6lb

Biography

Joe Worsley is rated as the best utility back row forward in the country, at home in any of the three positions. He joined Wasps at 16 and two years later set the record as the youngest player in the England U21 team.

In the England squad for the 1999 World Cup, Joe was a key player in the team that won the World Cup in 2003, though to the dismay of many was overlooked for the Lions squad in 2005. However, Joe let his playing do the talking in 2005-6, once again turning in top class displays week-in, week-out to prove his quality as one of the best in England.

Player Performance 05/06

Premiership Performance

Percentage of total possible time player was on pitch

position in league table at end of month

Month:	Sep	Oct	Nov	Dec	Jan	Feb	Mar	Apr	May	Total
% on pitch	100%	30%	0%	49%	100%	0%	48%	47%	94%	50%
League position	2	3	2	1	2	2	2	4	4	
League Pts:	16/20	0/5	13/20	10/10	4/10	8/15	5/10	3/15	5/10	64/115
Points F:	133	10	85	67	37	54	36	68	49	539
Points A:	83	18	66	44	34	44	37	89	54	469
Try Bonus:	2	0	0	2	0	0	1	1	1	7
Lose Bonus:	0	0	1	0	0	0	0	2	0	3
Total mins:	320	24	0	78	160	0	76	112	150	920
Starts (sub):	4	1	0	1	2	0	1	1 (1)	2	12 (1)
Points:	5	0	0	5	0	0	0	0	10	20
Tries:	1	0	0	1	0	0	0	0	2	4
Ball Carries:	46	4	0	8	12	0	4	15	9	98
Metres:	153	11	0	40	41	0	37	64	66	412
Tackles:	36	3	0	6	25	0	23	22	20	135

Prem. Performance Totals

Tries

Worsley:	4
Team-mates:	49
Total:	**53**

Points

Worsley:	20
Team-mates:	519
Total:	**539**

Cards

Worsley:	1
Team-mates:	8
Total:	**9**

Cup Games

	Apps	Pts
Heineken Cup	2	0
Powergen Cup	4	0
Total	**6**	**0**

Prem. Career History

Premiership Career Milestones

Club Debut:

vs Bristol (A), W, 38-21

30.08.97

First Try Scored for the Club:

vs Bath (A), L, 27-36

05.09.98

Time Spent at the Club:

9 Seasons

Full International:

England

Premiership Totals

97–06

Appearances	153
Points	135
Tries	27
Yellow Cards	5
Red Cards	0

Clubs

Year	Club	Apps	Pts
97-06	London Wasps	153	135

Off the Pitch

Age:

- Worsley: 28 years, 11 months
- Team: 26 years, 2 months
- League: 26 years, 10 months

Height:

- Worsley: 6'5"
- Team: 6'1"
- League: 6'1"

Weight:

- Worsley: 17st 6lb
- Team: 16st
- League: 15st 10lb

ABBOT ALE
ABBOT ALE
ABBOT ALE

GILBERT
SHARKS

RUGBY PREMIERSHIP

KICK OFF

2006/07

Premiership Roll of Honour

Season	Champions	Relegated	Promoted
2005/06 Premiership	Sale Sharks	Leeds Tykes	NEC Harlequins
2004/05 Premiership	London Wasps	NEC Harlequins	Bristol Rugby
2003/04 Premiership	London Wasps	Rotherham Titans	Worcester Warriors
2002/03 Premiership	London Wasps	Bristol Rugby	Rotherham Titans
2001/02 Premiership	Leicester Tigers	N/A	N/A
2000/01 Premiership	Leicester Tigers	Rotherham Titans	Leeds Tykes
1999/00 Premiership	Leicester Tigers	Bedford Blues	Rotherham Titans
1998/99 Premiership	Leicester Tigers	West Hartlepool	Bristol Rugby
1997/98 Premiership	Newcastle Falcons	Bristol Rugby	Bedford West Hartlepool London Scottish

RUGBY PREMIERSHIP

KICK OFF

2006/07

Season Statistics 2005/06

Final Premiership Table 2005/06

	RECORD			POINTS			ATTACK					DEFENCE					
Team	W	D	L	TB	LB	Tot	T	C	PG	DG	For	T	C	PG	DG	Agst	PD
1 Sale Sharks (C)	**16**	**1**	**5**	**6**	**2**	**74**	**52**	**38**	**73**	**6**	**573**	**42**	**27**	**56**	**4**	**444**	**129**
2 Leicester Tigers	14	3	5	5	1	68	51	34	64	1	518	24	20	78	7	415	103
3 London Irish	14	0	8	6	4	66	54	32	47	6	493	44	30	56	2	454	39
4 London Wasps	12	3	7	7	3	64	53	41	58	2	527	42	30	57	2	447	80
5 Gloucester Rugby	11	1	10	4	9	59	46	32	61	2	483	33	26	53	3	385	98
6 Northampton Saints	10	1	11	4	7	53	53	35	41	2	464	50	32	54	4	488	-24
7 Newcastle Falcons	9	1	12	3	6	47	42	25	45	7	416	44	30	50	1	433	-17
8 Worcester Warriors	9	1	12	3	6	47	40	28	61	4	451	56	32	48	2	494	-43
9 Bath Rugby	9	1	12	3	5	46	38	25	61	6	441	49	33	58	3	494	-53
10 Saracens	8	1	13	5	7	46	42	32	51	2	433	48	30	56	5	483	-50
11 Bristol Rugby	8	1	13	0	7	41	28	23	69	0	393	41	30	55	5	445	-52
12 Leeds Tykes (R)	5	0	17	1	7	28	36	24	42	3	363	62	49	52	3	573	-210

= Premiership Semi-Finalists = Qualified for European Cup = Relegated

Premiership Play-Off SF

14 May 2006 — **Sale Sharks 22-12 London Wasps** — **Edgeley Park**

Scoring sequence: 1' Hodgson (PG) 3-0, 5' Van Gisbergen (PG) 3-3, 16' Hodgson (PG) 6-3, 20' Hodgson (PG) 9-3, 31' Robinson (T) 14-3, Hodgson (C) 16-3, 43' Van Gisbergen (PG) 16-6, 45' Hodgson (PG) 19-6, 51' Van Gisbergen (PG) 19-9, 65' Van Gisbergen (PG) 19-12, 78' Hodgson (PG) 22-12.

Referee: Chris White (England)

Attendance: 10,641

Premiership Play-Off SF

14 May 2006 — **Leicester Tigers 40-8 London Irish** — **Welford Road**

Scoring sequence: 7' Goode (PG) 3-0, 15' Alesana Tuilagi (T) 8-0, Goode (C) 10-0, 25' Magne (T) 10-5, 32' Ellis (T) 15-5, Goode (C) 17-5, 40' Goode (PG) 20-5, 51' Catt (PG) 20-8, 56' Goode (PG) 23-8, 60' Lloyd (T) 28-8, 67' Murphy (T) 33-8, Goode (C) 35-8, 73' Lloyd (T) 40-8.

Referee: Dave Pearson (England)

Attendance: 14,069

Premiership Play-Off Final

27 May 2006 — **Sale Sharks 45-20 Leicester Tigers** — **Twickenham**

Scoring sequence: 3' Hodgson (PG) 3-0, 8' Cueto (T) 8-0, 9' Moody (T) 8-5, Goode (C) 8-7, 17' Lund (T) 13-7, 31' Hodgson (PG) 16-7, 36' Goode (PG) 16-10, 40' Ripol (T) 21-10, Hodgson (C) 23-10, 43' Goode (PG) 23-13, 45' Hodgson (PG) 26-13, 48' Hodgson (PG) 29-13, 63' Hodgson (PG) 32-13, 70' Hodgson (DG) 35-13, 74' Hamilton (T) 35-18, Goode (C) 35-20, 78' Hodgson (PG) 38-20, 80' Mayor (T) 43-20, Courrent (C) 45-20.

Referee: Dave Pearson (England)

Attendance: 58,000

Tries and Points

[includes play-off data]

Top Try Scorer

	Player	Team	Tries
1	**Tom Varndell**	**Leicester Tigers**	**14**
2	Tom Voyce	London Wasps	10
3	Delon Armitage	London Irish	8
4	Tom Biggs	Leeds Tykes	8
5	Matthew Burke	Newcastle Falcons	8
6	Anthony Elliott	Newcastle Falcons	8
7	David Lemi	Bristol Rugby	8
8	Paul Sackey	London Wasps	8

Top Points Scorer

	Player	Team	Points
1	**Charlie Hodgson**	**Sale Sharks**	**248**
2	Jason Strange	Bristol Rugby	244
3	Glen Jackson	Saracens	238
4	Shane Drahm	Worcester Warriors	233
5	Andy Goode	Leicester Tigers	225
6	Ludovic Mercier	Gloucester Rugby	213
7	Mark Van Gisbergen	London Wasps	211
8	Bruce Reihana	Northampton Saints	206

Premiership Records

Individual Game Records

	All Time	Best in 2005/06
Most points	32 – Niall Woods (Irish v Harlequins, 25 Apr 98) 32 – Dave Walder (Falcons v Saracens, 26 Nov 00) 32 – Tim Stimpson (Tigers v Falcons, 21 Sep 02)	27 – Andy Goode (Tigers v Sharks, 28 Jan)
Most tries	6 – Ryan Constable (Saracens at Bedford, 16 Apr 00)	4 – Sean Lamont (Saints v Saracens, 18 Feb)
Most conversions	13 – Richie Butland (Richmond at Bedford, 16 May 99)	6 – Valentin Courrent (Sharks at Warriors, 11 Feb) 6 – Bruce Reihana (Saints v Saracens, 18 Feb) 6 – Jonny Wilkinson (Falcons v Tykes, 6 May)
Most penalty goals	9 – Simon Mannix (Gloucester v Quins, 23 Sep 00) 9 – Luke Smith (Saracens v Gloucester, 8 Sep 01) 9 – Braam van Straaten (Tykes v Irish, 8 Sep 02) 9 – Alex King (Wasps v Falcons, 11 Nov 01)	8 – Andy Goode (Tigers v Sharks, 28 Jan)
Most drop goals	3 – Ludovic Mercier (Gloucester at Sharks, 22 Sep 01) 3 – Mark Mapletoft (Irish vs Saints, 27 Dec 04)	2 – Shane Drahm (Warriors at Irish, 11 Sep) 2 – Dave Walder (Falcons at Saints, 17 Sep) 2 – Barry Everitt (Irish v Tigers, 8 Jan)
Fastest try	9.63 secs – Tom Voyce (Wasps v Harlequins, 5 Nov 04)	28 secs – Tom Varndell (Tigers v Bath, 17 Sep)
Quickest bonus point try	14 mins – Mike Worsley (Quins v Saracens, 12 Nov 04)	20 mins – Sailosi Tagicakibau (Irish at Wasps, 30 Apr)

Team Records

	All Time	Best in 2005/06
Most points in a home game	77-19 – Bath v Harlequins (The Rec, 29 Apr 00)	58-17 – Saints v Saracens (Franklin's Gardens, 18 Feb)
Most points in an away game	106-12 – Richmond at Bedford (Goldington Road, 16 May 99)	56-37 – Irish at Wasps (Causeway Stadium, 30 Apr)
Highest aggregate of points in game	118pts – Bedford 12, Richmond 106 (Goldington Road, 16 May 99)	93pts – Wasps 37, Irish 56 (Causeway Stadium, 30 Apr)
Biggest home win	76pts – Sale 76, Bristol 0 (Heywood Road, 9 Nov 97)	41pts – Saints 58, Saracens 17 (Franklin's Gardens, 18 Feb)
Biggest away win	94pts – Bedford 12, Richmond 106 (Goldington Road, 16 May 99)	32pts – Bristol 9, Gloucester 41 (Memorial Stadium, 18 Sep)
Highest attendance (non-Twickenham)	20,840 – Irish v Bath (Madejski Stadium, 21 Mar 04)	19,884 – Irish v Sharks (Madejski Stadium, 25 Mar)

Bath Rugby

Season Summary 2005/06

Position	Won	Drawn	Lost	For	Against	Bonus Points	Total Points
9	9	1	12	441	494	8	46

Despite pre-season optimism, this was another disappointing Premiership campaign for the West Country side. Three consecutive defeats in the opening games left John Connolly's side playing catch up. Connolly's departure opened the way for the return of Rec favourite Brian Ashton and performances improved. However, despite reaching the semi-finals of both the Heineken and Powergen Cups, ninth in the league was ultimately disappointing for a club that sets such high standards. The season ended with the club looking to appoint a new coaching set-up following the summer departures of Ashton, Michael Foley and Richard Graham.

Forwards Coach: Mark Bakewell
Backs Coach: Steve Meehan

Club Honours

Courage League / Zurich Premiership: 1988-89, 1990-91, 1991-92, 1992-93, 1993-94, 1995-96, 2003-04 (lost play-offs)

John Player Cup / Pilkington Cup: 1984, 1985, 1986, 1987 1989, 1990, 1992, 1994, 1995, 1996

Heineken Cup: 1997-1998

Season Squad

Stats 2005-06

Position	Player	Height	Weight	Apps	Rep	Tries	Points
FB/W	N.Abendanon	5'10"	13st 0lb	1	3	-	-
FH/C	O.Barkley	5'10"	14st 6lb	12	-	-	118
P	D.Barnes	6'0"	17st 10lb	11	1	-	-
SH	M.Baxter	5'10"	13st 10lb	-	1	-	-
BR	A.Beattie	6'5"	18st 8lb	20	-	2	10
P	D.Bell	6'2"	19st 8lb	17	4	1	5
FB/W	L.Best	6'3"	15st 2lb	4	2	1	5
L	S.Borthwick	6'6"	17st 5lb	13	-	-	-
W	D.Bory	5'11"	14st 9lb	14	-	2	10
C	T.Cheeseman	6'0"	14st 2lb	2	1	-	-
C	A.Crockett	5'11"	14st 9lb	14	-	2	10
C	S.Davey	6'1"	15st 2lb	-	1	-	-
FB/FH/C	R.Davis	5'6"	13st 12lb	1	7	-	-
BR	G.Delve	6'3"	18st 0lb	7	10	3	15
H	P.Dixon	5'11"	16st 7lb	8	5	-	-
FH	A.Dunne	5'8"	12st 8lb	4	1	-	20
L	J.Fa'amatuainu	6'4"	16st 4lb	1	1	-	-
8	Z.Feau'nati	6'2"	18st 8lb	17	3	3	15
L	R.Fidler	6'5"	18st 4lb	4	7	-	-
P	T.Filise	6'2"	19st 7lb	4	3	1	5
W	S.Finau	6'0"	16st 0lb	6	2	2	10
P	D.Flatman	6'1"	18st 12lb	6	3	-	-
FH	E.Fuimaono-Sapolu	6'1"	16st 0lb	3	1	1	5
BR	C.Goodman	6'2"	16st 5lb	1	1	-	-
L	D.Grewcock	6'6"	18st 10lb	14	-	-	-
H	R.Hawkins	6'0"	16st 4lb	-	3	-	-
C	A.Higgins	5'11"	13st 12lb	15	2	1	5
L	J.Hudson	6'7"	17st 10lb	6	-	2	10
BR	M.Lipman	6'1"	15st 7lb	11	2	2	10
P	C.Loader	5'10"	18st 6lb	-	3	-	-
FB/W	J.Maddock	5'8"	13st 5lb	16	1	3	15
FH	C.Malone	6'0"	14st 9lb	17	-	4	130
H	L.Mears	5'9"	15st 8lb	14	1	2	10
FB	M.Perry	6'1"	13st 12lb	7	-	-	-
BR	J.Scaysbrook	6'3"	15st 6lb	8	4	1	5
BR/L	P.Short	6'5"	18st 8lb	8	5	-	-
W	M.Stephenson	6'0"	13st 0lb	9	4	1	8
P	M.Stevens	6'0"	19st 0lb	6	3	1	5
SH	N.Walshe	5'10"	13st 6lb	11	2	-	-
W/C	F.Welsh	6'1"	15st 6lb	7	1	2	10
SH	A.Williams	5'11"	13st 12lb	6	8	-	-
SH	M.Wood	5'10"	14st 11lb	5	-	1	5

Last Season Form 2005/06

Season Progression

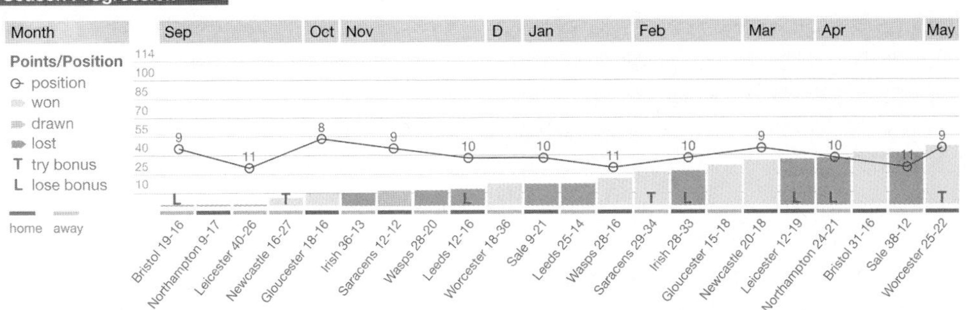

Home Matches

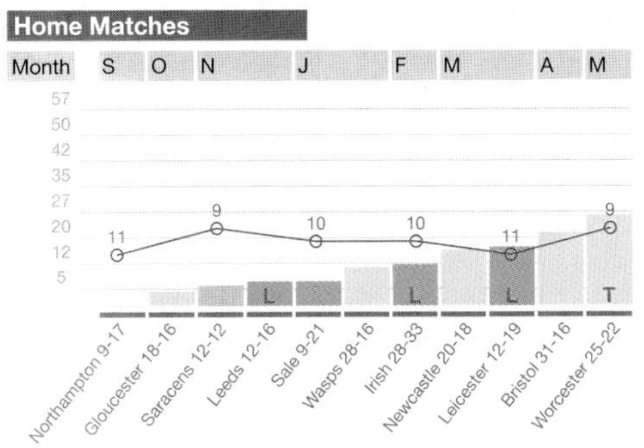

Away Matches

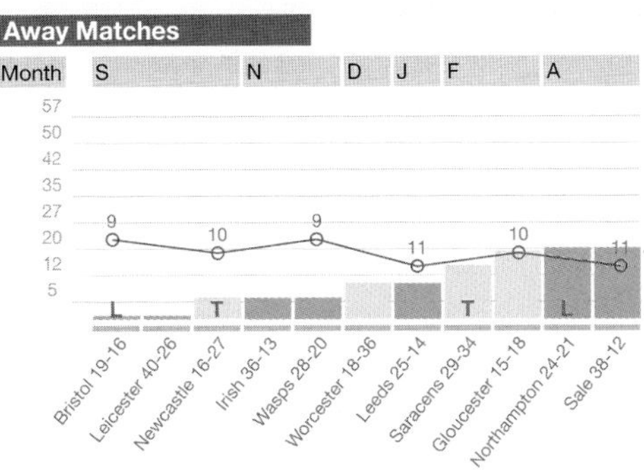

Premiership Statistics

Premiership Statistics	Total	Home	Away
Tries	38	15	23
Coversions	25	9	16
Penalty goals	61	35	26
Drop goals	6	2	4
Kick %	67%	69%	66%
Yellow/Red cards	16/1	10/1	6/0
Powerplay tries	4	1	3
Shorthand tries	1	1	0

Powerplay tries are scored when your side are playing with a man or more advantage due to yellow or red cards.

Shorthand tries are scored when your side are playing with a man or more fewer due to yellow or red cards.

Team Performance

Position	Team	% total points won	% won at home	% won away
1	Sale			
2	Leicester	4%	7%	0%
3	Irish			
4	Wasps			
5	Gloucester	24%	26%	20%
6	Northampton			
7	Newcastle			
8	Worcester	49%	44%	55%
9	**Bath**			
10	Saracens			
11	Bristol	23%	23%	25%
12	Leeds			

Bath Rugby

Top Scorer

Chris Malone

Points Facts

Total points	% team points	Home	Away
130	29	73	57

Points by Time Period

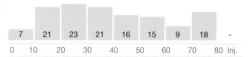

0–10	10–20	20–30	30–40	40–50	50–60	60–70	70–80	Inj.
7	21	23	21	16	15	9	18	-

Team Tries and Points

Tries by Time Period

scored
conceded

	0–10min	10–20min	20–30min	30–40min	40–50min	50–60min	60–70min	70–80	Injury time
scored	3	5	3	8	6	5	3	4	1
conceded	5	1	5	7	4	8	5	14	0

Tries by Halves

scored
conceded

	Total	1st half	2nd half	1st half %	2nd half %
scored	38	19	19	50%	50%
conceded	49	18	31	37%	63%

How Points were Scored

- tries: 190
- conversions: 50
- pen goals: 183
- drop goals: 18

How Points were Conceded

- tries: 245
- conversions: 66
- pen goals: 174
- drop goals: 9

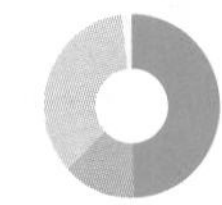

Tries Scored by Player

- backs: 20
- forwards: 18

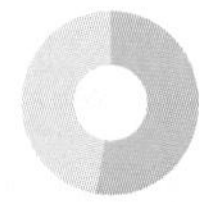

Tries Conceded by Player

- backs: 36
- forwards: 10

Eight-Season Form 1998-2006

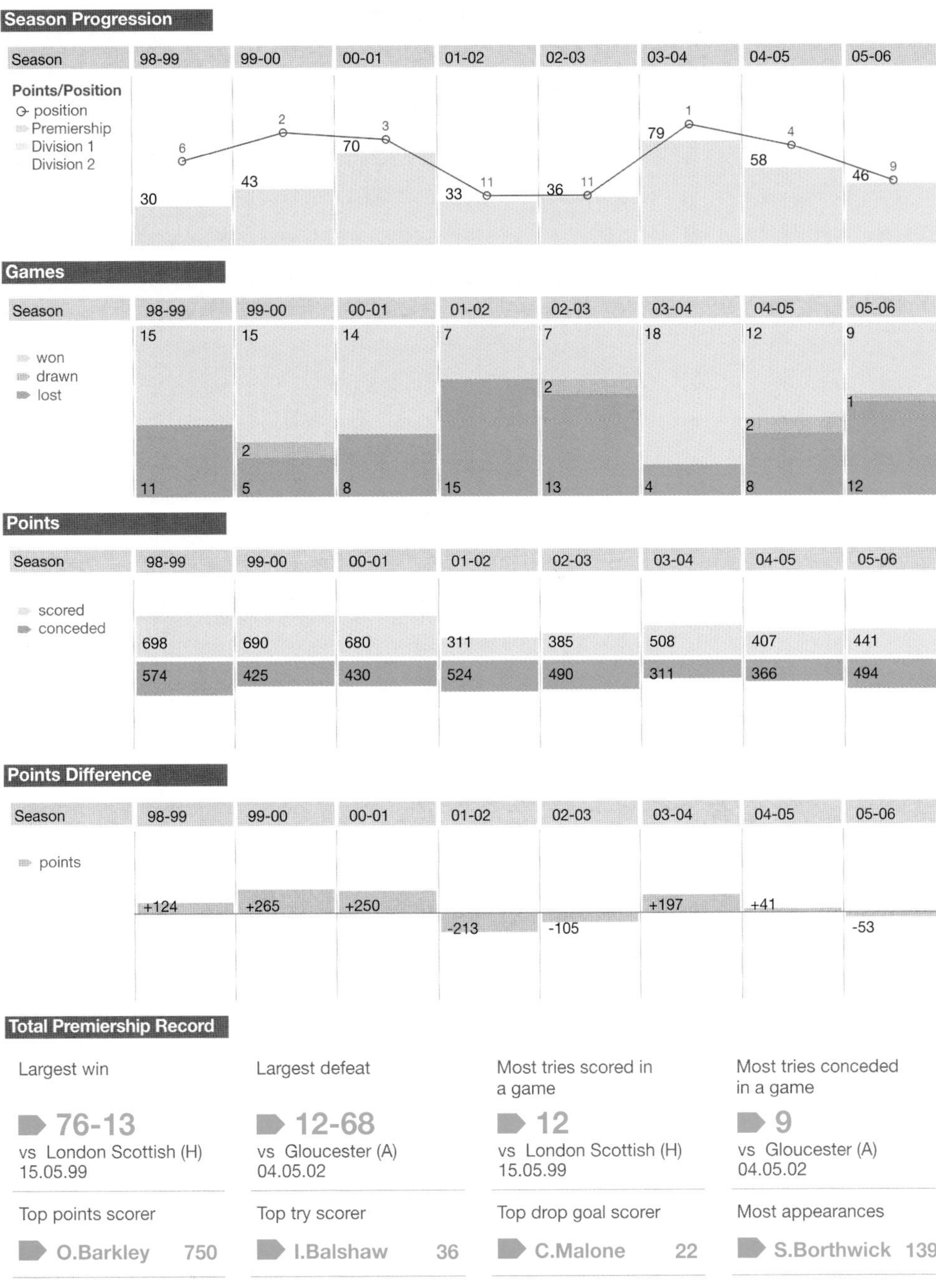

Total Premiership Record

Largest win
76-13
vs London Scottish (H)
15.05.99

Largest defeat
12-68
vs Gloucester (A)
04.05.02

Most tries scored in a game
12
vs London Scottish (H)
15.05.99

Most tries conceded in a game
9
vs Gloucester (A)
04.05.02

Top points scorer
O.Barkley 750

Top try scorer
I.Balshaw 36

Top drop goal scorer
C.Malone 22

Most appearances
S.Borthwick 139

Longest winning sequence
10 wins from 22.01.00 to 06.05.00

Longest losing sequence
6 defeats from 31.10.98 to 02.01.99

Bath Rugby EFL

ENHANCED FIXTURE LIST

[does not include play-off data]

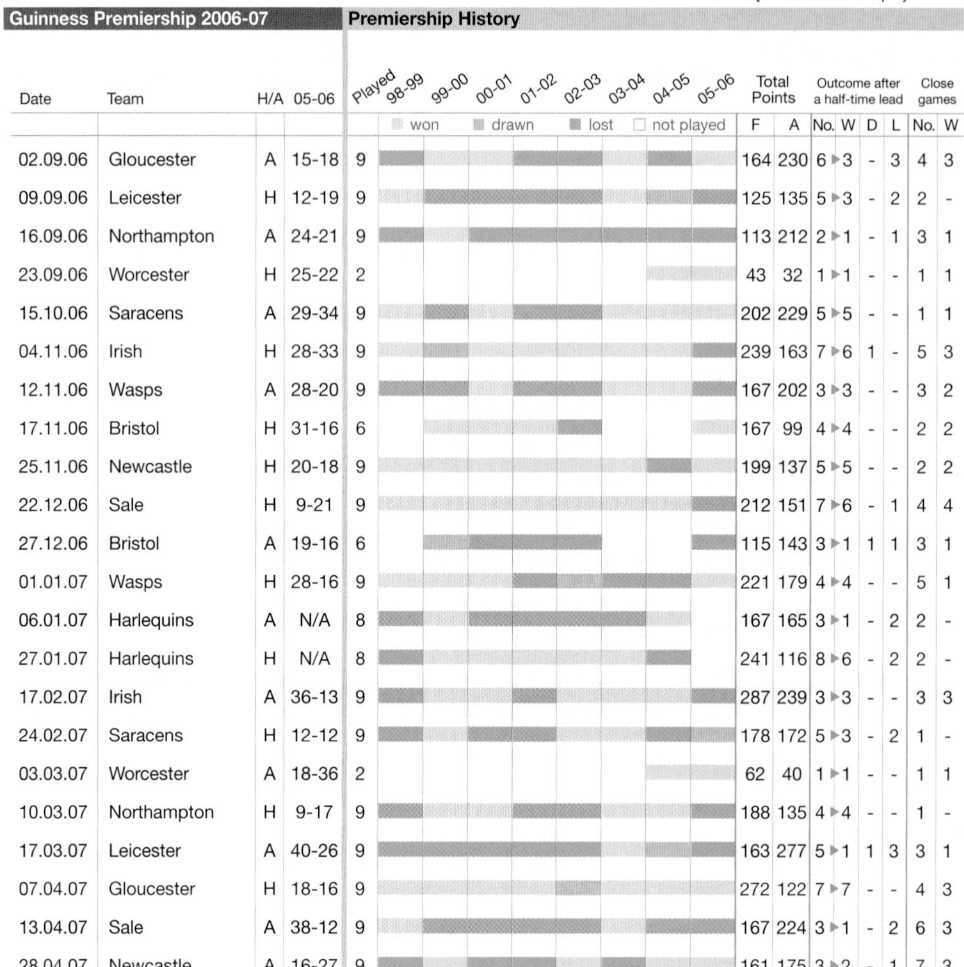

Guinness Premiership 2006-07 | **Premiership History**

won / drawn / lost / not played

Date	Team	H/A	05-06	Played	Total Points F	Total Points A	Outcome after a half-time lead No.	W	D	L	Close games No.	W
02.09.06	Gloucester	A	15-18	9	164	230	6	3	-	3	4	3
09.09.06	Leicester	H	12-19	9	125	135	5	3	-	2	2	-
16.09.06	Northampton	A	24-21	9	113	212	2	1	-	1	3	1
23.09.06	Worcester	H	25-22	2	43	32	1	1	-	-	1	1
15.10.06	Saracens	A	29-34	9	202	229	5	5	-	-	1	1
04.11.06	Irish	H	28-33	9	239	163	7	6	1	-	5	3
12.11.06	Wasps	A	28-20	9	167	202	3	3	-	-	3	2
17.11.06	Bristol	H	31-16	6	167	99	4	4	-	-	2	2
25.11.06	Newcastle	H	20-18	9	199	137	5	5	-	-	2	2
22.12.06	Sale	H	9-21	9	212	151	7	6	-	1	4	4
27.12.06	Bristol	A	19-16	6	115	143	3	1	1	1	3	1
01.01.07	Wasps	H	28-16	9	221	179	4	4	-	-	5	1
06.01.07	Harlequins	A	N/A	8	167	165	3	1	-	2	2	-
27.01.07	Harlequins	H	N/A	8	241	116	8	6	-	2	2	-
17.02.07	Irish	A	36-13	9	287	239	3	3	-	-	3	3
24.02.07	Saracens	H	12-12	9	178	172	5	3	-	2	1	-
03.03.07	Worcester	A	18-36	2	62	40	1	1	-	-	1	1
10.03.07	Northampton	H	9-17	9	188	135	4	4	-	-	1	-
17.03.07	Leicester	A	40-26	9	163	277	5	1	1	3	3	1
07.04.07	Gloucester	H	18-16	9	272	122	7	7	-	-	4	3
13.04.07	Sale	A	38-12	9	167	224	3	1	-	2	6	3
28.04.07	Newcastle	A	16-27	9	161	175	3	2	-	1	7	3

Club Information

Useful Information

Founded
1865

Address
The Recreation Ground
Bath
BA2 6PW

Capacity
10,600 (5,740 seated)

Main switchboard
01225 325200

Website
www.bathrugby.com

Travel Information

Car
(Lambridge Park & Ride):
Leave the M4 at Junction 18 and follow the A46 to Bath. Follow the signs for the town centre. The Park & Ride is at Bath Rugby's training ground on your left after the first set of traffic lights.
The Park & Ride is open for all 1st XV weekend fixtures. To go direct to the stadium, carry on past the training ground until you reach the junction on London Road with Bathwick Street. Turn left and then right down Sydney Place. Go straight on at the roundabout then turn left down North Parade. The ground is on your right.

Train
Bath has direct links to London, Bristol, Cardiff, Salisbury and Southampton. From Birmingham and the Midlands, there are connecting services at Bristol Temple Meads. National Rail enquiries: 08457 48 49 50.

Coach
National Express services operate between most major towns and cities in Britain.
For further information contact Bath Bus Station on 01225 464446 or National Express direct on 08705 80 80 80 or visit www.nationalexpress.com

Maps

Area Map

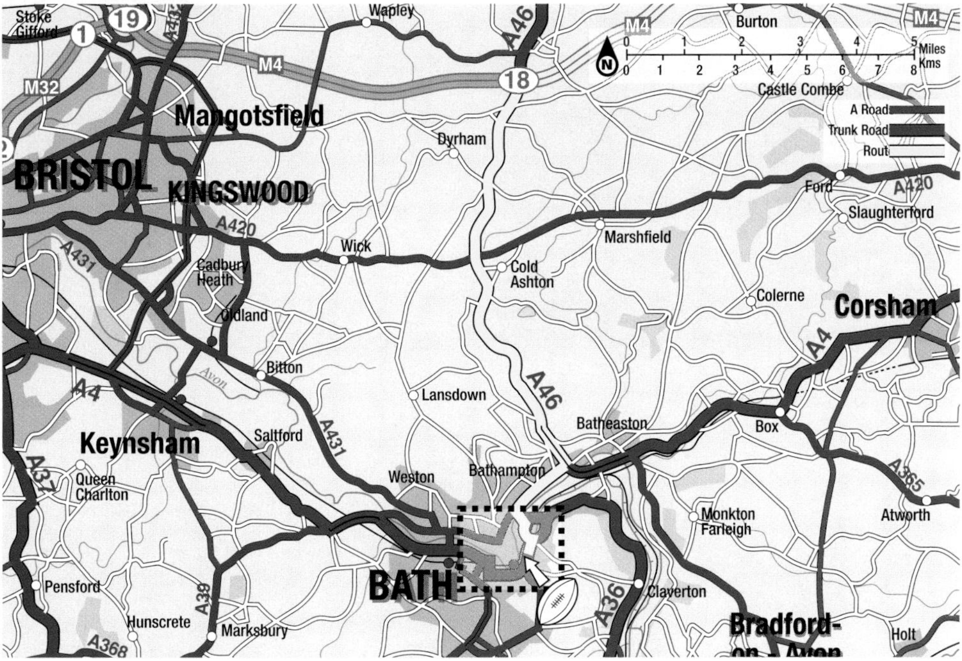

Local Map

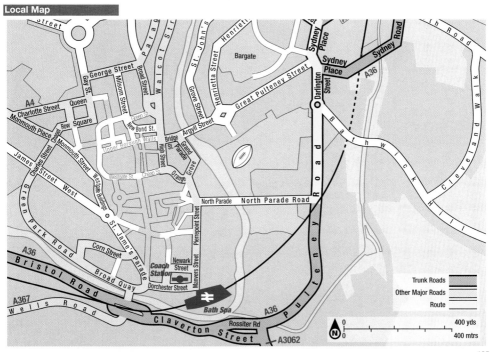

Bristol Rugby

Season Summary 2005/06

Position	Won	Drawn	Lost	For	Against	Bonus Points	Total Points
11	8	1	13	393	445	7	41

As with Worcester the previous year, there are few that would have wanted to see Bristol fall at the first hurdle. Head coach Richard Hill made a series of shrewd signings to ensure his side was no easy proposition and they proved to be a hard team to beat, enjoying victories against Tigers, Sale and Saracens. Fly half Jason Strange formed a successful pairing with newcomer Shaun Perry, with Strange finishing the season as the Premiership's top points scorer. The West Country side finished the season in 11th place with 41 points.

Head Coach: Richard Hill

Club Honours
John Player Cup: 1983

Season Squad

Stats 2005-06

Position	Player	Height	Weight	Apps	Rep	Tries	Points
BR	N.Budgett	6'5"	17st 0lb	8	-	-	-
H	N.Clark	5'11"	16st 0lb	-	6	-	-
P	A.Clarke	5'11"	17st 0lb	-	8	-	-
C	M.Contepomi	6'2"	14st 2lb	4	2	-	-
C	S.Cox	6'0"	13st 10lb	16	-	1	5
P	D.Crompton	6'2"	18st 0lb	22	-	1	5
C	M.Denney	6'0"	17st 4lb	-	5	-	-
FL	J.El Abd	6'2"	16st 0lb	14	-	2	10
FB	V.Going	5'11"	14st 2lb	14	1	-	-
FH	D.Gray	5'10"	13st 0lb	-	5	-	-
FH	T.Hayes	6'0"	14st 4lb	1	5	1	19
C	R.Higgitt	6'2"	14st 7lb	17	1	-	-
P	D.Hilton	5'11"	16st 10lb	21	-	-	-
L	O.Hodge	6'8"	16st 10lb	-	1	-	-
P	M.Irish	6'0"	16st 0lb	1	4	-	-
W	D.Lemi	5'9"	11st 11lb	12	-	8	40
BR	G.Lewis	6'3"	15st 8lb	13	6	1	5
W	B.Lima	6'0"	15st 4lb	11	2	2	10

Position	Player	Height	Weight	Apps	Rep	Tries	Points
L	G.Llewellyn	6'6"	17st 7lb	19	-	-	-
BR	R.Martin-Redman	6'3"	17st 0lb	-	1	-	-
FL	C.Morgan	6'2"	16st 4lb	-	2	-	-
H	S.Nelson	5'10"	14st 9lb	4	4	-	-
SH	G.Nicholls	5'8"	12st 0lb	1	1	-	-
SH	S.Perry	5'10"	15st 0lb	19	-	4	20
SH	J.Rauluni	5'11"	14st 6lb	2	2	-	-
H	M.Regan	5'10"	15st 2lb	18	-	1	5
W	L.Robinson	6'2"	17st 1lb	17	-	3	15
BR	M.Salter	6'4"	16st 4lb	21	-	-	-
L	M.Sambucetti	6'5"	17st 1lb	6	6	-	-
BR	C.Short	6'2"	16st 0lb	8	1	-	-
W	M.Stanojevic	5'11"	12st 7lb	5	1	2	10
FB	B.Stortoni	6'1"	14st 4lb	14	-	-	-
FH	J.Strange	5'10"	13st 3lb	21	1	1	244
8	D.Ward-Smith	6'4"	17st 8lb	10	8	-	-
L	R.Winters	6'4"	17st 10lb	11	5	1	5

Bristol Rugby

Last Season Form 2005/06

Season Progression

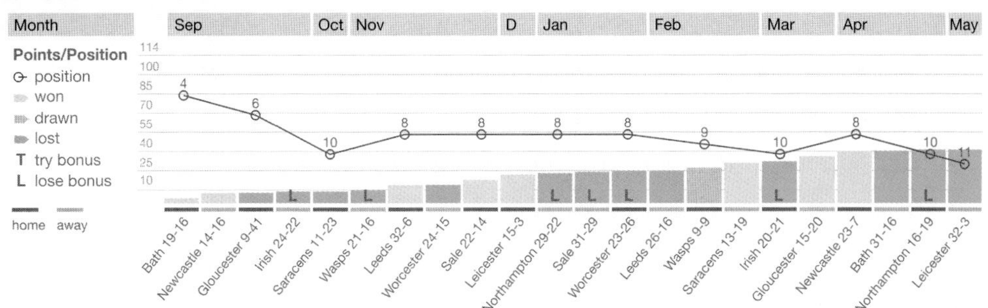

Home Matches

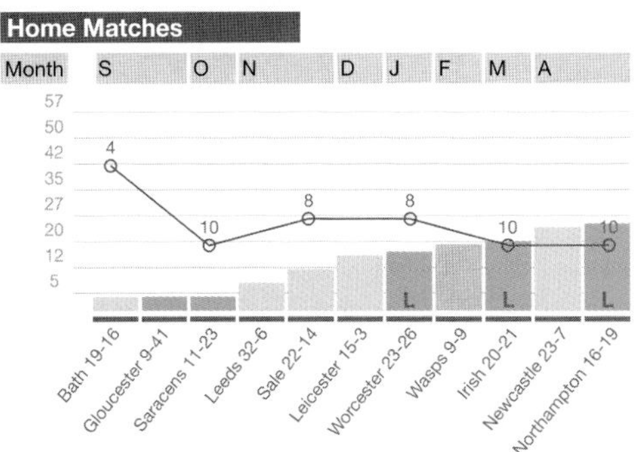

Away Matches

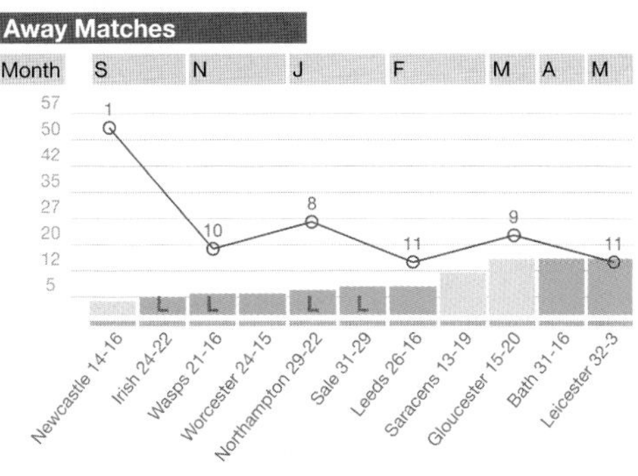

Premiership Statistics

	Total	Home	Away
Tries	28	12	16
Coversions	23	11	12
Penalty goals	69	39	30
Drop goals	0	0	0
Kick %	77%	77%	76%
Yellow/Red cards	17/0	4/0	13/0
Powerplay tries	3	2	1
Shorthand tries	1	0	1

Powerplay tries are scored when your side are playing with a man or more advantage due to yellow or red cards.

Shorthand tries are scored when your side are playing with a man or more fewer due to yellow or red cards.

Team Performance

Position	Team	% total points won	% won at home	% won away
1	Sale			
2	Leicester	24%	33%	11%
3	Irish			
4	Wasps			
5	Gloucester	20%	11%	33%
6	Northampton			
7	Newcastle			
8	Worcester	29%	33%	22%
9	Bath			
10	Saracens			
11	**Bristol**	27%	23%	34%
12	Leeds			

Bristol Rugby

Top Scorer

Jason Strange

Points Facts

Total points	% team points	Home	Away
244	62	138	106

Points by Time Period

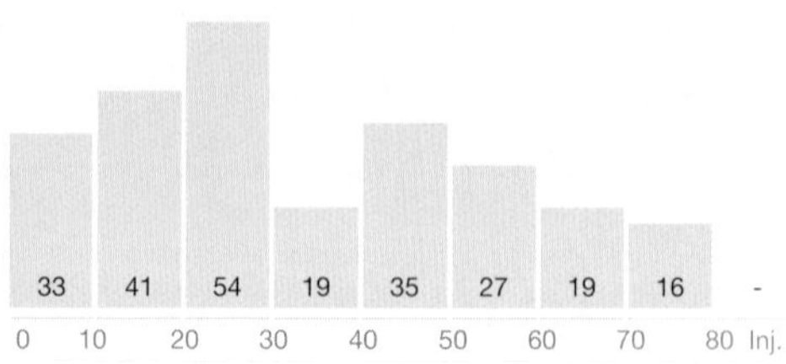

Team Tries and Points

Tries by Time Period

scored
conceded

Tries by Halves

scored
conceded

	Total	1st half	2nd half	1st half %	2nd half %
scored	28	12	16	43%	57%
conceded	41	21	20	51%	49%

How Points were Scored

tries:	140
conversions:	46
pen goals:	207
drop goals:	0

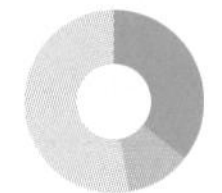

How Points were Conceded

tries:	205
conversions:	60
pen goals:	165
drop goals:	15

Tries Scored by Player

backs:	22
forwards:	6

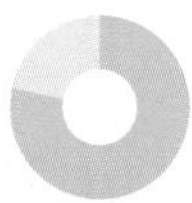

Tries Conceded by Player

backs:	25
forwards:	16

Bristol Rugby

Eight-Season Form 1998-2006

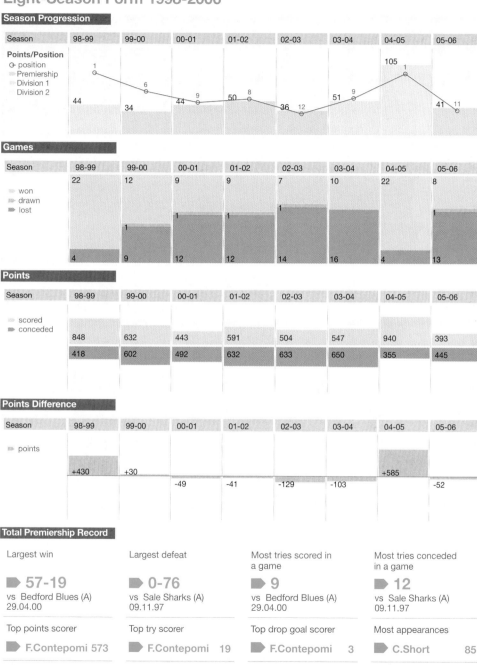

Season Progression

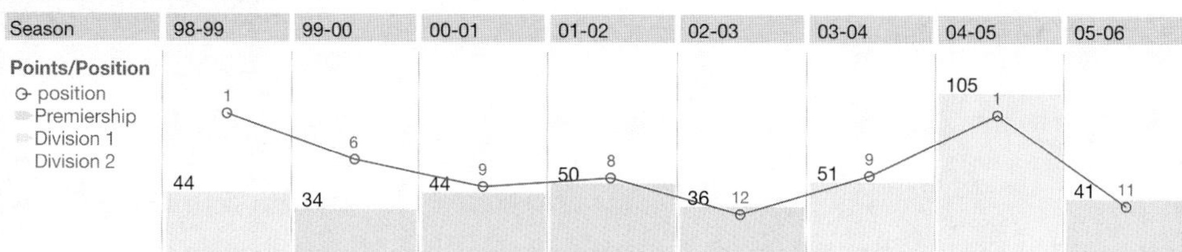

Games

Season	98-99	99-00	00-01	01-02	02-03	03-04	04-05	05-06
won	22	12	9	9	7	10	22	8
drawn		1	1	1	1			1
lost	4	9	12	12	14	16	4	13

Points

Season	98-99	99-00	00-01	01-02	02-03	03-04	04-05	05-06
scored	848	632	443	591	504	547	940	393
conceded	418	602	492	632	633	650	355	445

Points Difference

Season	98-99	99-00	00-01	01-02	02-03	03-04	04-05	05-06
points	+430	+30	-49	-41	-129	-103	+585	-52

Total Premiership Record

Largest win

57-19
vs Bedford Blues (A)
29.04.00

Largest defeat

0-76
vs Sale Sharks (A)
09.11.97

Most tries scored in a game

9
vs Bedford Blues (A)
29.04.00

Most tries conceded in a game

12
vs Sale Sharks (A)
09.11.97

Top points scorer

F.Contepomi 573

Top try scorer

F.Contepomi 19

Top drop goal scorer

F.Contepomi 3

Most appearances

C.Short 85

Longest winning sequence

4 wins from 19.04.00 to 10.05.00

Longest losing sequence

13 defeats from 18.01.98 to 10.05.98

Bristol Rugby EFL

ENHANCED FIXTURE LIST

[does not include play-off data]

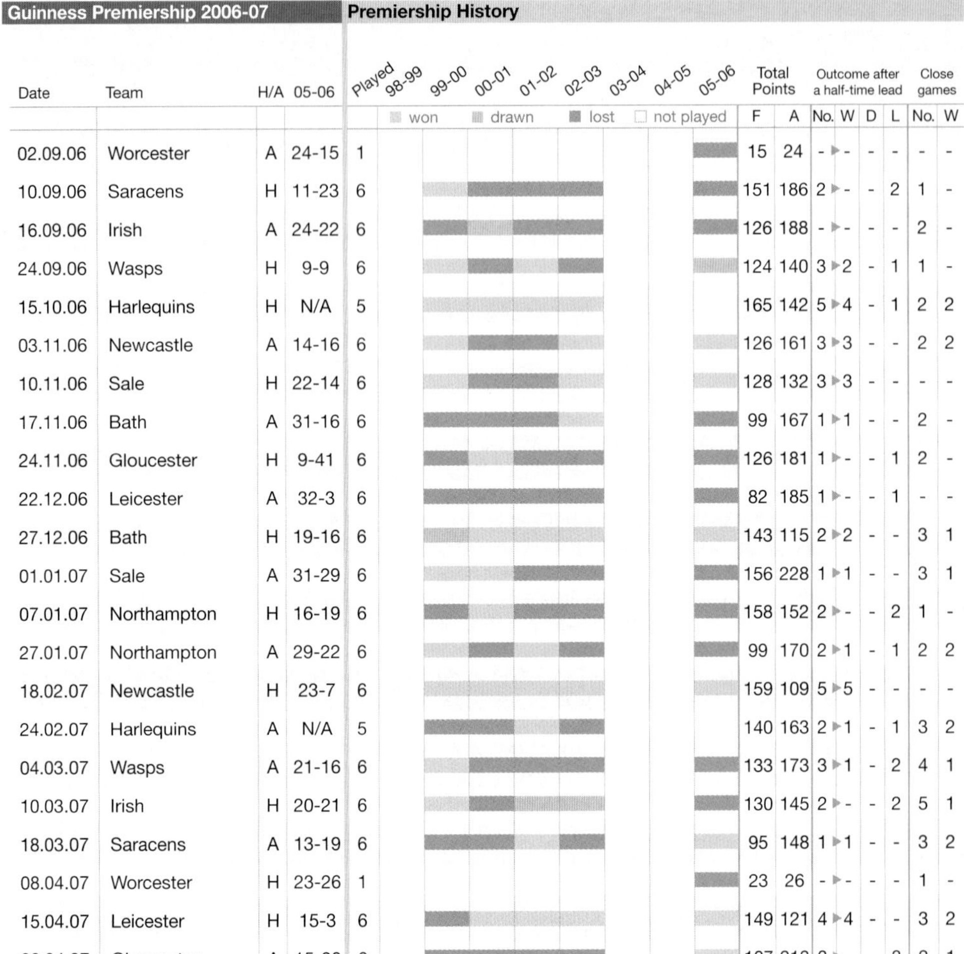

Guinness Premiership 2006-07				Premiership History																	
Date	Team	H/A	05-06	Played	98-99	99-00	00-01	01-02	02-03	03-04	04-05	05-06	Total Points		Outcome after a half-time lead				Close games	
													F	A	No.	W	D	L	No.	W
02.09.06	Worcester	A	24-15	1									15	24	-	-	-	-	-	-
10.09.06	Saracens	H	11-23	6									151	186	2	-	-	2	1	-
16.09.06	Irish	A	24-22	6									126	188	-	-	-	-	2	-
24.09.06	Wasps	H	9-9	6									124	140	3	2	-	1	1	-
15.10.06	Harlequins	H	N/A	5									165	142	5	4	-	1	2	2
03.11.06	Newcastle	A	14-16	6									126	161	3	3	-	-	2	2
10.11.06	Sale	H	22-14	6									128	132	3	3	-	-	-	-
17.11.06	Bath	A	31-16	6									99	167	1	1	-	-	2	-
24.11.06	Gloucester	H	9-41	6									126	181	1	-	-	1	2	-
22.12.06	Leicester	A	32-3	6									82	185	1	-	-	1	-	-
27.12.06	Bath	H	19-16	6									143	115	2	2	-	-	3	1
01.01.07	Sale	A	31-29	6									156	228	1	1	-	-	3	1
07.01.07	Northampton	H	16-19	6									158	152	2	-	-	2	1	-
27.01.07	Northampton	A	29-22	6									99	170	2	1	-	1	2	2
18.02.07	Newcastle	H	23-7	6									159	109	5	5	-	-	-	-
24.02.07	Harlequins	A	N/A	5									140	163	2	1	-	1	3	2
04.03.07	Wasps	A	21-16	6									133	173	3	1	-	2	4	1
10.03.07	Irish	H	20-21	6									130	145	2	-	-	2	5	1
18.03.07	Saracens	A	13-19	6									95	148	1	1	-	-	3	2
08.04.07	Worcester	H	23-26	1									23	26	-	-	-	-	1	-
15.04.07	Leicester	H	15-3	6									149	121	4	4	-	-	3	2
28.04.07	Gloucester	A	15-20	6									107	213	3	-	-	3	2	1

won · drawn · lost · not played

Club Information

Useful Information

Founded
1888

Address
The Memorial Stadium
Filton Avenue
Horfield
Bristol
BS7 0AQ

Stadium capacity
12,000 (3,000 seated)

Main switchboard
0117 952 0500

Website
www.bristolrugby.co.uk

Travel Information

Car

From the M4: Exit at junction 19 and follow signs onto the M32. Leave the M32 at junction 2 and at the roundabout turn right towards Horfield and the B4469. Continue for 1.4 miles, then after passing the bus garage (on your right) turn left at the second set of traffic lights into Filton Avenue. Take the first left into the club car park.

From the M5: Exit at junction 16 and join the A38 towards Bristol City Centre. After 5 miles turn left at traffic lights onto B4469. Turn right at the next traffic lights into Filton Avenue and then first left into car park.

Train

Nearest mainline rail stations are Bristol Parkway or Bristol Temple Meads.

Maps

Area Map

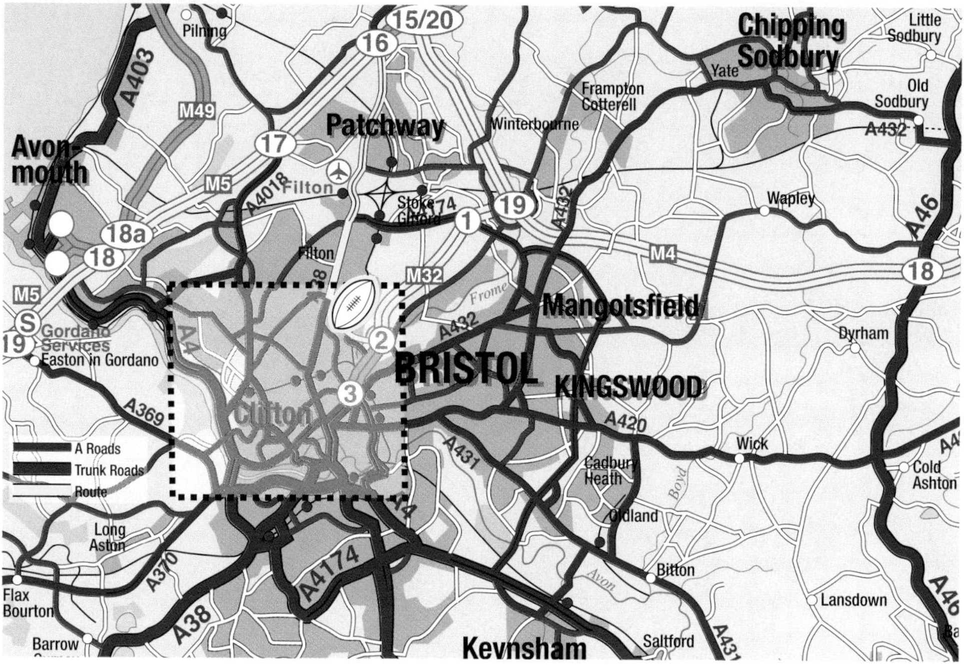

Local Map

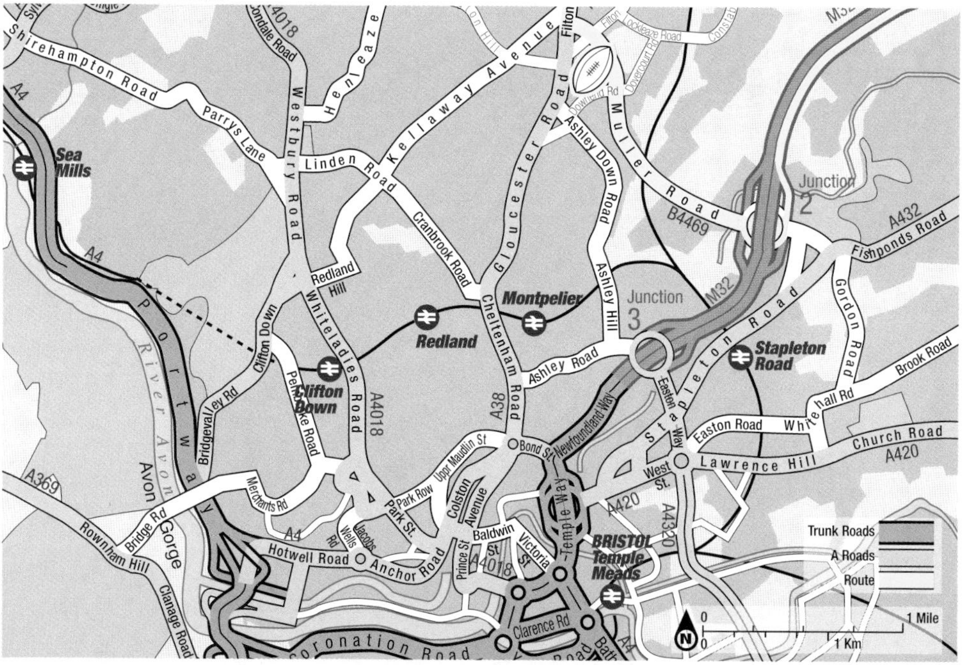

Gloucester Rugby

Season Summary 2005/06

Position	Won	Drawn	Lost	For	Against	Bonus Points	Total Points
5	11	1	10	483	385	13	59

The Kingsholm faithful had high expectations at the start of the season and welcomed new boy Mike Tindall from Bath. However, it was the young fly half Ryan Lamb who really stole the show throughout the season, especially for his performance against Worcester in the semi-final of the European Challenge Cup. Despite a positive start to their league campaign – winning four out of their first six matches – Dean Ryan's side failed to display that kind of consistency throughout the season. They did enjoy success in the European Challenge Cup, beating London Irish in the final thanks to a moment of inspirational attacking instinct from James Forrester to score what proved to be the winning try.

Head Coach: Dean Ryan

Club Honours
Zurich Premiership: 2002-03 (playoffs won by Wasps)
John Player Cup: 1972, 1978, 1982, 2003
European Challenge Cup: 2006

Season Squad

Stats 2005-06

Position	Player	Height	Weight	Apps	Rep	Tries	Points
C	J.Adams	6'0"	16st 5lb	-	2	-	-
C	A.Allen	5'11"	14st 2lb	8	1	4	20
FH/SH	S.Amor	5'7"	12st 0lb	1	3	-	-
H	O.Azam	6'0"	18st 0lb	3	3	1	5
W	J.Bailey	5'11"	13st 0lb	10	2	5	25
8	A.Balding	6'2"	17st 7lb	8	5	-	-
FL	J.Boer	6'1"	16st 8lb	9	3	1	5
L	A.Brown	6'7"	17st 5lb	18	-	-	-
BR	P.Buxton	6'3"	17st 9lb	16	3	-	-
P	P.Collazo	6'1"	17st 4lb	19	-	-	-
L	M.Cornwell	6'7"	18st 2lb	1	2	-	-
L	Q.Davids	6'6"	19st 4lb	2	1	-	-
FH	B.Davies	5'9"	14st 1lb	1	4	-	-
H	M.Davies	5'10"	15st 0lb	13	3	-	-
H	R.Elloway	6'0"	15st 6lb	4	2	-	-
L	A.Eustace	6'4"	17st 0lb	14	8	-	-
C	T.Fanolua	6'0"	14st 10lb	5	5	1	5
8	J.Forrester	6'5"	15st 9lb	14	2	3	15
P	J.Forster	6'1"	17st 11lb	4	3	-	-
W	M.Foster	6'0"	14st 4lb	19	-	5	25
W	M.Garvey	5'8"	13st 7lb	2	1	-	-
FB	J.Goodridge	6'1"	13st 8lb	9	1	1	5
FL	A.Hazell	6'0"	14st 9lb	17	1	1	5
C	R.Keil	6'1"	13st 5lb	3	1	-	-
FH	R.Lamb	5'10"	12st 10lb	4	1	1	49
FH/FB	D.McRae	5'7"	12st 10lb	-	2	-	-
FH	L.Mercier	5'10"	14st 2lb	18	4	2	213
FL	J.Merriman	6'0"	14st 7lb	1	-	-	-
FB	O.Morgan	6'2"	14st 0lb	12	-	1	5
BR	L.Narraway	6'3"	15st 10lb	2	8	-	-
H	J.Parkes	5'10"	15st 6lb	2	4	-	-
C	H.Paul	5'11"	14st 10lb	5	-	-	-
L	J.Pendlebury	6'7"	16st 5lb	8	3	-	-
P	G.Powell	6'0"	17st 9lb	7	5	-	-
SH	P.Richards	5'9"	14st 10lb	14	4	6	30
P	T.Sigley	6'2"	19st 4lb	3	8	-	-
W/C	J.Simpson-Daniel	6'0"	12st 7lb	16	-	6	30
W	R.Thirlby	6'1"	14st 0lb	7	3	1	5
SH	H.Thomas	5'8"	12st 4lb	7	7	1	5
C	M.Tindall	6'2"	16st 8lb	13	1	1	11
P	P.Vickery	6'3"	18st 4lb	8	-	-	-
P	N.Wood	6'1"	17st 0lb	3	4	-	-

Gloucester Rugby

Last Season Form 2005/06

Season Progression

Month: Sep, Oct, Nov, D, Jan, Feb, Mar, Apr, May

Points/Position
- position
- won
- drawn
- lost
- T try bonus
- L lose bonus

home away

Worcester 15-15, Sale 21-18, Bristol 9-41 (T), Northampton 28-24, Bath 18-16 (L), Newcastle 27-20, Leicester 25-20 (L), Irish 25-10, Saracens 19-8, Wasps 32-25 (L), Leeds 31-7 (T), Saracens 9-19, Irish 9-13 (L), Leicester 34-16, Newcastle 9-13, Bath 15-18 (L), Northampton 21-20 (L), Bristol 15-20 (L), Sale 18-15 (L), Worcester 27-16, Leeds 7-31 (T), Wasps 32-37 (TL)

Position: 7, 3, 4, 4, 5, 4, 4, 3, 5, 5, 5, 5

Home Matches

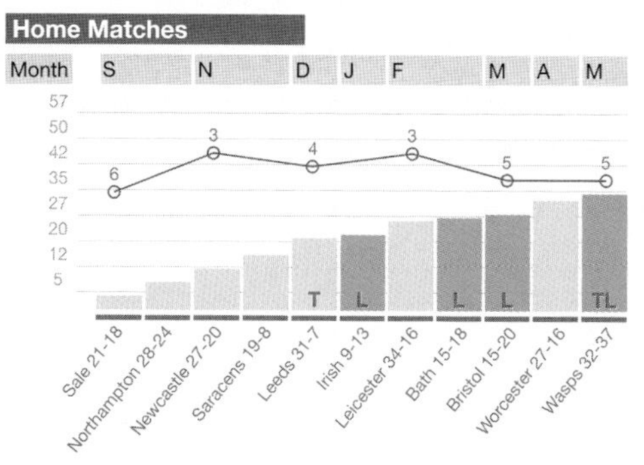

Away Matches

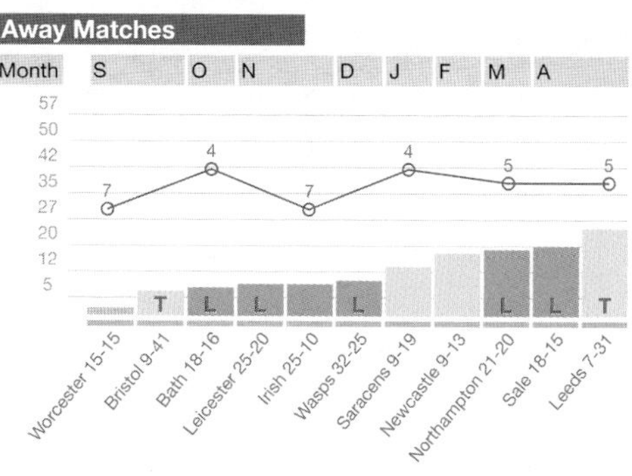

Premiership Statistics

	Total	Home	Away
Tries	46	27	19
Coversions	32	15	17
Penalty goals	61	30	31
Drop goals	2	1	1
Kick %	70%	63%	77%
Yellow/Red cards	15/1	4/1	11/0
Powerplay tries	11	7	4
Shorthand tries	3	3	0

Powerplay tries are scored when your side are playing with a man or more advantage due to yellow or red cards.

Shorthand tries are scored when your side are playing with a man or more fewer due to yellow or red cards.

Team Performance

Position	Team	% total points won	% won at home	% won away
1	Sale			
2	Leicester	17%	24%	8%
3	Irish			
4	Wasps			
5	**Gloucester**	19%	24%	12%
6	Northampton			
7	Newcastle			
8	Worcester	25%	24%	27%
9	Bath			
10	Saracens			
11	Bristol	39%	28%	53%
12	Leeds			

Gloucester Rugby

Top Scorer

Ludovic Mercier

Points Facts

Total points	% team points	Home	Away
213	47	104	109

Points by Time Period

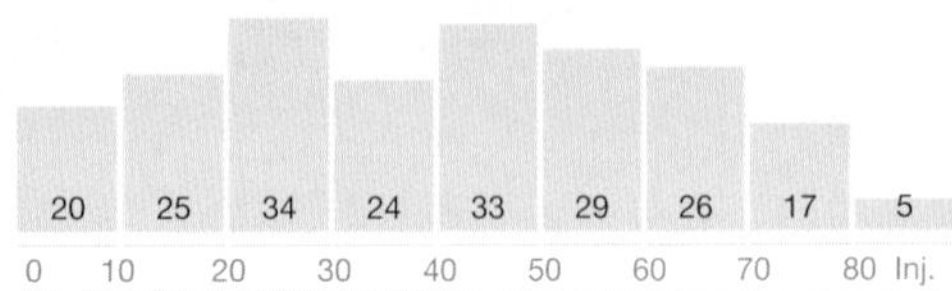

Team Tries and Points

Tries by Time Period

scored
conceded

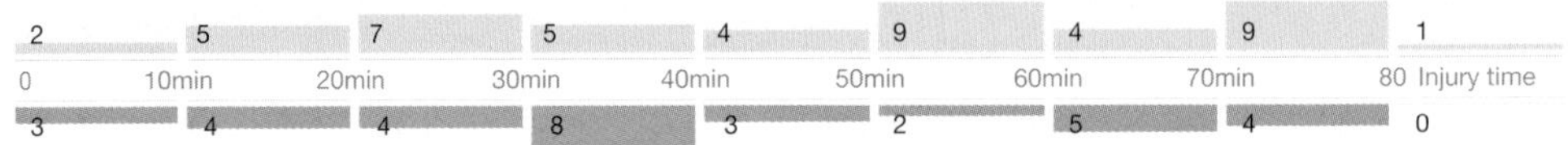

Tries by Halves

scored
conceded

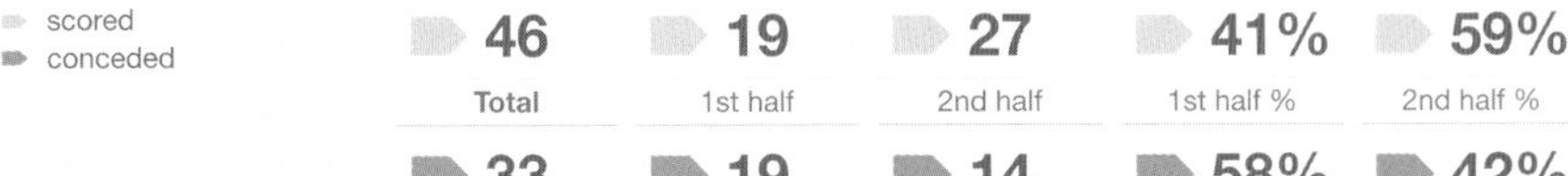

How Points were Scored

- tries: 230
- conversions: 64
- pen goals: 183
- drop goals: 6

How Points were Conceded

- tries: 165
- conversions: 52
- pen goals: 159
- drop goals: 9

Tries Scored by Player

- backs: 35
- forwards: 6

Tries Conceded by Player

- backs: 14
- forwards: 18

Gloucester Rugby

Eight-Season Form 1998-2006

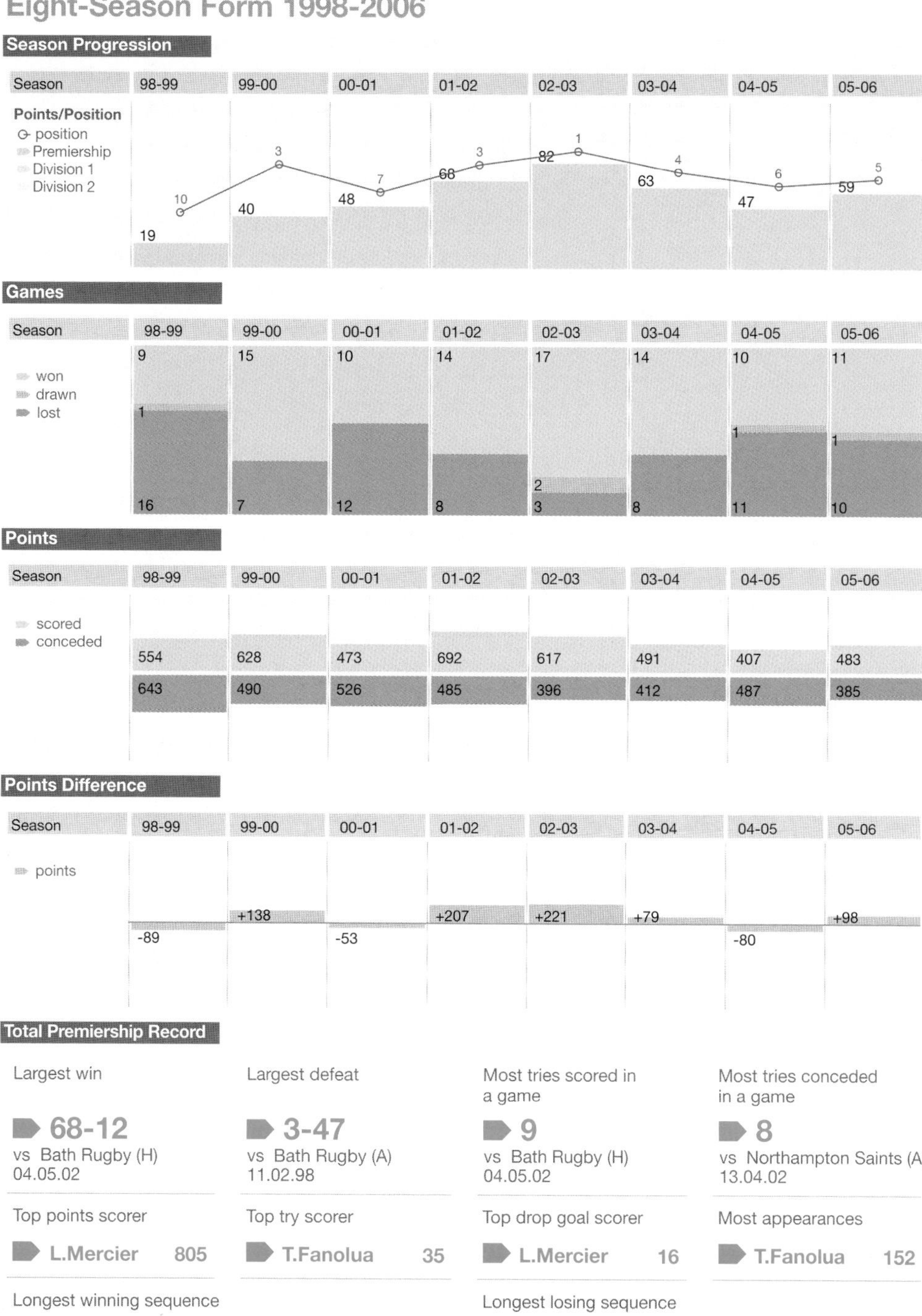

Total Premiership Record

Largest win
68-12
vs Bath Rugby (H)
04.05.02

Largest defeat
3-47
vs Bath Rugby (A)
11.02.98

Most tries scored in a game
9
vs Bath Rugby (H)
04.05.02

Most tries conceded in a game
8
vs Northampton Saints (A)
13.04.02

Top points scorer
L.Mercier 805

Top try scorer
T.Fanolua 35

Top drop goal scorer
L.Mercier 16

Most appearances
T.Fanolua 152

Longest winning sequence
8 wins from 24.11.02 to 12.04.03

Longest losing sequence
8 defeats from 23.01.99 to 07.05.99

Gloucester Rugby EFL

ENHANCED FIXTURE LIST

[does not include play-off data]

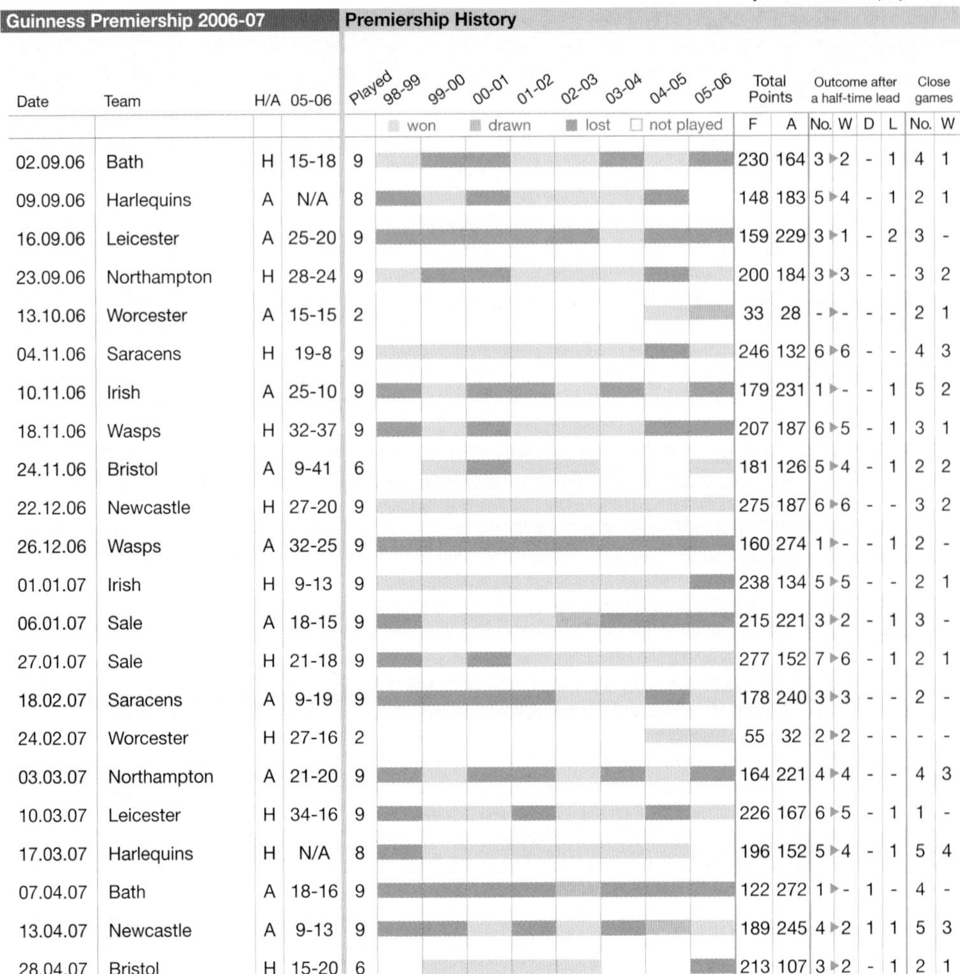

Guinness Premiership 2006-07 / Premiership History

Date	Team	H/A	05-06	Played	Total Points F	Total Points A	Outcome after a half-time lead No.	W	D	L	Close games No.	W
02.09.06	Bath	H	15-18	9	230	164	3	2	-	1	4	1
09.09.06	Harlequins	A	N/A	8	148	183	5	4	-	1	2	1
16.09.06	Leicester	A	25-20	9	159	229	3	1	-	2	3	-
23.09.06	Northampton	H	28-24	9	200	184	3	3	-	-	3	2
13.10.06	Worcester	A	15-15	2	33	28	-	-	-	-	2	1
04.11.06	Saracens	H	19-8	9	246	132	6	6	-	-	4	3
10.11.06	Irish	A	25-10	9	179	231	1	-	-	1	5	2
18.11.06	Wasps	H	32-37	9	207	187	6	5	-	1	3	1
24.11.06	Bristol	A	9-41	6	181	126	5	4	-	1	2	2
22.12.06	Newcastle	H	27-20	9	275	187	6	6	-	-	3	2
26.12.06	Wasps	A	32-25	9	160	274	1	-	-	1	2	-
01.01.07	Irish	H	9-13	9	238	134	5	5	-	-	2	1
06.01.07	Sale	A	18-15	9	215	221	3	2	-	1	3	-
27.01.07	Sale	H	21-18	9	277	152	7	6	-	1	2	1
18.02.07	Saracens	A	9-19	9	178	240	3	3	-	-	2	-
24.02.07	Worcester	H	27-16	2	55	32	2	2	-	-	-	-
03.03.07	Northampton	A	21-20	9	164	221	4	4	-	-	4	3
10.03.07	Leicester	H	34-16	9	226	167	6	5	-	1	1	-
17.03.07	Harlequins	H	N/A	8	196	152	5	4	-	1	5	4
07.04.07	Bath	A	18-16	9	122	272	1	-	1	-	4	-
13.04.07	Newcastle	A	9-13	9	189	245	4	2	1	1	5	3
28.04.07	Bristol	H	15-20	6	213	107	3	2	-	1	2	1

Club Information

Useful Information

Founded
1873

Address
Kingsholm
Kingsholm Road
Gloucester
GL1 3AX

Capacity
13,000 (1,498 seated)

Main switchboard
01452 381087

Website
www.gloucesterrugbyclub.com

Travel Information

Car

From Midlands: From the M5 southbound, exit at junction 11 (Cheltenham south and Gloucester north). Follow A40 to Gloucester/ Ross and Northern Bypass. Turn left at Longford roundabout (where A40 crosses A38) towards the City Centre. Go straight over the Tewkesbury Road roundabout and the ground is on your right after a quarter of a mile.

From South: From the M4 westbound, exit at junction 15 (Swindon) and follow the A419/417 to Gloucester. At Zoons Court roundabout follow the signs A40 to Ross and continue along Northern Bypass until you reach Longford roundabout. The as route for Midlands.

From West Country: Exit the M5 northbound at junction 11A (Gloucester) until you reach Zoons Court roundabout. Then as above.

Parking is available approx 5 minutes from the ground. Turn right at the Tewkesbury Road roundabout and follow the signs for the Park and Ride Car Park.

Train

Gloucester station is a 5 minute walk from the ground, and is well sign-posted.

Virgin Trains, Great Western and Central Trains all serve Gloucester from the Midlands, and there are direct services from all regions.

Maps

Area Map

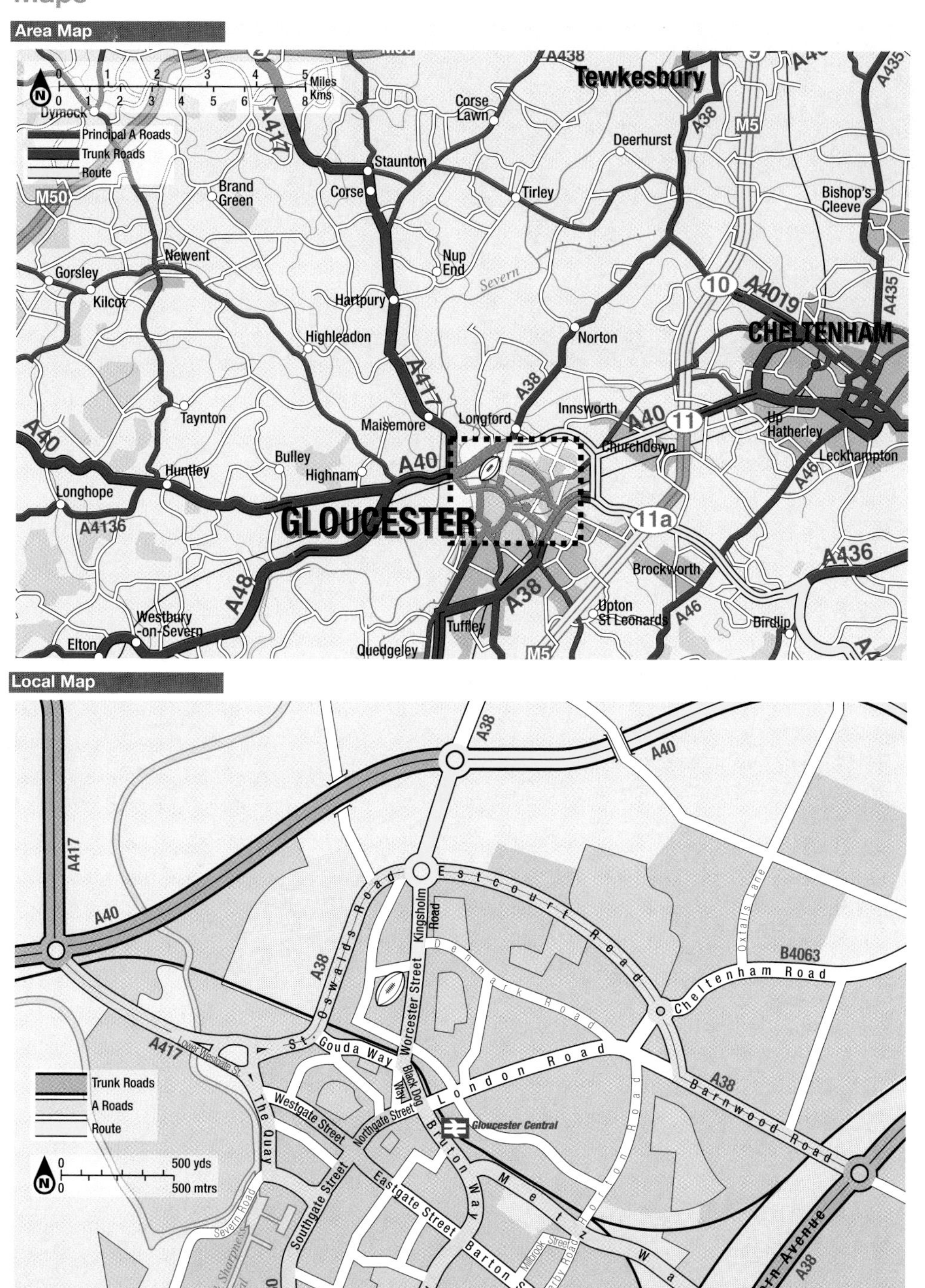

Leicester Tigers

Season Summary 2005/06

Position	Won	Drawn	Lost	For	Against	Bonus Points	Total Points
2	14	3	5	518	415	6	68

Despite being out-classed in the Premiership final, Pat Howard will reflect on the 2005/06 season with a great deal of satisfaction. After an indifferent start, Tigers ended the season as the competition's form side. The Heineken Cup quarter-final defeat to Bath Rugby at the Walkers Stadium was a watershed, as Leicester went on an unbeaten run that resulted in them cruising into the Premiership semi-finals where they defeated London Irish. Much had been made of the recent retirement of influential players, but Tigers remain a force in the domestic game. Welford Road is still one of the toughest places to earn a win, while the Midlands team will be looking to appease fans by winning some silverware.

Head Coach: Pat Howard

Club Honours

Courage League / Allied Dunbar Premiership / Zurich Premiership: 1987-88, 1994-95, 1998-99 1999-2000, 2000-01, 2001-02, 2004-05 (lost in play-offs)

John Player Cup / Pilkington Cup: 1979, 1980, 1981, 1993, 1997

Heineken Cup: 2000-01 2001-02

Season Squad

Stats 2005-06

Position	Player	Height	Weight	Apps	Rep	Tries	Points
FL/H	L.Abraham	6'2"	16st 5lb	5	6	-	-
SH	S.Bemand	5'11"	13st 5lb	4	4	-	-
FH	R.Broadfoot	5'11"	13st 2lb	4	4	-	28
H	J.Buckland	5'11"	16st 11lb	6	9	1	5
H	G.Chuter	5'10"	15st 12lb	17	2	3	15
SH	N.Cole	5'11"	12st 6lb	1	2	-	-
C/FB	M.Cornwell	6'1"	15st 0lb	3	3	3	15
FL	M.Corry	6'5"	17st 10lb	13	1	-	-
L	T.Croft	6'5"	16st 4lb	2	-	-	-
L	L.Cullen	6'6"	17st 5lb	14	6	-	-
FL	B.Deacon	6'4"	17st 0lb	10	-	-	-
L	L.Deacon	6'5"	17st 10lb	14	4	1	5
C	A.Dodge	6'2"	15st 0lb	-	2	-	-
SH	H.Ellis	5'10"	13st 4lb	10	2	2	10
C	D.Gibson	5'11"	15st 6lb	8	2	-	-
FH	A.Goode	5'11"	13st 9lb	15	4	-	225
L	J.Hamilton	6'8"	19st 4lb	7	10	3	15
UB	A.Healey	5'10"	13st 9lb	14	8	1	5
C	D.Hipkiss	5'10"	14st 2lb	12	1	1	5
P	M.Holford	5'11"	16st 1lb	8	11	4	20
FH	I.Humphreys	5'11"	13st 1lb	2	1	-	15
FL	S.Jennings	6'0"	16st 1lb	16	3	1	5
BR	W.Johnson	6'4"	17st 0lb	10	4	1	5
L	B.Kay	6'6"	17st 9lb	18	2	1	5
W/C	L.Lloyd	6'4"	15st 2lb	16	5	4	20
FL	L.Moody	6'3"	16st 8lb	8	-	1	5
P	A.Moreno	6'1"	17st 5lb	6	1	-	-
P	D.Morris	6'1"	19st 10lb	8	6	1	5
FB/W	G.Murphy	6'1"	13st 3lb	13	-	2	13
C/W	S.Rabeni	6'2"	15st 0lb	2	1	-	-
P	G.Rowntree	6'0"	17st 3lb	13	-	-	-
FL	W.Skinner	5'11"	14st 2lb	3	6	2	10
C/W	O.Smith	6'1"	14st 7lb	17	4	2	10
H	E.Taukafa	5'11"	17st 0lb	1	6	1	5
W/C	A.Tuilagi	6'1"	17st 7lb	14	4	5	25
BR	H.Tuilagi	6'1"	18st 10lb	-	2	1	5
W	T.Varndell	6'3"	14st 13lb	18	3	14	70
FH/FB	S.Vesty	6'0"	14st 2lb	15	5	2	27
P	J.White	6'1"	18st 0lb	13	2	-	-

Leicester Tigers

Last Season Form 2005/06

Season Progression

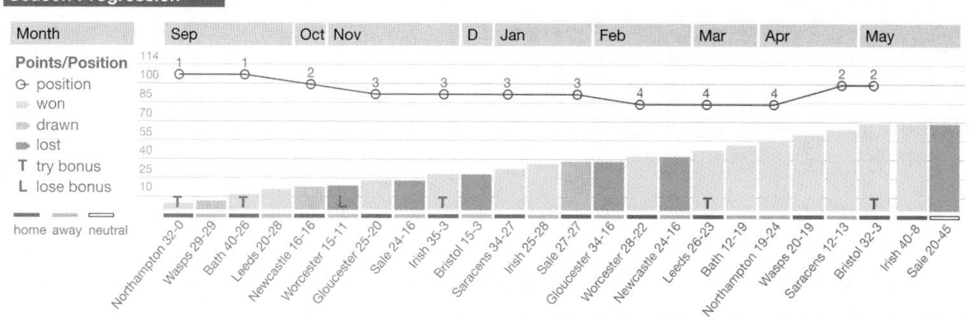

Home Matches

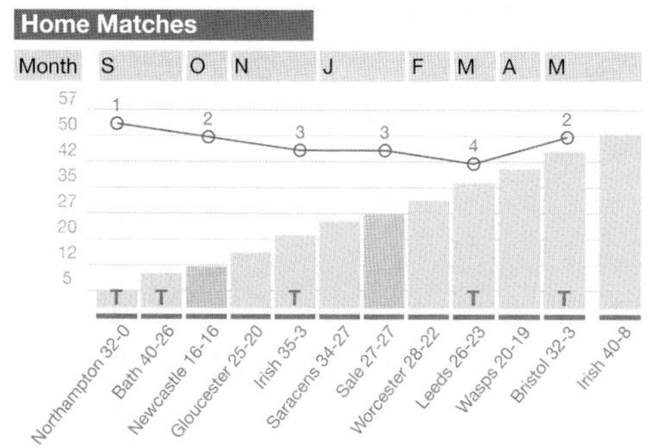

Away Matches

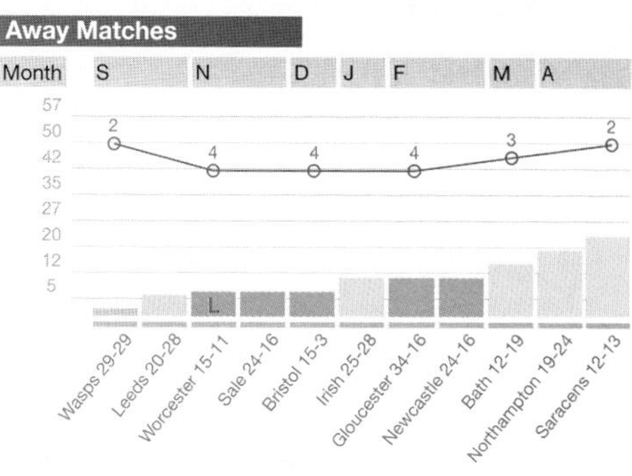

Premiership Stats

Premiership Stats	Home	Away	Neutral
Tries 58	40	16	2
Coversions 39	25	12	2
Penalty goals 69	34	33	2
Drop goals 1	1	0	0
Kick % 68%	66%	69%	80%
Yellow/Red cards 18/1	6/1	12/0	0/0
Powerplay tries 7	4	3	0
Shorthand tries 2	1	1	0

Powerplay tries are scored when your side are playing with a man or more advantage due to yellow or red cards.

Shorthand tries are scored when your side are playing with a man or more fewer due to yellow or red cards.

Team Performance

Position	Team	% total points won	% won at home	% won away
1	Sale			
2	**Leicester**	22%	22%	24%
3	Irish			
4	Wasps			
5	Gloucester	26%	27%	24%
6	Northampton			
7	Newcastle			
8	Worcester	22%	23%	20%
9	Bath			
10	Saracens			
11	Bristol	30%	28%	32%
12	Leeds			

Leicester Tigers

Top Scorer

Andy Goode

Points Facts

Total points	% team points	Home	Away	Neutral
225	39	144	71	10

Points by Time Period

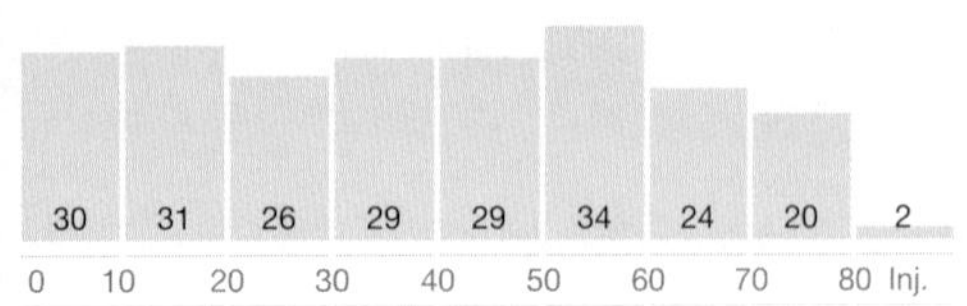

0–10	10–20	20–30	30–40	40–50	50–60	60–70	70–80	Inj.
30	31	26	29	29	34	24	20	2

Team Tries and Points

Tries by Time Period

- scored
- conceded

	0–10min	10–20min	20–30min	30–40min	40–50min	50–60min	60–70min	70–80	Injury time
scored	9	6	9	9	6	4	4	10	1
conceded	2	5	4	6	2	3	1	6	0

Tries by Halves

- scored
- conceded

	Total	1st half	2nd half	1st half %	2nd half %
scored	58	33	25	57%	43%
conceded	29	17	12	59%	41%

How Points were Scored

- tries: 290
- conversions: 78
- pen goals: 207
- drop goals: 3

How Points were Conceded

- tries: 145
- conversions: 44
- pen goals: 255
- drop goals: 24

Tries Scored by Player

- backs: 35
- forwards: 21

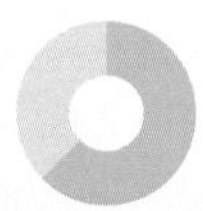

Tries Conceded by Player

- backs: 17
- forwards: 11

Eight-Season Form 1998-2006

Season Progression

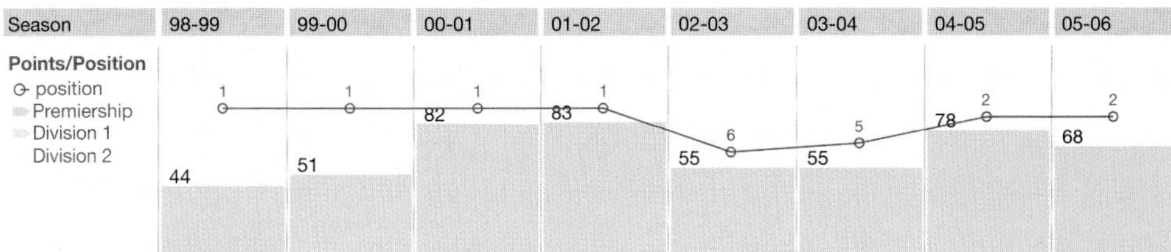

Games

Season	98-99	99-00	00-01	01-02	02-03	03-04	04-05	05-06
won	22	18	18	18	12	11	15	14
drawn		1	1			3	3	3
lost	4	3	3	4	10	8	4	5

Points

Season	98-99	99-00	00-01	01-02	02-03	03-04	04-05	05-06
scored	771	687	571	658	448	537	665	518
conceded	423	425	346	349	396	430	323	415

Points Difference

Season	98-99	99-00	00-01	01-02	02-03	03-04	04-05	05-06
points	+348	+262	+225	+309	+52	+107	+342	+103

Total Premiership Record

Largest win

83-10
vs Newcastle Falcons (H)
19.02.05

Largest defeat

6-34
vs Gloucester (A)
01.10.99

Most tries scored in a game

12
vs West Hartlepool (H)
16.05.99

Most tries conceded in a game

6
vs Northampton Saints (A)
11.09.99

Top points scorer

T.Stimpson 1180

Top try scorer

N.Back 59

Top drop goal scorer

A.Goode 15

Most appearances

G.Rowntree 150

Longest winning sequence

17 wins from 26.12.99 to 06.09.00

Longest losing sequence

5 defeats from 04.10.03 to 01.11.03

Leicester Tigers EFL

ENHANCED FIXTURE LIST

[does not include play-off data]

Guinness Premiership 2006-07 | **Premiership History**

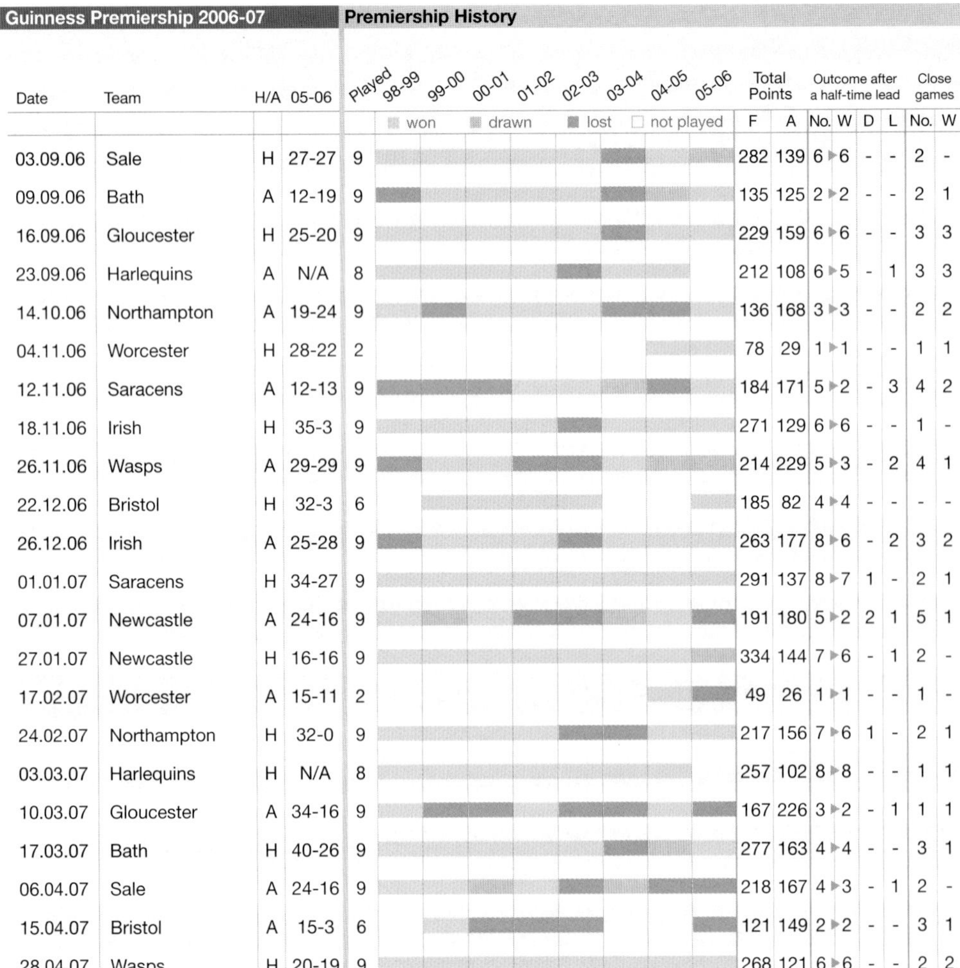

Date	Team	H/A	05-06	Played	Total Points F	Total Points A	Outcome after a half-time lead No.	W	D	L	Close games No.	Close games W
03.09.06	Sale	H	27-27	9	282	139	6	6	-	-	2	-
09.09.06	Bath	A	12-19	9	135	125	2	2	-	-	2	1
16.09.06	Gloucester	H	25-20	9	229	159	6	6	-	-	3	3
23.09.06	Harlequins	A	N/A	8	212	108	6	5	-	1	3	3
14.10.06	Northampton	A	19-24	9	136	168	3	3	-	-	2	2
04.11.06	Worcester	H	28-22	2	78	29	1	1	-	-	1	1
12.11.06	Saracens	A	12-13	9	184	171	5	2	-	3	4	2
18.11.06	Irish	H	35-3	9	271	129	6	6	-	-	1	-
26.11.06	Wasps	A	29-29	9	214	229	5	3	-	2	4	1
22.12.06	Bristol	H	32-3	6	185	82	4	4	-	-	-	-
26.12.06	Irish	A	25-28	9	263	177	8	6	-	2	3	2
01.01.07	Saracens	H	34-27	9	291	137	8	7	1	-	2	1
07.01.07	Newcastle	A	24-16	9	191	180	5	2	2	1	5	1
27.01.07	Newcastle	H	16-16	9	334	144	7	6	-	1	2	-
17.02.07	Worcester	A	15-11	2	49	26	1	1	-	-	1	-
24.02.07	Northampton	H	32-0	9	217	156	7	6	1	-	2	1
03.03.07	Harlequins	H	N/A	8	257	102	8	8	-	-	1	1
10.03.07	Gloucester	A	34-16	9	167	226	3	2	-	1	1	1
17.03.07	Bath	H	40-26	9	277	163	4	4	-	-	3	1
06.04.07	Sale	A	24-16	9	218	167	4	3	-	1	2	-
15.04.07	Bristol	A	15-3	6	121	149	2	2	-	-	3	1
28.04.07	Wasps	H	20-19	9	268	121	6	6	-	-	2	2

Club Information

Useful Information

Founded
1888

Address
Welford Road Stadium
Aylestone Road
Leicester LE2 7TR

Capacity
16,815 (12,411 seated)

Main switchboard
08701 283 430

Website
www.leicestertigers.com

Travel Information

Car

From M1 (North and South) and M69 (East): Exit the motorway at Junction 21 (M1). Follow the signs for the city centre via Narborough Road (A5460). After 3 miles, at the crossroad junction with Upperton Road, turn right. The stadium is 1/2 mile ahead (past Leicester City Football ground on the right).

From A6 (South): Follow the signs for the city centre, coming in via London Road. At the main set of lights opposite the entrance to the railway station (on the right), turn left onto the Waterloo Way. The stadium is 1/2 mile further on.

From A47 (East): Follow the signs for the city centre, coming in via Uppingham Road. At the St Georges Retail Park roundabout, take the second exit into St Georges Way (A594). Carry on past the Leicester Mercury offices on the right, and then filter off right into Waterloo Way just before the Railway Station. The stadium is 1/2 mile further on.

Train

Leicester Station is a ten minute walk away, along Waterloo Way.

Maps

Area Map

Local Map

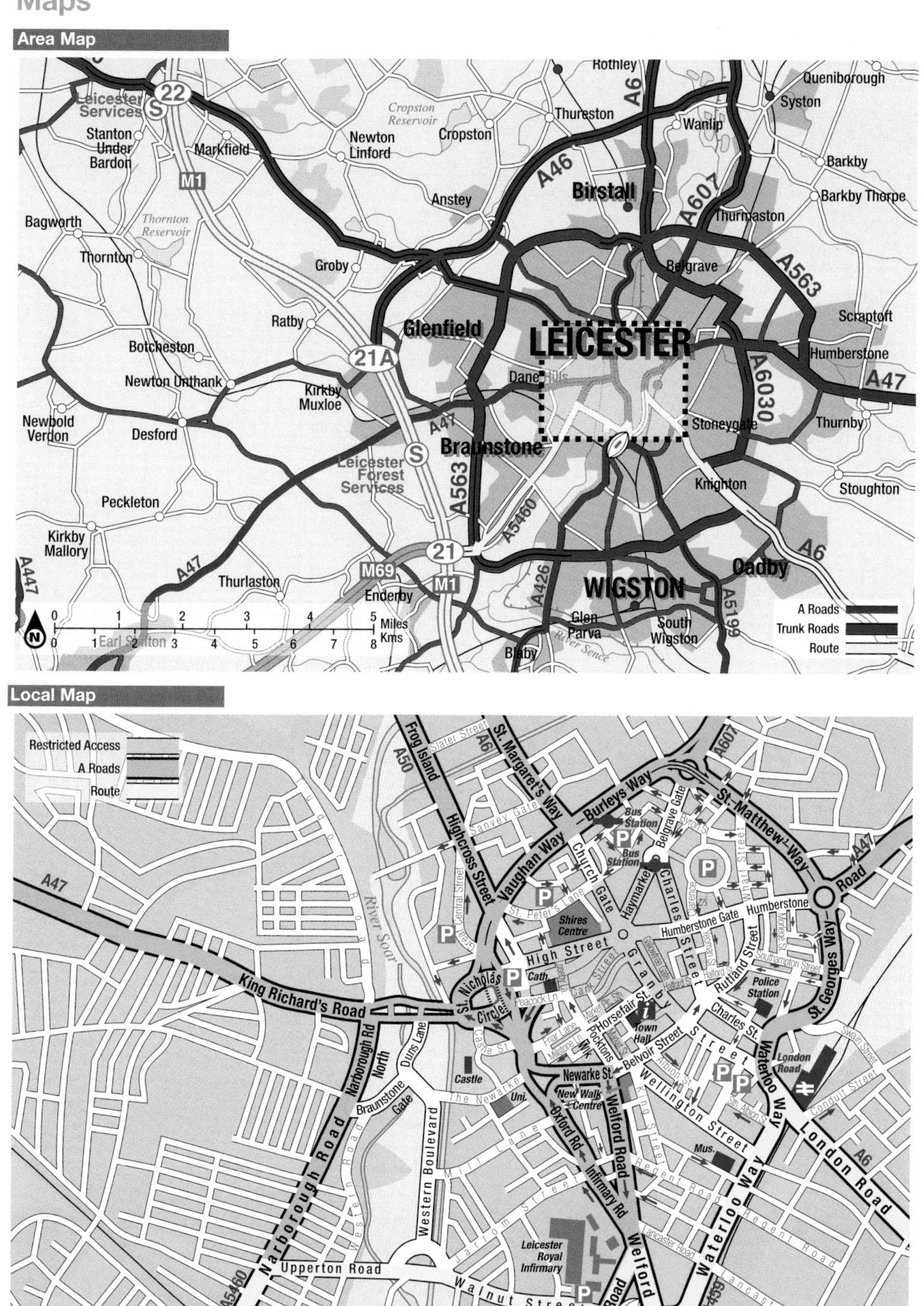

London Irish

Season Summary 2005/06

Position	Won	Drawn	Lost	For	Against	Bonus Points	Total Points
3	14	0	8	493	454	10	66

If the Premiership title was decided by a style of play, London Irish would have been worthy champions in 2005/06. In a remarkable close season turn around, Brian Smith's side went from the lowest try-scoring Premiership side to the competition's most prolific. Key to that success was an ambition to play open, attacking rugby which suited the Exiles' talented and pacey back line. While players such as Tipsy Ojo and Delon Armitage set the Premiership alight, it was Mike Catt who was to prove most influential for Irish. The veteran World Cup winner enjoyed an Indian summer of a season, winning an England recall and sparking everything that was good about Irish.

Director of Rugby: Brian Smith

Club Honours
Powergen Cup: 2002

Season Squad

Stats 2005-06

Position	Player	Height	Weight	Apps	Rep	Tries	Points
W/FB	D.Armitage	6'1"	12st 8lb	21	1	8	40
W/C	J.Bishop	6'1"	13st 10lb	9	2	1	5
L	B.Casey	6'7"	19st 3lb	21	1	2	10
C/FH	M.Catt	5'10"	13st 8lb	19	1	2	33
H	D.Coetzee	6'1"	17st 5lb	8	2	-	-
P	M.Collins	5'10"	17st 9lb	2	11	-	-
BR	D.Danaher	6'4"	16st 3lb	13	1	1	5
FL	K.Dawson	6'1"	15st 3lb	11	4	1	5
SH	D.Edwards	5'8"	12st 9lb	1	3	-	-
FH	B.Everitt	5'9"	12st 13lb	9	4	-	109
W	D.Feau'nati	6'1"	17st 5lb	5	-	2	10
H	A.Flavin	5'10"	16st 7lb	5	3	-	-
FH	R.Flutey	5'11"	13st 9lb	16	-	7	112
C	P.Franze	6'1"	15st 6lb	2	1	-	-
FH	S.Geraghty	5'11"	13st 0lb	2	5	1	5
BR	P.Gustard	6'4"	17st 0lb	2	9	1	5
P	R.Hardwick	5'11"	18st 10lb	3	1	-	-
P	N.Hatley	6'1"	18st 11lb	21	2	-	-
SH	P.Hodgson	5'8"	12st 9lb	15	5	2	10
FB	M.Horak	6'3"	14st 6lb	10	2	1	5
L	N.Kennedy	6'8"	17st 10lb	12	3	-	-
FH	R.Laidlaw	5'10"	13st 2lb	1	1	-	17
BR	J.Leguizamon	6'2"	16st 1lb	10	6	1	5
FL	O.Magne	6'2"	15st 0lb	11	-	2	10
C	N.Mordt	6'1"	14st 12lb	6	1	1	5
8	P.Murphy	6'5"	17st 3lb	12	8	2	10
W	T.Ojo	5'11"	13st 1lb	8	3	7	35
H	D.Paice	6'1"	15st 12lb	4	9	2	10
C	R.Penney	6'0"	14st 7lb	12	-	1	5
P	F.Rautenbach	6'2"	18st 0lb	13	2	-	-
L/BR	K.Roche	6'7"	18st 2lb	20	1	1	5
H	R.Russell	5'10"	15st 4lb	6	7	-	-
P	R.Skuse	5'11"	18st 2lb	7	6	-	-
W/FB	S.Staniforth	6'2"	15st 11lb	7	-	3	15
C	J.Storey	6'3"	14st 5lb	-	1	-	-
L	R.Strudwick	6'5"	17st 0lb	2	11	1	5
W/FB	S.Tagicakibau	6'3"	14st 12lb	9	1	4	20
FL	R.Thorpe	6'1"	15st 7lb	1	2	-	-
C	G.Tiesi	6'1"	13st 12lb	2	4	1	5
P	T.Warren	6'1"	17st 0lb	-	1	-	-
P	D.Wheatley	6'2"	18st 12lb	-	2	-	-
SH	B.Willis	5'9"	13st 8lb	7	7	-	-

London Irish

Last Season Form 2005/06

Season Progression

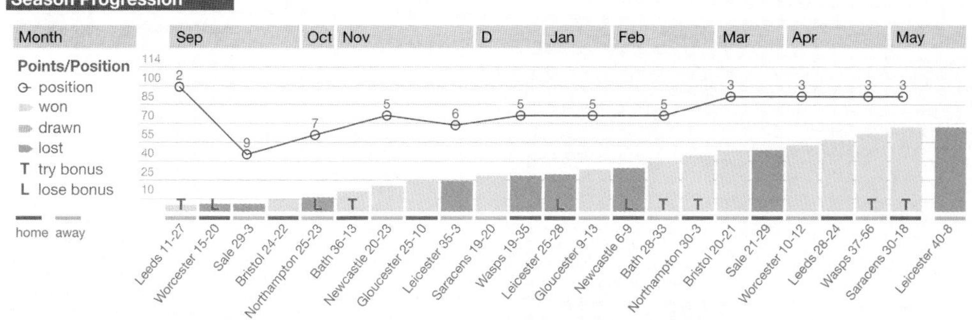

Home Matches

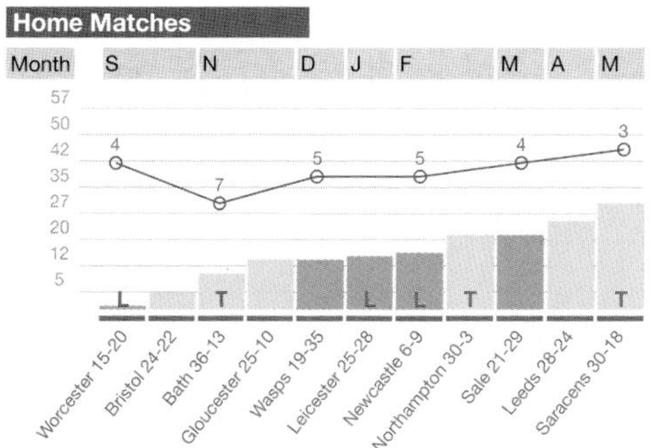

Away Matches

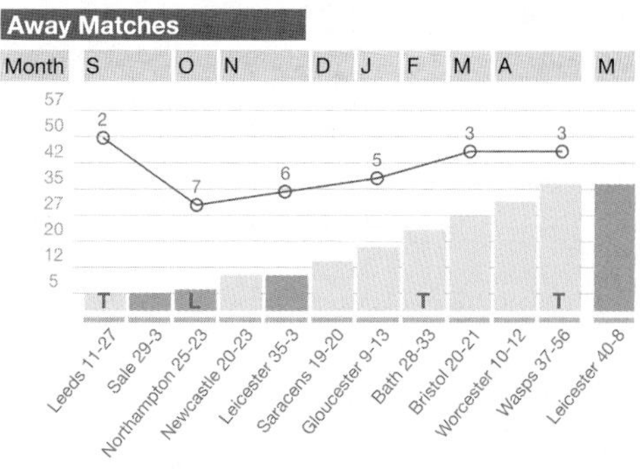

Premiership Statistics

Premiership Statistics		Home	Away
Tries	55	25	30
Coversions	32	13	19
Penalty goals	48	31	17
Drop goals	6	5	1
Kick %	63%	61%	67%
Yellow/Red cards	15/0	7/0	8/0
Powerplay tries	4	3	1
Shorthand tries	4	3	1

Powerplay tries are scored when your side are playing with a man or more advantage due to yellow or red cards.

Shorthand tries are scored when your side are playing with a man or more fewer due to yellow or red cards.

Team Performance

Position	Team	% total points won	% won at home	% won away
1	Sale			
2	Leicester	2%	5%	0%
3	**Irish**			
4	Wasps			
5	Gloucester	29%	30%	28%
6	Northampton			
7	Newcastle			
8	Worcester	30%	23%	36%
9	Bath			
10	Saracens			
11	Bristol	39%	42%	36%
12	Leeds			

London Irish

Top Scorer

Riki Flutey

Points Facts

Total points	% team points	Home	Away
112	22	47	65

Points by Time Period

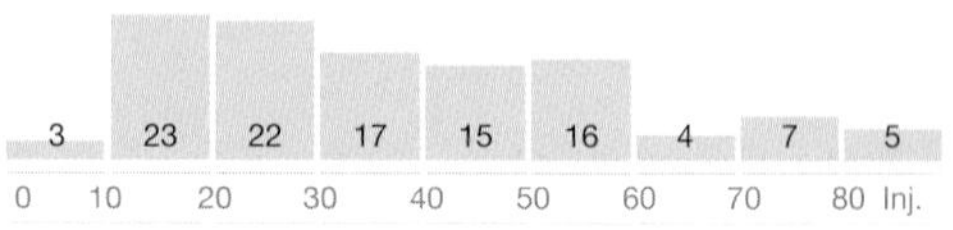

0–10	10–20	20–30	30–40	40–50	50–60	60–70	70–80	80–Inj.
3	23	22	17	15	16	4	7	5

Team Tries and Points

Tries by Time Period

scored
conceded

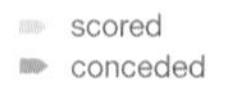

	0–10min	10–20min	20–30min	30–40min	40–50min	50–60min	60–70min	70–80min	Injury time
scored	5	10	11	11	3	5	4	5	1
conceded	8	2	9	2	9	1	6	10	2

Tries by Halves

scored
conceded

	Total	1st half	2nd half	1st half %	2nd half %
scored	55	37	18	67%	33%
conceded	49	21	28	43%	57%

How Points were Scored

- tries: 275
- conversions: 64
- pen goals: 144
- drop goals: 18

How Points were Conceded

- tries: 245
- conversions: 66
- pen goals: 177
- drop goals: 6

Tries Scored by Player

- backs: 41
- forwards: 14

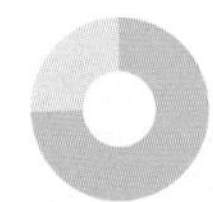

Tries Conceded by Player

- backs: 31
- forwards: 16

London Irish

Eight-Season Form 1998-2006

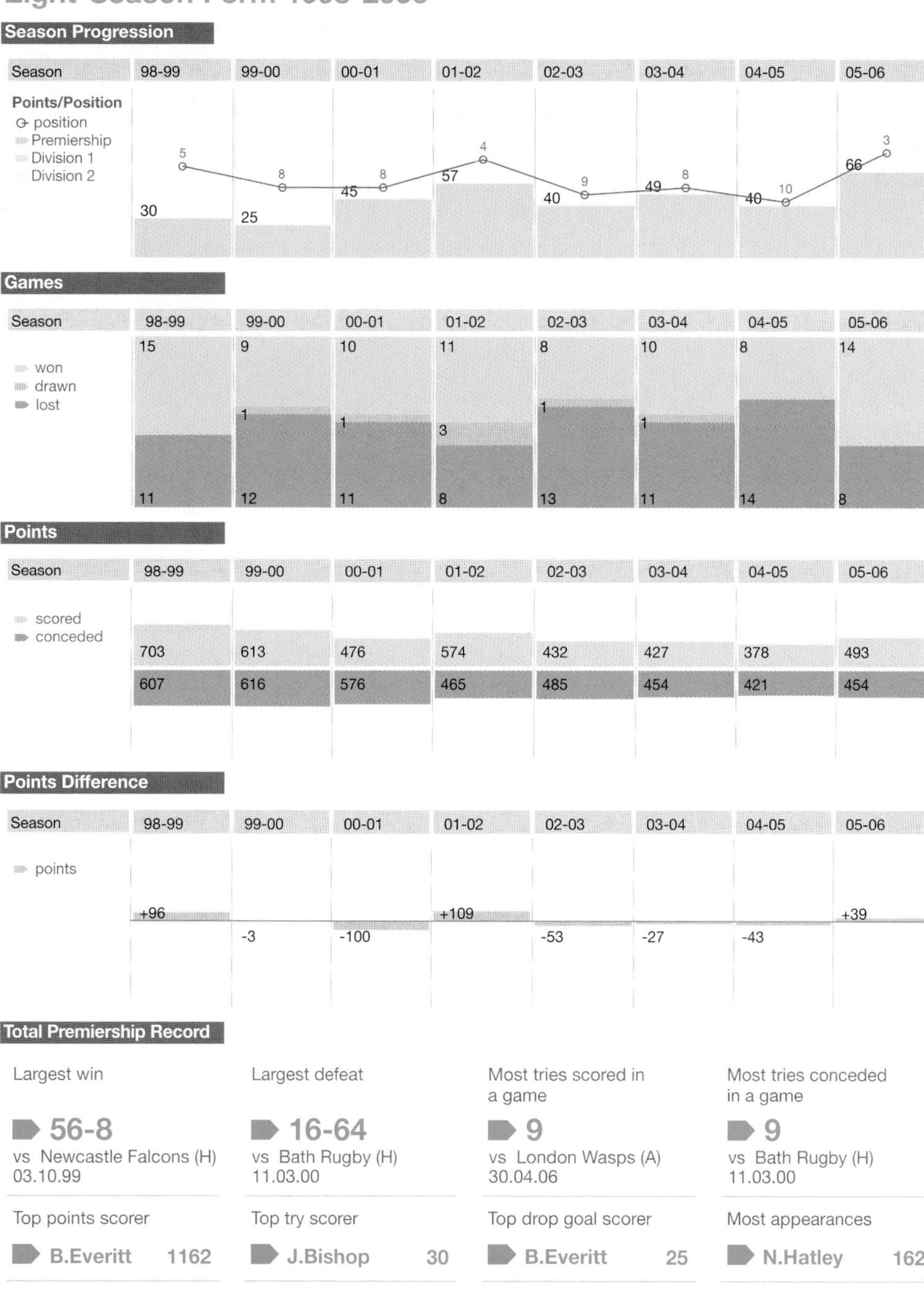

Total Premiership Record

Largest win
56-8
vs Newcastle Falcons (H)
03.10.99

Largest defeat
16-64
vs Bath Rugby (H)
11.03.00

Most tries scored in a game
9
vs London Wasps (A)
30.04.06

Most tries conceded in a game
9
vs Bath Rugby (H)
11.03.00

Top points scorer
B.Everitt 1162

Top try scorer
J.Bishop 30

Top drop goal scorer
B.Everitt 25

Most appearances
N.Hatley 162

Longest winning sequence
7 wins from 19.12.98 to 07.02.99

Longest losing sequence
8 defeats from 01.11.97 to 14.02.98

London Irish EFL

ENHANCED FIXTURE LIST

[does not include play-off data]

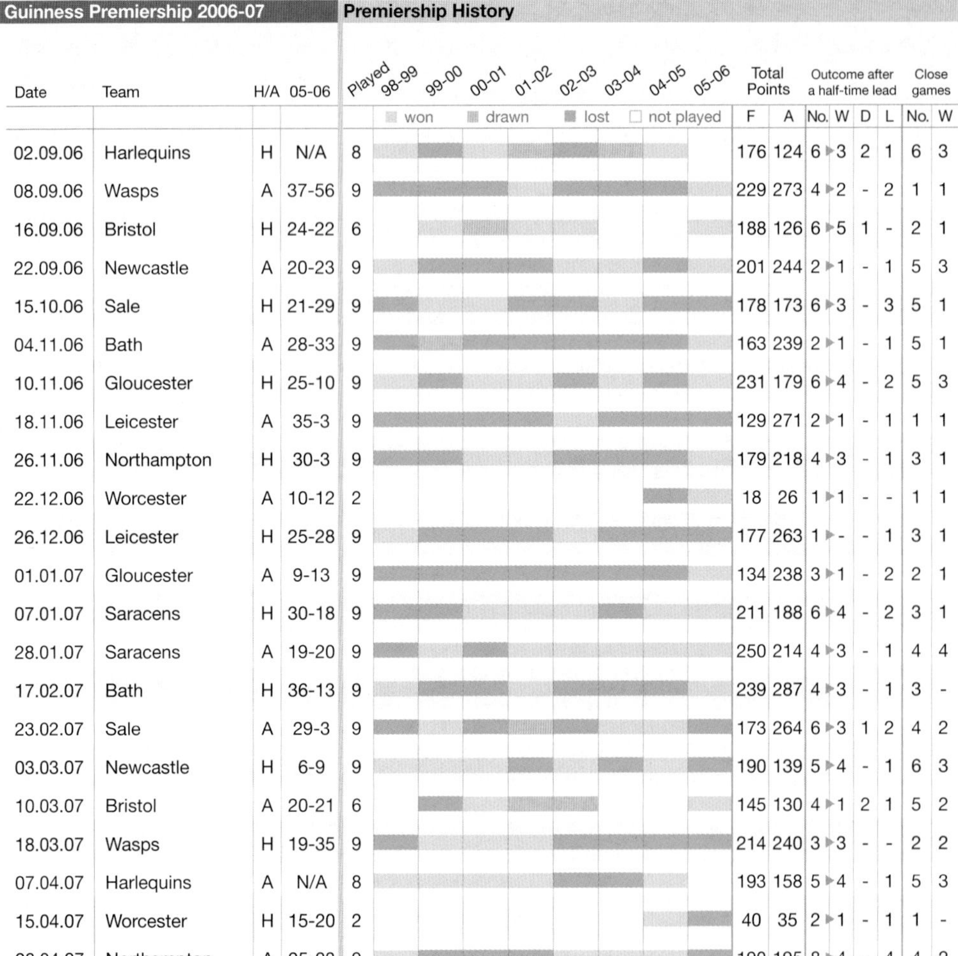

Date	Team	H/A	05-06	Played	Total Points F	Total Points A	Outcome after a half-time lead No.	W	D	L	Close games No.	W
02.09.06	Harlequins	H	N/A	8	176	124	6	3	2	1	6	3
08.09.06	Wasps	A	37-56	9	229	273	4	2	-	2	1	1
16.09.06	Bristol	H	24-22	6	188	126	6	5	1	-	2	1
22.09.06	Newcastle	A	20-23	9	201	244	2	1	-	1	5	3
15.10.06	Sale	H	21-29	9	178	173	6	3	-	3	5	1
04.11.06	Bath	A	28-33	9	163	239	2	1	-	1	5	1
10.11.06	Gloucester	H	25-10	9	231	179	6	4	-	2	5	3
18.11.06	Leicester	A	35-3	9	129	271	2	1	-	1	1	1
26.11.06	Northampton	H	30-3	9	179	218	4	3	-	1	3	1
22.12.06	Worcester	A	10-12	2	18	26	1	1	-	-	1	1
26.12.06	Leicester	H	25-28	9	177	263	1	-	-	1	3	1
01.01.07	Gloucester	A	9-13	9	134	238	3	1	-	2	2	1
07.01.07	Saracens	H	30-18	9	211	188	6	4	-	2	3	1
28.01.07	Saracens	A	19-20	9	250	214	4	3	-	1	4	4
17.02.07	Bath	H	36-13	9	239	287	4	3	-	1	3	-
23.02.07	Sale	A	29-3	9	173	264	6	3	1	2	4	2
03.03.07	Newcastle	H	6-9	9	190	139	5	4	-	1	6	3
10.03.07	Bristol	A	20-21	6	145	130	4	1	2	1	5	2
18.03.07	Wasps	H	19-35	9	214	240	3	3	-	-	2	2
07.04.07	Harlequins	A	N/A	8	193	158	5	4	-	1	5	3
15.04.07	Worcester	H	15-20	2	40	35	2	1	-	1	1	-
28.04.07	Northampton	A	25-23	9	190	195	8	4	-	4	4	2

Club Information

Useful Information

Founded
1898

Address
Madejski Stadium
Reading
Berkshire
RG2 OFL

Capacity
24,105 (all seated)

Main switchboard
0118 987 9730

Website
www.london-irish.com

Travel Information

Car
Approaching on the M4, exit at junction 11 onto the A33 towards Reading. When you reach a roundabout, take the 2nd exit onto the Reading Relief Road, the stadium is on your left.
For parking, carry on past the stadium and turn left onto Northern Way and follow the signs for the car parks.

Train
Trains run from London Paddington and London Waterloo to Reading station. A shuttle bus runs from Reading station to the ground on matchdays, costing £2 for adults and £1 for children.

Coach
National Express coaches run from London Victoria station approx every half hour.
Visit www.nationalexpress.com for further information.

Maps

Area Map

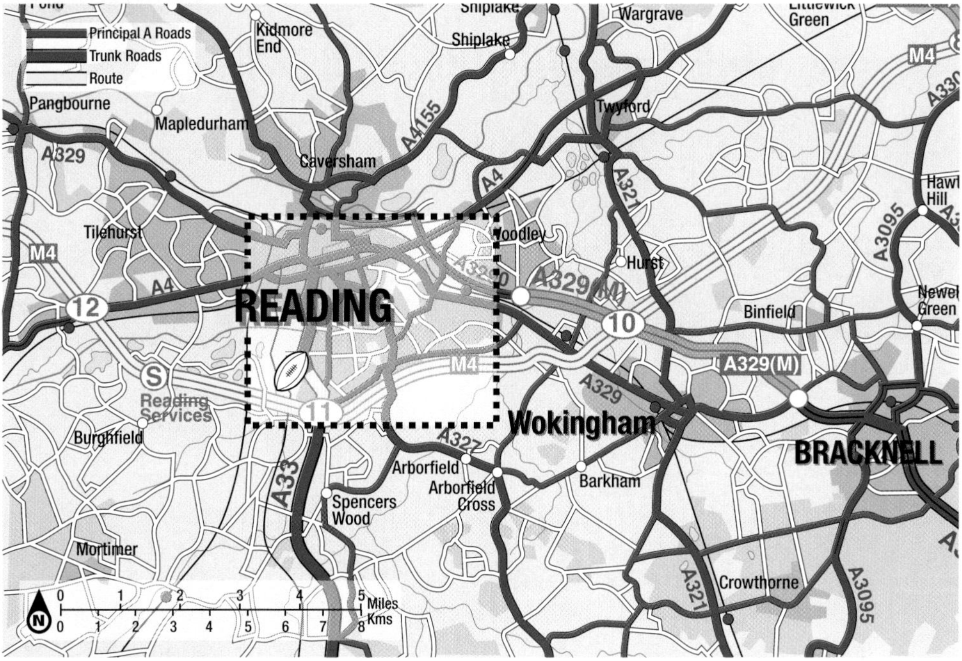

Local Map

London Wasps

Season Summary 2005/06

Position	Won	Drawn	Lost	For	Against	Bonus Points	Total Points
4	12	3	7	527	447	10	64

London Wasps' vice-like grip on the Premiership ended with Sale Sharks' first Premiership league title. For a club whose name has become a byword for winning, the 2005/06 Premiership campaign was ultimately a disappointment. In previous victorious Premiership campaigns, Wasps were the masters of peaking for the season's climax, but captain Lawrence Dallaglio and his side looked tired this term, eventually having to settle for fourth place. Winning the Powergen Cup in a rather one-sided game against Llanelli Scarlets ensured that Ian McGeechan's side did at least add some silverware, but even the celebrations at Twickenham couldn't mask what was a far from satisfactory Premiership campaign.

Director of Rugby: Ian McGeechan

Club Honours

Courage League / Zurich Premiership: 1989-90, 1996-97, 2002-03, 2003-04, 2004-05
Tetley's Bitter Cup: 1998-99, 1999-2000
Heineken Cup: 2003-04
Parker Pen Shield: 2002-03
Powergen Cup: 2005-06

Season Squad

Stats 2005-06

Position	Player	Height	Weight	Apps	Rep	Tries	Points
C	S.Abbott	6'0"	14st 2lb	20	1	-	-
H	J.Barrett	5'10"	16st 4lb	3	3	-	-
W	N.Baxter	6'2"	13st 12lb	1	1	2	10
SH	H.Biljon	5'11"	13st 2lb	-	1	-	-
L	R.Birkett	6'3"	17st 1lb	17	2	1	5
P	P.Bracken	6'2"	18st 7lb	11	5	-	-
FH	J.Brooks	5'9"	13st 9lb	1	5	-	-
FL	G.Chamberlain	6'2"	14st 2lb	-	1	-	-
L	M.Corker	6'6"	17st 6lb	-	1	-	-
8	L.Dallaglio	6'3"	17st 8lb	16	2	-	-
P	J.Dawson	5'10"	18st 7lb	8	3	-	-
SH	M.Dawson	5'10"	14st 2lb	6	8	1	5
C	A.Erinle	6'3"	17st 4lb	12	7	2	10
W	T.Evans	6'1"	14st 8lb	1	-	-	-
SH	W.Fury	6'0"	13st 7lb	-	1	-	-
H	B.Gotting	6'0"	16st 7lb	2	7	-	-
BR	J.Hart	6'4"	17st 10lb	11	2	2	10
BR	J.Haskell	6'3"	17st 6lb	1	4	-	-
C	R.Hoadley	6'0"	13st 13lb	7	5	2	10
SH	J.Honeyben	6'0"	14st 4lb	2	1	-	-
H	R.Ibanez	6'0"	15st 10lb	10	5	4	20
FH	A.King	6'0"	14st 6lb	11	4	-	55
FB	R.Laird	6'0"	14st 2lb	-	1	-	-
L/BR	D.Leo	6'6"	17st 8lb	8	2	-	-
W	J.Lewsey	5'10"	13st 9lb	9	1	3	15
BR	M.Lock	6'2"	16st 2lb	6	4	-	-
P	A.McKenzie	6'3"	18st 12lb	5	4	-	-
FL	J.O'Connor	5'10"	15st 10lb	7	3	-	-
P	T.Payne	6'0"	18st 3lb	21	-	1	5
L	M.Purdy	6'6"	17st 8lb	3	2	-	-
SH	E.Reddan	5'7"	12st 8lb	15	3	1	5
FL	T.Rees	5'11"	15st 10lb	10	3	4	20
W	P.Sackey	6'1"	14st 4lb	23	-	8	40
L	S.Shaw	6'7"	19st 0lb	12	3	1	5
L	G.Skivington	6'6"	17st 6lb	12	-	1	5
FH/FB	J.Staunton	6'0"	15st 1lb	12	3	2	33
P	J.Va'a	6'0"	21st 3lb	1	8	-	-
FB	M.Van Gisbergen	5'10"	13st 13lb	19	-	3	211
W	T.Voyce	6'0"	14st 13lb	18	1	10	50
H	J.Ward	6'0"	17st 8lb	8	4	-	-
C	F.Waters	6'0"	14st 10lb	4	7	1	5
FL	J.Worsley	6'5"	17st 6lb	12	1	4	20

London Wasps

Last Season Form 2005/06

Season Progression

Month: Sep, Oct, Nov, D, Jan, Feb, Mar, Apr, May

Points/Position
- position
- won
- drawn
- lost
- T try bonus
- L lose bonus

home away

Saracens 23-11, Leicester 29-29, Leeds 23-47, Worcester 34-20, Sale 18-10, Bristol 21-16, Northampton 13-21, Bath 28-20, Newcastle 17-15, Gloucester 32-25, Irish 19-35, Newcastle 21-6, Bath 28-16, Northampton 19-19, Bristol 9-9, Sale 26-16, Worcester 37-8, Leeds 28-0, Saracens 13-12, Leicester 20-19, Irish 37-56, Gloucester 32-37, Sale 22-12

Home Matches

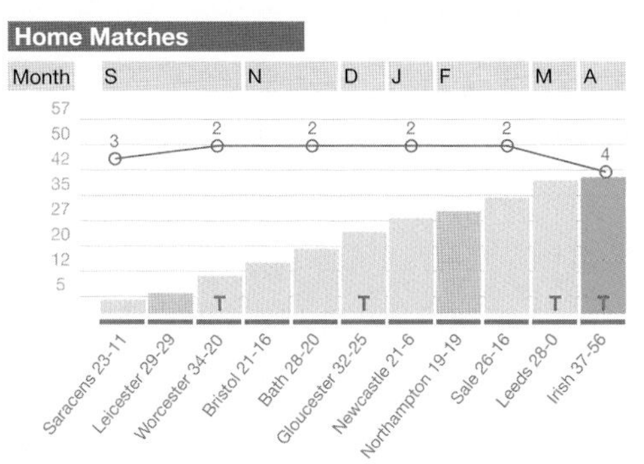

Away Matches

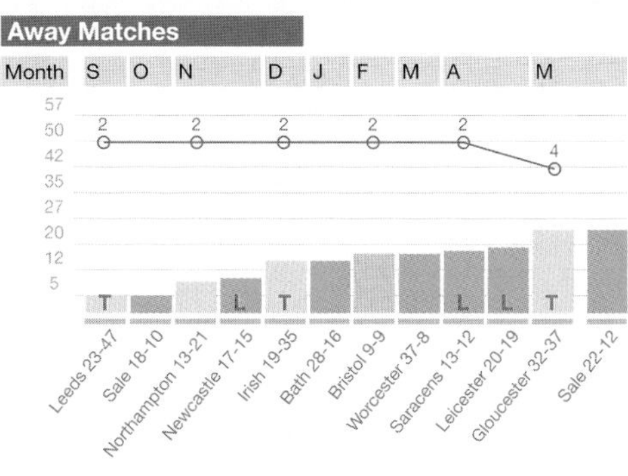

Premiership Statistics

	Total	Home	Away
Tries	53	32	21
Coversions	41	24	17
Penalty goals	62	29	33
Drop goals	2	1	1
Kick %	76%	77%	76%
Yellow/Red cards	9/0	2/0	7/0
Powerplay tries	7	7	0
Shorthand tries	0	0	0

Powerplay tries are scored when your side are playing with a man or more advantage due to yellow or red cards.

Shorthand tries are scored when your side are playing with a man or more fewer due to yellow or red cards.

Team Performance

Position	Team	% total points won	% won at home	% won away
1	Sale			
2	Leicester	18%	16%	21%
3	Irish			
4	**Wasps**			
5	Gloucester	33%	24%	47%
6	Northampton			
7	Newcastle			
8	Worcester	19%	30%	4%
9	Bath			
10	Saracens			
11	Bristol	30%	30%	28%
12	Leeds			

London Wasps

Top Scorer

Mark Van Gisbergen

Points Facts

Total points	% team points	Home	Away
211	39	101	110

Points by Time Period

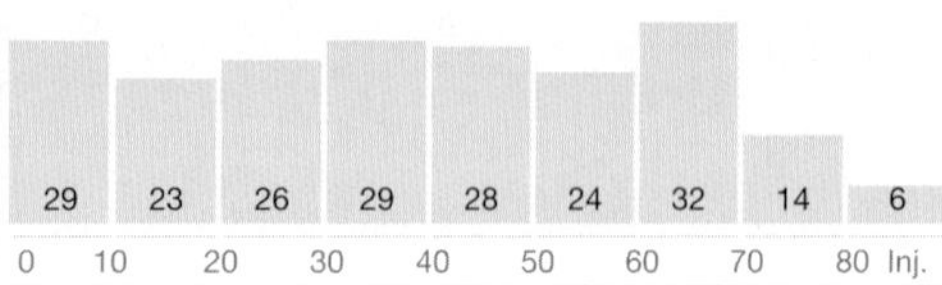

Team Tries and Points

Tries by Time Period

scored
conceded

	0–10min	10–20min	20–30min	30–40min	40–50min	50–60min	60–70min	70–80	Injury time
scored	10	3	5	5	6	10	4	7	3
conceded	11	4	3	5	7	6	0	7	0

Tries by Halves

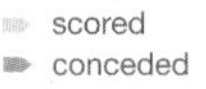

	Total	1st half	2nd half	1st half %	2nd half %
scored	53	23	30	43%	57%
conceded	43	23	20	53%	47%

How Points were Scored

- tries: 265
- conversions: 82
- pen goals: 186
- drop goals: 6

How Points were Conceded

- tries: 215
- conversions: 62
- pen goals: 186
- drop goals: 6

Tries Scored by Player

- backs: 35
- forwards: 18

Tries Conceded by Player

- backs: 31
- forwards: 10

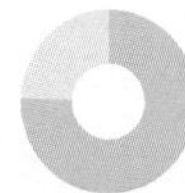

London Wasps

Eight-Season Form 1998-2006

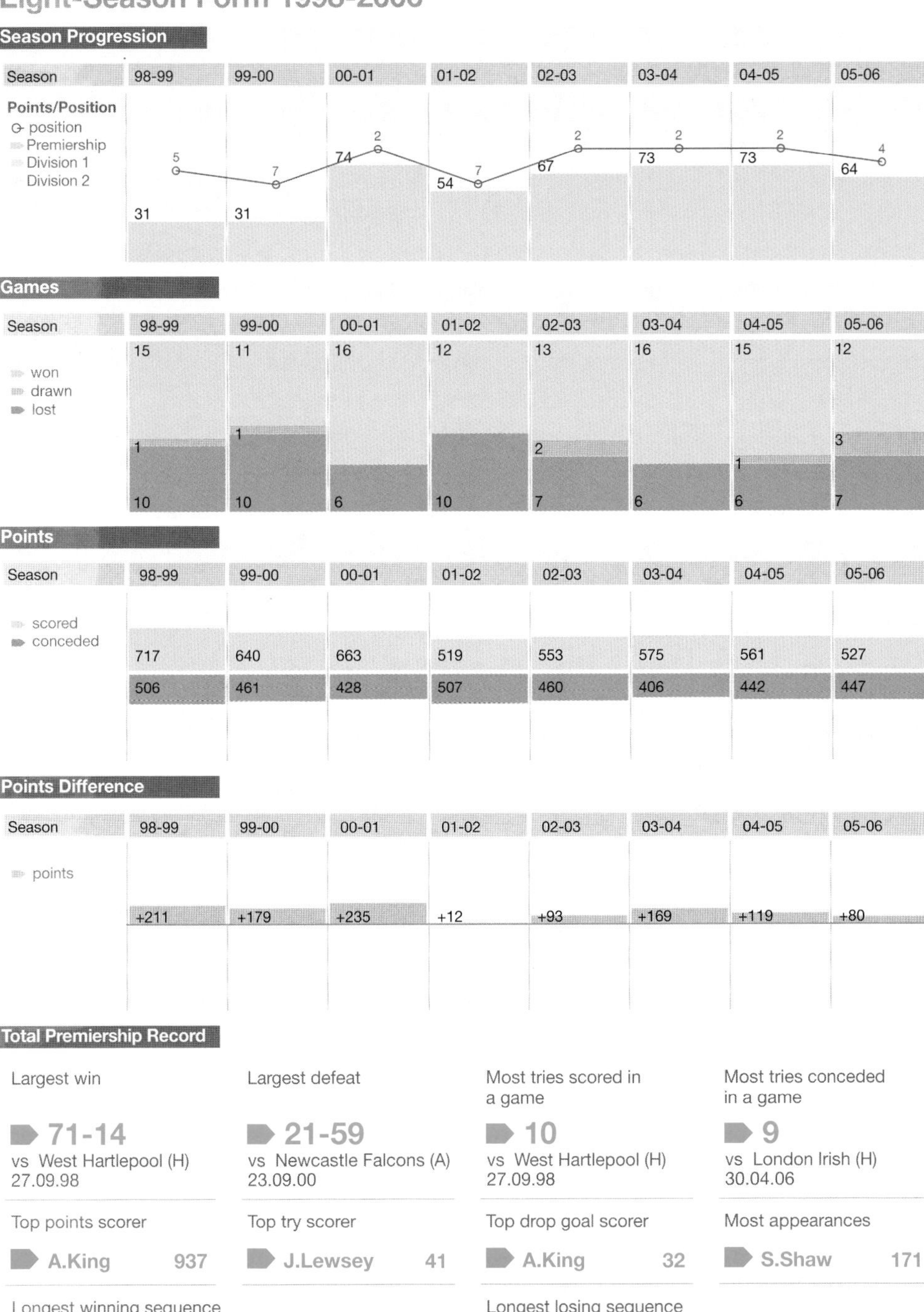
Season Progression
Season
98-99
99-00
00-01
01-02
02-03
03-04
04-05
05-06
Points/Position
position
Premiership
Division 1
Division 2
5
7
2
7
2
2
2
4
31
31
74
54
67
73
73
64
Games
won
drawn
lost
15
11
16
12
13
16
15
12
1
1
2
1
3
10
10
6
10
7
6
6
7
Points
scored
conceded
717
640
663
519
553
575
561
527
506
461
428
507
460
406
442
447
Points Difference
points
+211
+179
+235
+12
+93
+169
+119
+80
Total Premiership Record
Largest win
71-14
vs West Hartlepool (H)
27.09.98
Largest defeat
21-59
vs Newcastle Falcons (A)
23.09.00
Most tries scored in a game
10
vs West Hartlepool (H)
27.09.98
Most tries conceded in a game
9
vs London Irish (H)
30.04.06
Top points scorer
A.King 937
Top try scorer
J.Lewsey 41
Top drop goal scorer
A.King 32
Most appearances
S.Shaw 171
Longest winning sequence
11 wins from 21.11.03 to 18.04.04
Longest losing sequence
6 defeats from 08.09.01 to 11.11.01

London Wasps EFL

ENHANCED FIXTURE LIST

[does not include play-off data]

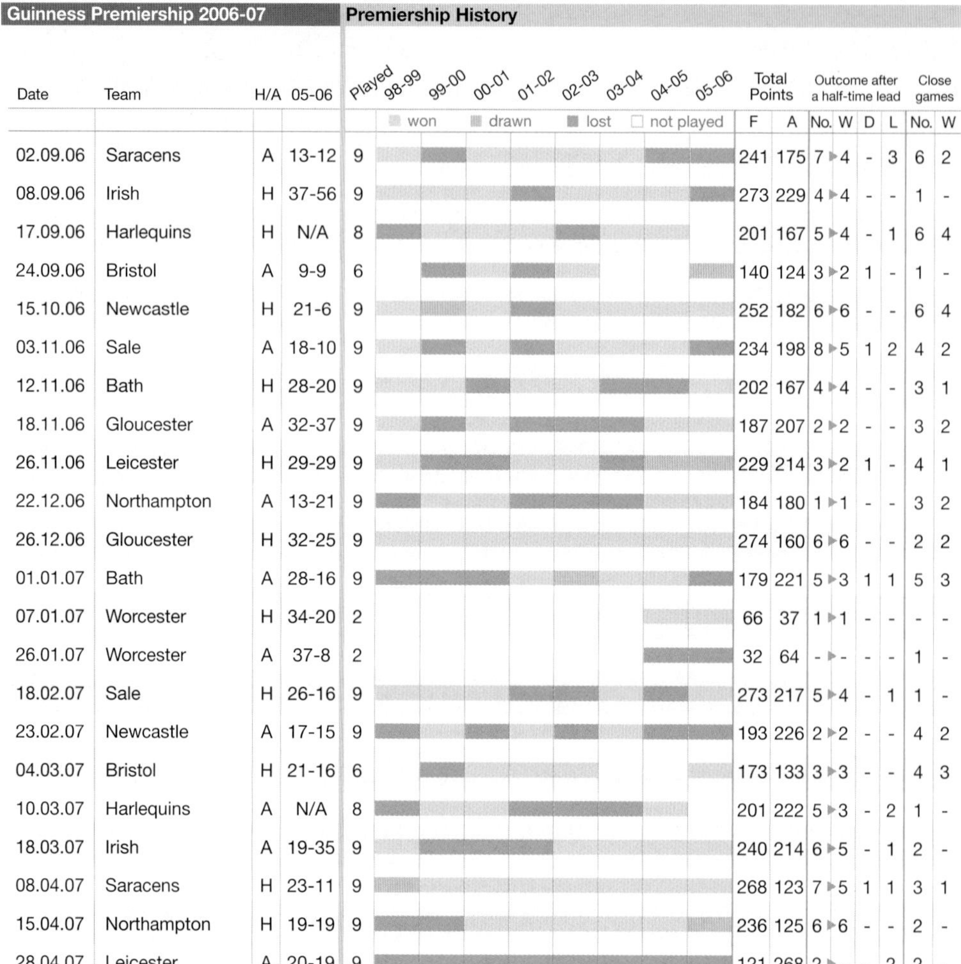

Guinness Premiership 2006-07 | **Premiership History**

Date	Team	H/A	05-06	Played	Total Points F	Total Points A	Outcome after a half-time lead No.	W	D	L	Close games No.	W
02.09.06	Saracens	A	13-12	9	241	175	7	4	-	3	6	2
08.09.06	Irish	H	37-56	9	273	229	4	4	-	-	1	-
17.09.06	Harlequins	H	N/A	8	201	167	5	4	-	1	6	4
24.09.06	Bristol	A	9-9	6	140	124	3	2	1	-	1	-
15.10.06	Newcastle	H	21-6	9	252	182	6	6	-	-	6	4
03.11.06	Sale	A	18-10	9	234	198	8	5	1	2	4	2
12.11.06	Bath	H	28-20	9	202	167	4	4	-	-	3	1
18.11.06	Gloucester	A	32-37	9	187	207	2	2	-	-	3	2
26.11.06	Leicester	H	29-29	9	229	214	3	2	1	-	4	1
22.12.06	Northampton	A	13-21	9	184	180	1	1	-	-	3	2
26.12.06	Gloucester	H	32-25	9	274	160	6	6	-	-	2	2
01.01.07	Bath	A	28-16	9	179	221	5	3	1	1	5	3
07.01.07	Worcester	H	34-20	2	66	37	1	1	-	-	-	-
26.01.07	Worcester	A	37-8	2	32	64	-	-	-	-	1	-
18.02.07	Sale	H	26-16	9	273	217	5	4	-	1	1	-
23.02.07	Newcastle	A	17-15	9	193	226	2	2	-	-	4	2
04.03.07	Bristol	H	21-16	6	173	133	3	3	-	-	4	3
10.03.07	Harlequins	A	N/A	8	201	222	5	3	-	2	1	-
18.03.07	Irish	A	19-35	9	240	214	6	5	-	1	2	-
08.04.07	Saracens	H	23-11	9	268	123	7	5	1	1	3	1
15.04.07	Northampton	H	19-19	9	236	125	6	6	-	-	2	-
28.04.07	Leicester	A	20-19	9	121	268	2	-	-	2	2	-

Club Information

Useful Information

Founded
1867

Address
Adam's Park
Hillbottom Road
Sands
High Wycombe
Buckinghamshire
HP12 4HJ

Capacity
10,200 (all seated)

Main switchboard
0208 993 8298

Website
www.wasps.co.uk

Travel Information

Car

From North

Approaching on the M1, exit onto the M25 at junction 6a (anti-clockwise). Continue on the M25 until junction 16 (M40), then head to junction 4 for the A404 High Wycombe. When you reach the junction take the slip road and turn right, taking the exit for the A4010 John Hall Way. Continue on this road, which becomes New Road, until you reach a mini roundabout with a left turn on to Lane End Road. Take this left turning and continue straight ahead onto Hillbottom Road, which leads to Causeway Stadium.

Train

Train services run from London Marylebone to High Wycombe.

Maps

Area Map

Local Map

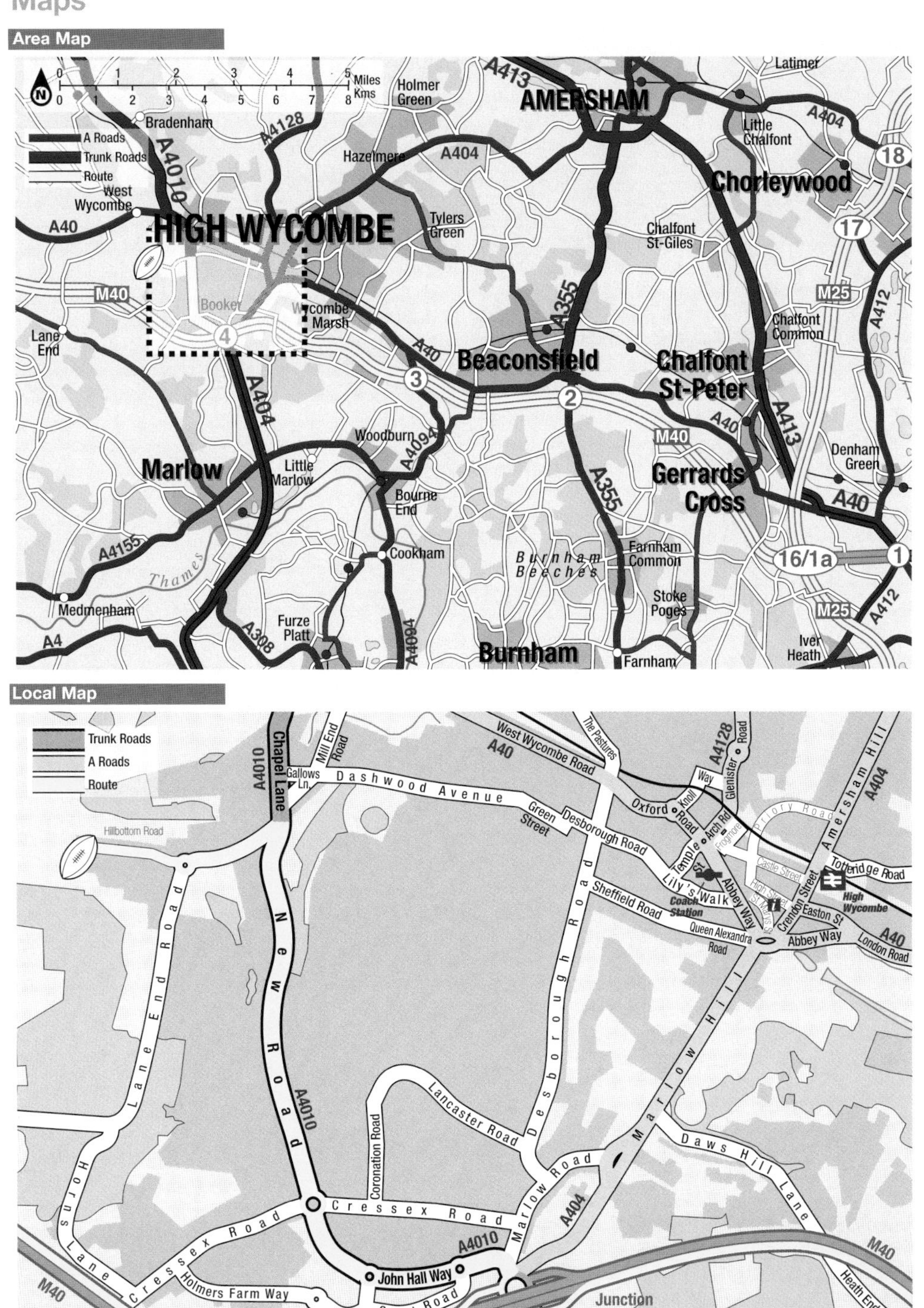

NEC Harlequins

Season Summary 2005/06 (National Division One)

Position	Won	Drawn	Lost	For	Against	Bonus Points	Total Points
1	25	0	1	1001	337	21	121

NEC Harlequins returned to the Premiership at the first attempt after completely dominating National Division One, losing only once along the way. Key to this success was the club's ability to retain the majority of their big name players, while the signing of former All Blacks legend Andrew Mehrtens gave Quins the direction and impetus they lacked during 2004/05's relegation season. With Dean Richards back at the helm of a Premiership club and a plethora of summer signings, Quins will be looking to challenge for silverware in their return season.

Director of Rugby: Andy Friend

Club Honours
John Player Cup / Pilkington Cup: 1988, 1991
European Shield / Parker Pen Challenge Cup: 2001, 2004
National Division One: 2006
Powergen National Trophy: 2006

Season Squad

Stats 2005-06

Position	Player	Height	Weight	Apps	Rep	Tries	Points
W	C.Amesbury	N/A	N/A	4	2	3	15
BR	P.Bouza	6'4"	15st 10lb	2	10	1	5
FB	M.Brown	6'0"	14st 5lb	7	6	7	37
L	K.Burke	6'6"	19st 3lb	-	6	-	-
BR	D.Clayton	N/A	N/A	-	1	-	-
P	A.Croall	6'0"	16st 7lb	2	3	-	-
C	M.Deane	5'10"	13st 8lb	9	12	2	10
8	T.Diprose	6'5"	17st 8lb	5	1	1	5
FB	G.Duffy	6'1"	14st 2lb	24	1	6	30
BR	N.Easter	6'4"	18st 2lb	23	2	16	80
L	J.Evans	6'7"	16st 2lb	24	1	6	30
H	T.Fuga	5'11"	14st 8lb	16	3	3	15
C	W.Greenwood	6'4"	15st 12lb	15	1	4	22
BR	T.Guest	6'4"	16st 0lb	7	10	5	25
W/C	G.Harder	6'1"	14st 9lb	6	3	4	20
H	J.Hayter	6'2"	15st 10lb	1	4	1	5
L	J.Inglis	N/A	N/A	-	1	-	-
FH	A.Jarvis	6'2"	13st 0lb	10	9	3	138
P	C.Jones	6'0"	16st 7lb	18	-	5	25
SH/W	S.Keogh	5'9"	12st 9lb	24	1	18	90
P	M.Lambert	6'3"	19st 1lb	-	3	-	-
C	T.Masson	N/A	N/A	8	2	3	15
FH	A.Mehrtens	5'10"	13st 2lb	16	4	1	194
L	S.Miall	6'4"	16st 6lb	26	-	3	15
W	U.Monye	6'1"	13st 4lb	16	2	16	80
P	R.Nebbett	5'11"	17st 8lb	20	3	-	-
H	J.Richards	5'9"	15st 10lb	9	12	-	-
W	K.Richards	N/A	N/A	-	1	-	-
BR	C.Robshaw	6'2"	14st 7lb	6	4	2	10
L	G.Robson	N/A	N/A	-	3	-	-
P	A.Rogers	6'3"	18st 5lb	4	1	2	10
FL	L.Sherriff	6'4"	15st 10lb	14	6	4	20
SH	S.So'oialo	5'10"	14st 6lb	19	1	6	30
C	J.Turner-Hall	N/A	N/A	4	1	-	-
SH	I.Vass	5'11"	15st 2lb	7	7	1	5
FL	A.Vos	6'5"	16st 1lb	23	-	1	5
P	L.Ward	N/A	N/A	7	17	-	-
FB/W	T.Williams	5'11"	13st 2lb	13	5	12	60
P	M.Worsley	6'0"	17st 2lb	1	1	-	-

NEC Harlequins

Last Season Form 2005/06

Season Progression

Month: Sep | Oct | Nov | D | Jan | Feb | Mar | Apr | May

Points/Position
- position
- won
- drawn
- lost
- T try bonus
- L lose bonus

home away

114 100 85 70 55 40 25 10

Birm & S 9-35, Otley 15-18, Newbury 52-13, Nottingham 10-32, Doncaster 27-7, Coventry 18-36, Exeter 70-5, Rotherham 7-22, Sedgley 22-29, Penzance 50-6, Bedford 20-26, Plymouth 16-23, Welsh 47-23, Birm & S 42-3, Otley 43-3, Newbury 25-57, Nottingham 31-16, Doncaster 0-45, Coventry 52-12, Exeter 13-8, Rotherham 50-10, Penzance 8-29, Sedgley 65-8, Welsh 17-28, Bedford 45-36, Plymouth 39-15

Home Matches

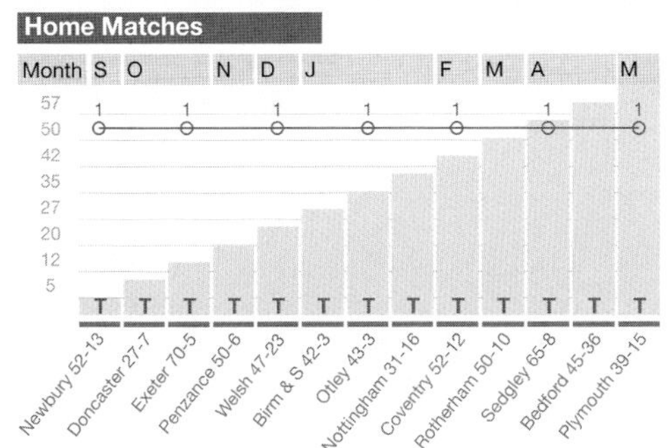

Away Matches

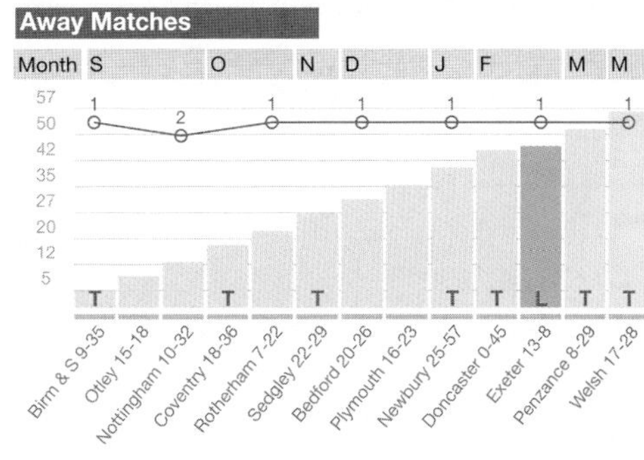

Division 1 Statistics

	Total	Home	Away
Tries	137	88	49
Coversions	101	64	37
Penalty goals	38	15	23
Drop goals	0	0	0
Yellow/Red cards	9/0	1/0	8/0
Powerplay tries	18	13	5
Shorthand tries	3	1	2

Powerplay tries are scored when your side are playing with a man or more advantage due to yellow or red cards.

Shorthand tries are scored when your side are playing with a man or more fewer due to yellow or red cards.

Team Performance

Position	Team	% total points won	% won at home	% won away
1	**Harlequins**			
2	Bedford			
3	Penzance			
4	Rotherham	47%	50%	43%
5	Plymouth			
6	Exeter			
7	Nottingham			
8	Otley			
9	Doncaster			
10	Coventry			
11	Newbury	53%	50%	57%
12	Welsh			
13	Sedgley			
14	Birm & S			

NEC Harlequins

Top Scorer

Andrew Mehrtens

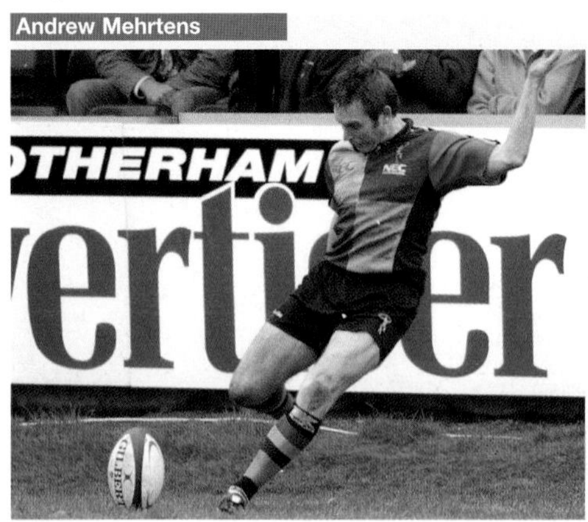

Points Facts

Total points	% team points	Home	Away
194	19	84	110

Points by Time Period

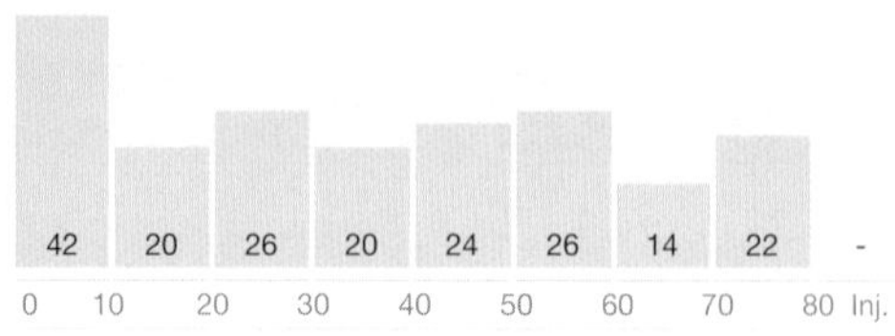

Team Tries and Points

Tries by Time Period

- scored
- conceded

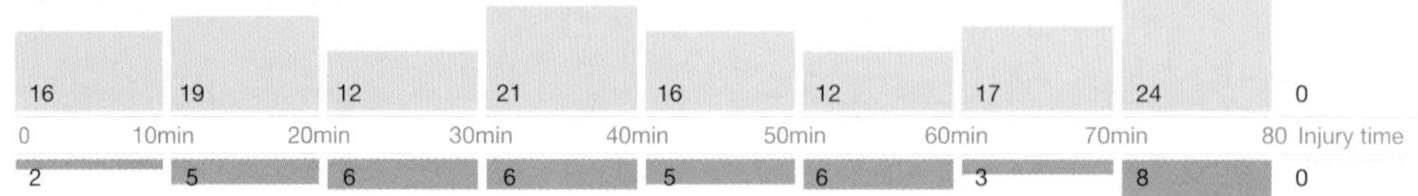

Tries by Halves

- scored
- conceded

	Total	1st half	2nd half	1st half %	2nd half %
scored	137	68	69	50%	50%
conceded	41	19	22	46%	54%

How Points were Scored

- tries: 685
- conversions: 202
- pen goals: 114
- drop goals: 0

How Points were Conceded

- tries: 205
- conversions: 42
- pen goals: 87
- drop goals: 3

Tries Scored by Player

- backs: 86
- forwards: 50

Tries Conceded by Player

- backs: 26
- forwards: 14

NEC Harlequins

Eight-Season Form 1998-2006

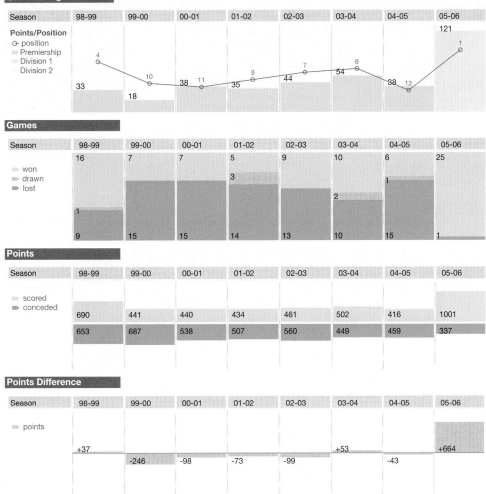

Season Progression

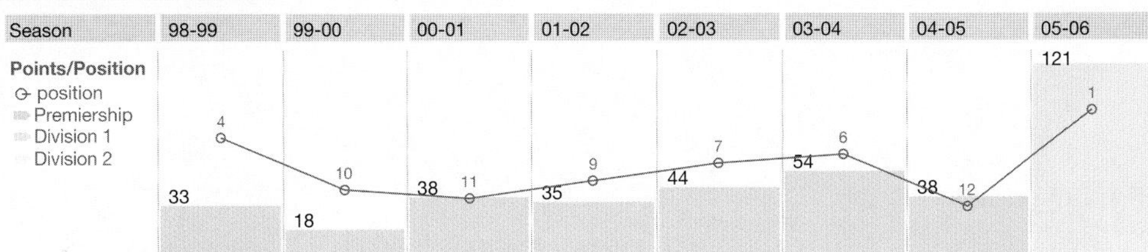

Games

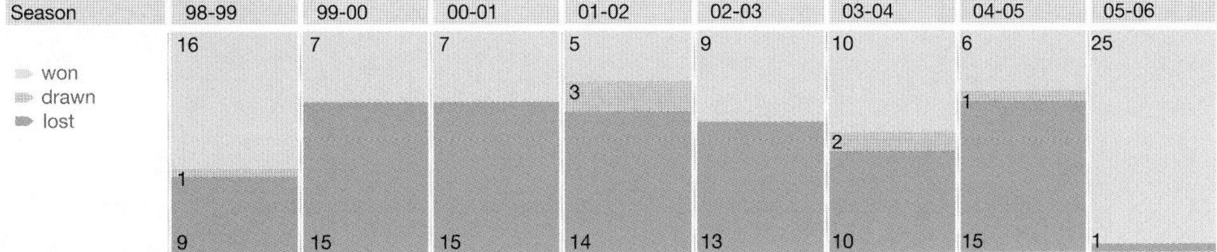

Points

Season	98-99	99-00	00-01	01-02	02-03	03-04	04-05	05-06
scored	690	441	440	434	461	502	416	1001
conceded	653	687	538	507	560	449	459	337

Points Difference

Season	98-99	99-00	00-01	01-02	02-03	03-04	04-05	05-06
points	+37	-246	-98	-73	-99	+53	-43	+664

Total Premiership Record

Largest win

43-6
vs Saracens (H)
16.11.01

Largest defeat

19-77
vs Bath Rugby (A)
29.04.00

Most tries scored in a game

7
vs Sale Sharks (H)
25.10.97

Most tries conceded in a game

10
vs Bath Rugby (A)
29.04.00

Top points scorer

P.Burke 707

Top try scorer

D.O'Leary 24

Top drop goal scorer

P.Burke 16

Most appearances

J.Leonard 110

Longest winning sequence

6 wins from 17.10.98 to 21.11.98

Longest losing sequence

9 defeats from 08.05.04 to 05.11.04

NEC Harlequins EFL

ENHANCED FIXTURE LIST

[does not include play-off data]

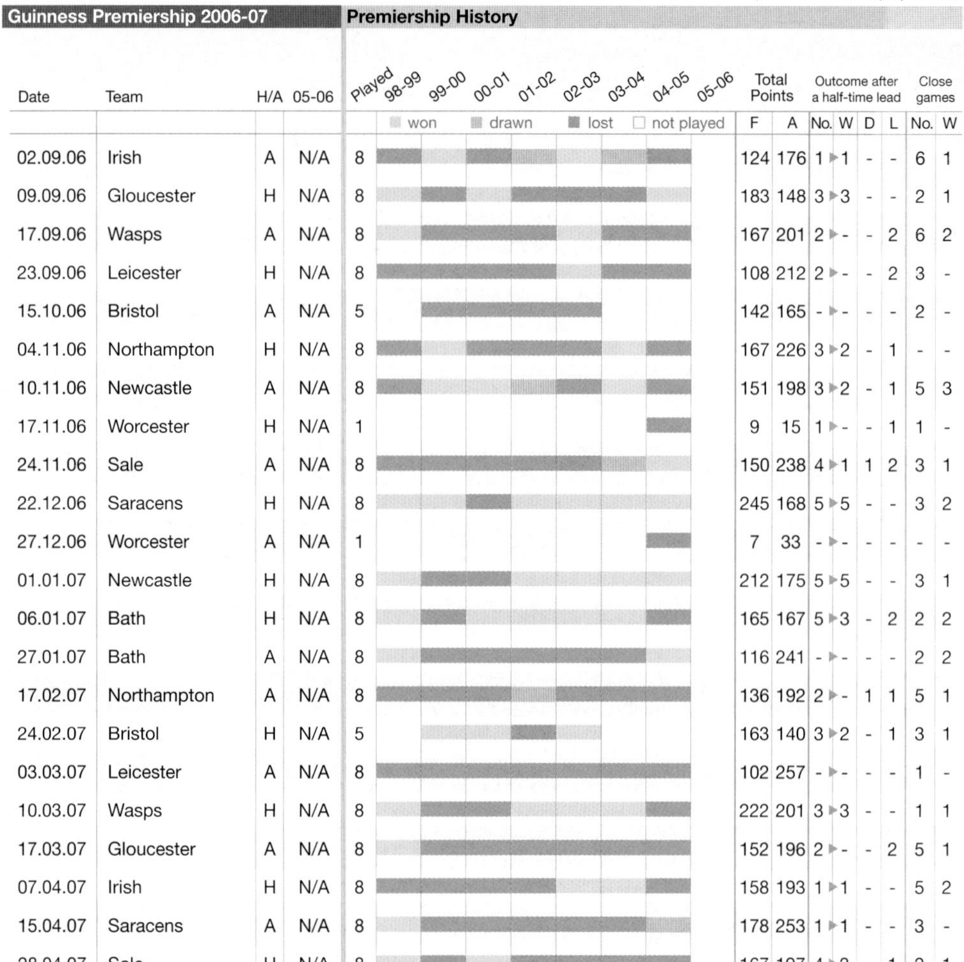

Guinness Premiership 2006-07 / **Premiership History**

Date	Team	H/A	05-06	Played	Total Points F	Total Points A	Outcome after a half-time lead No.	W	D	L	Close games No.	W
02.09.06	Irish	A	N/A	8	124	176	1	1	-	-	6	1
09.09.06	Gloucester	H	N/A	8	183	148	3	3	-	-	2	1
17.09.06	Wasps	A	N/A	8	167	201	2	-	-	2	6	2
23.09.06	Leicester	H	N/A	8	108	212	2	-	-	2	3	-
15.10.06	Bristol	A	N/A	5	142	165	-	-	-	-	2	-
04.11.06	Northampton	H	N/A	8	167	226	3	2	-	1	-	-
10.11.06	Newcastle	A	N/A	8	151	198	3	2	-	1	5	3
17.11.06	Worcester	H	N/A	1	9	15	1	-	-	1	1	-
24.11.06	Sale	A	N/A	8	150	238	4	1	1	2	3	1
22.12.06	Saracens	H	N/A	8	245	168	5	5	-	-	3	2
27.12.06	Worcester	A	N/A	1	7	33	-	-	-	-	-	-
01.01.07	Newcastle	H	N/A	8	212	175	5	5	-	-	3	1
06.01.07	Bath	H	N/A	8	165	167	5	3	-	2	2	2
27.01.07	Bath	A	N/A	8	116	241	-	-	-	-	2	2
17.02.07	Northampton	A	N/A	8	136	192	2	-	1	1	5	1
24.02.07	Bristol	H	N/A	5	163	140	3	2	-	1	3	1
03.03.07	Leicester	A	N/A	8	102	257	-	-	-	-	1	-
10.03.07	Wasps	H	N/A	8	222	201	3	3	-	-	1	1
17.03.07	Gloucester	A	N/A	8	152	196	2	-	-	2	5	1
07.04.07	Irish	H	N/A	8	158	193	1	1	-	-	5	2
15.04.07	Saracens	A	N/A	8	178	253	1	1	-	-	3	-
28.04.07	Sale	H	N/A	8	167	197	4	3	-	1	2	1

Club Information

Useful Information

Founded
1866

Address
Twickenham Stoop
Langhorn Drive
Twickenham
Middlesex
TW2 7SX

Stadium capacity
12,400

Main switchboard
020 8410 6000

Website
www.quins.co.uk

Travel Information

Car

From the M4:
Leave the M4 at Junction 3. Take the 3rd exit of the Roundabout for the A312, towards Feltham (A3006). Continue along the A312 for 4.5 miles. At the A305 / A316 roundabout, turn left onto the A316. Follow the A316 Chertsey Road, over three roundabouts. Continue for 2 miles. With Twickenham Rugby Stadium on your left, Quins' ground is on the right. U-turn at the RFU roundabout. Enter the Stoop via Langhorn Drive, 450 yards on your left.

Train

Twickenham station is served by trains from London Waterloo and Reading, with more services and routes accessible via Clapham Junction. After the match (and after a warming pint or two in the East Stand) there are plenty of trains to return you home safely. Upon leaving the station, turn right towards Twickenham Rugby Stadium and left at the mini-roundabout. Take the first left into Court Way and then turn left into Craneford Way and continue on until you reach the stadium.The Twickenham Stoop is at the end of the road on the right.

NEC Harlequins

Maps

Area Map

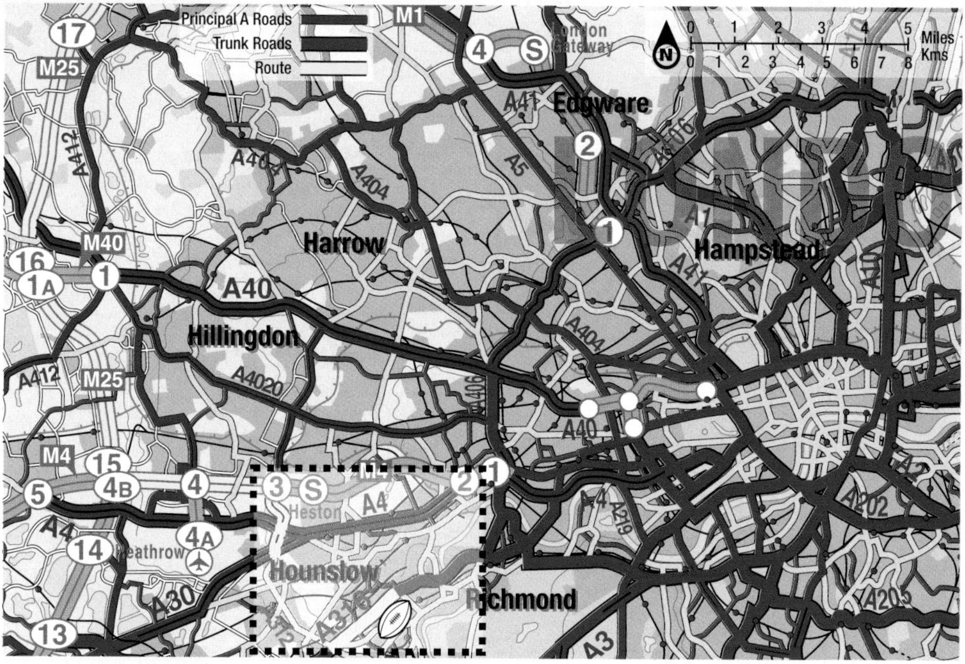

Local Map

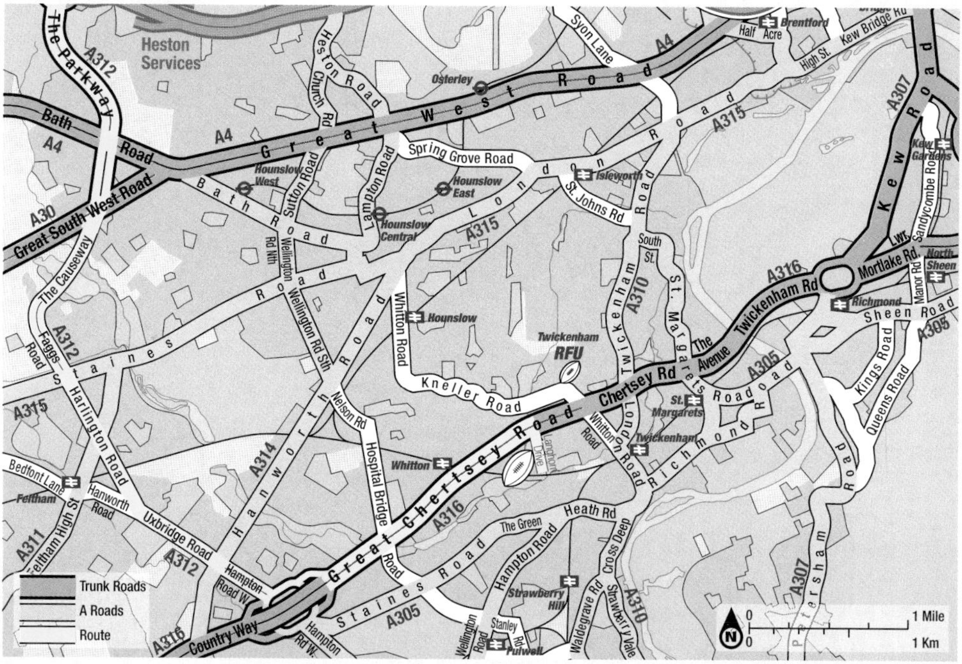

Newcastle Falcons

Season Summary 2005/06

Position	Won	Drawn	Lost	For	Against	Bonus Points	Total Points
7	9	1	12	416	433	9	47

The 2005/06 season was a landmark for long-serving Newcastle Falcon's director of rugby Rob Andrew, who celebrated 10 years at the helm of the club. Andrew, though, had little to celebrate, as his side once again flattered to deceive in the Premiership. Without the services of playmaker Jonny Wilkinson for most of the campaign and lacking in fire power, Newcastle were always going to struggle. However, it wasn't all doom and gloom. The coming-of-age of talented youngsters Toby Flood and Matthew Tait, the return of Wilkinson and the emergence of some promising young players gave reason for optimism.

Director of Rugby: Rob Andrew

Club Honours
Allied Dunbar Premiership: 1997-98
John Player Cup / Powergen Cup: 1976, 1977, 2001, 2004

Season Squad

Stats 2005-06

Position	Player	Height	Weight	Apps	Rep	Tries	Points
P	G.Anderson	6'0"	18st 8lb	1	-	-	-
L	A.Buist	6'6"	17st 0lb	8	4	-	-
FB	M.Burke	6'0"	14st 10lb	20	-	8	142
SH	H.Charlton	5'11"	14st 4lb	9	5	-	-
BR	C.Charvis	6'3"	16st 10lb	13	-	-	-
SH	L.Dickson	5'11"	12st 6lb	-	3	-	-
8	P.Dowson	6'3"	16st 10lb	2	-	-	-
W/FB	A.Elliott	6'3"	14st 9lb	12	1	8	42
FL/L	O.Finegan	6'6"	18st 12lb	13	4	1	5
FH/FB	T.Flood	6'2"	15st 0lb	12	4	1	7
L	S.Grimes	6'5"	17st 3lb	4	5	-	-
SH	J.Grindal	5'9"	13st 4lb	13	7	-	-
L	L.Gross	6'9"	19st 8lb	2	4	-	-
FL	C.Harris	6'0"	17st 0lb	12	1	1	5
W/C	J.Hoyle	6'1"	13st 4lb	3	-	1	5
8	G.Irvin	N/A	N/A	-	1	-	-
H	A.Long	5'11"	16st 3lb	17	4	1	5
W	T.May	5'10"	14st 5lb	18	-	4	23
C	M.Mayerhofler	6'0"	15st 2lb	14	1	-	-
FL	M.McCarthy	6'4"	17st 0lb	9	10	3	15
P	R.Morris	6'2"	18st 11lb	20	2	1	5
C	J.Noon	5'10"	13st 5lb	12	3	2	10
P	T.Paoletti	6'0"	20st 0lb	1	5	-	-
L/FL	G.Parling	6'5"	16st 5lb	16	2	1	5
P	I.Peel	5'11"	18st 0lb	1	1	-	-
L	A.Perry	6'7"	18st 7lb	19	-	-	-
W	O.Phillips	5'11"	14st 7lb	5	-	2	10
FB/C	J.Shaw	6'0"	15st 2lb	5	4	2	10
8	J.Smithson	6'2"	11st 13lb	2	1	-	-
C/W	M.Tait	5'11"	13st 4lb	16	-	2	10
H	M.Thompson	6'2"	18st 0lb	5	12	-	-
FH	D.Walder	5'10"	12st 9lb	11	2	2	56
P	M.Ward	5'11"	18st 9lb	19	3	-	-
FH	J.Wilkinson	5'10"	13st 5lb	4	3	1	56
C	M.Wilkinson	6'3"	17st 0lb	-	1	-	-
P	J.Williams	6'0"	15st 5lb	2	6	-	-
FL	E.Williamson	6'2"	14st 9lb	-	1	-	-
P	D.Wilson	6'1"	18st 7lb	-	7	-	-
FL	B.Woods	6'2"	16st 5lb	10	7	1	5

Newcastle Falcons

Last Season Form 2005/06

Season Progression

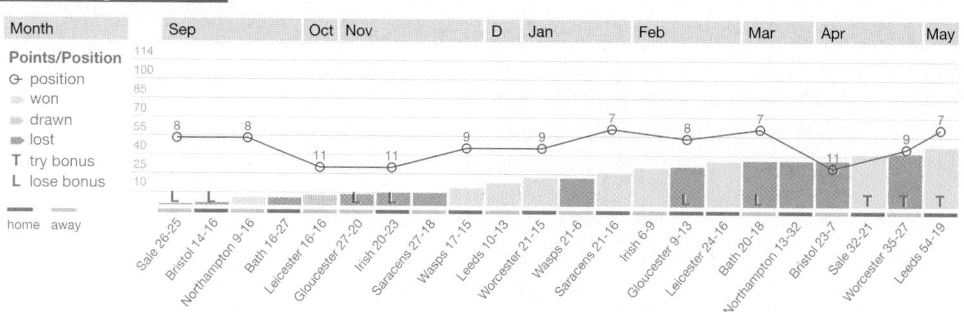

Home Matches

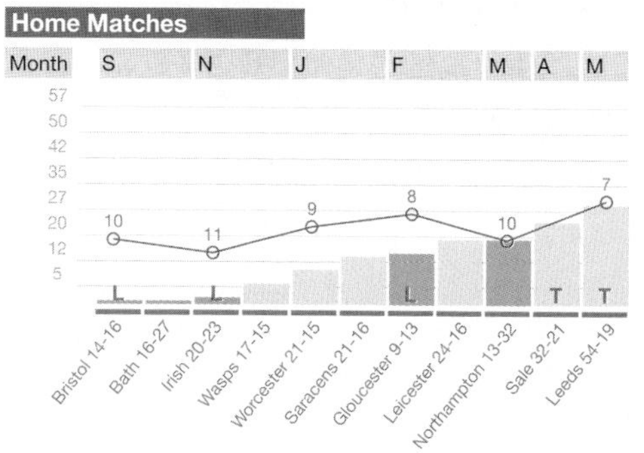

Away Matches

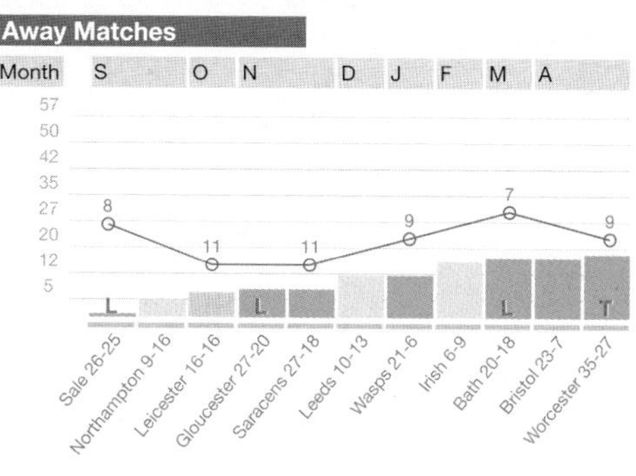

Premiership Statistics

Premiership Statistics	Home	Away
Tries 42	23	19
Coversions 25	15	10
Penalty goals 45	29	16
Drop goals 7	3	4
Kick % 63%	68%	57%
Yellow/Red cards 9/1	3/0	6/1
Powerplay tries 3	2	1
Shorthand tries 3	1	2

Powerplay tries are scored when your side are playing with a man or more advantage due to yellow or red cards.

Shorthand tries are scored when your side are playing with a man or more fewer due to yellow or red cards.

Team Performance

Position	Team	% total points won	% won at home	% won away
1	Sale			
2	Leicester	34%	32%	37%
3	Irish			
4	Wasps			
5	Gloucester	20%	16%	26%
6	Northampton			
7	**Newcastle**			
8	Worcester	18%	19%	16%
9	Bath			
10	Saracens			
11	Bristol	28%	33%	21%
12	Leeds			

Newcastle Falcons

Top Scorer

Matthew Burke

Points Facts

Total points	% team points	Home	Away
142	34	80	62

Points by Time Period

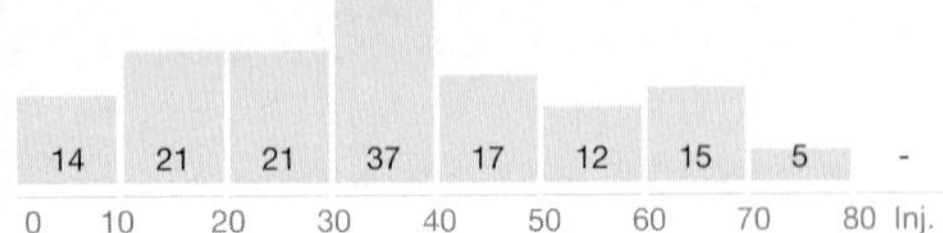

Team Tries and Points

Tries by Time Period

scored
conceded

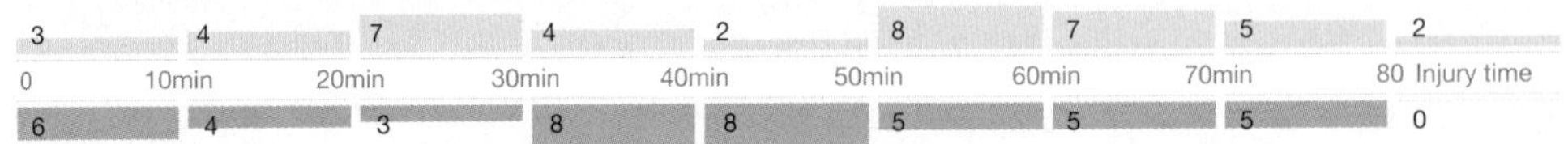

Tries by Halves

scored
conceded

	Total	1st half	2nd half	1st half %	2nd half %
scored	42	18	24	43%	57%
conceded	44	21	23	48%	52%

How Points were Scored

- tries: 210
- conversions: 50
- pen goals: 135
- drop goals: 21

How Points were Conceded

- tries: 220
- conversions: 60
- pen goals: 150
- drop goals: 3

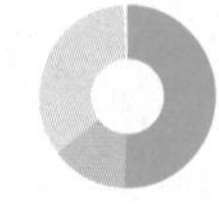

Tries Scored by Player

- backs: 33
- forwards: 9

Tries Conceded by Player

- backs: 29
- forwards: 15

Newcastle Falcons

Eight-Season Form 1998-2006

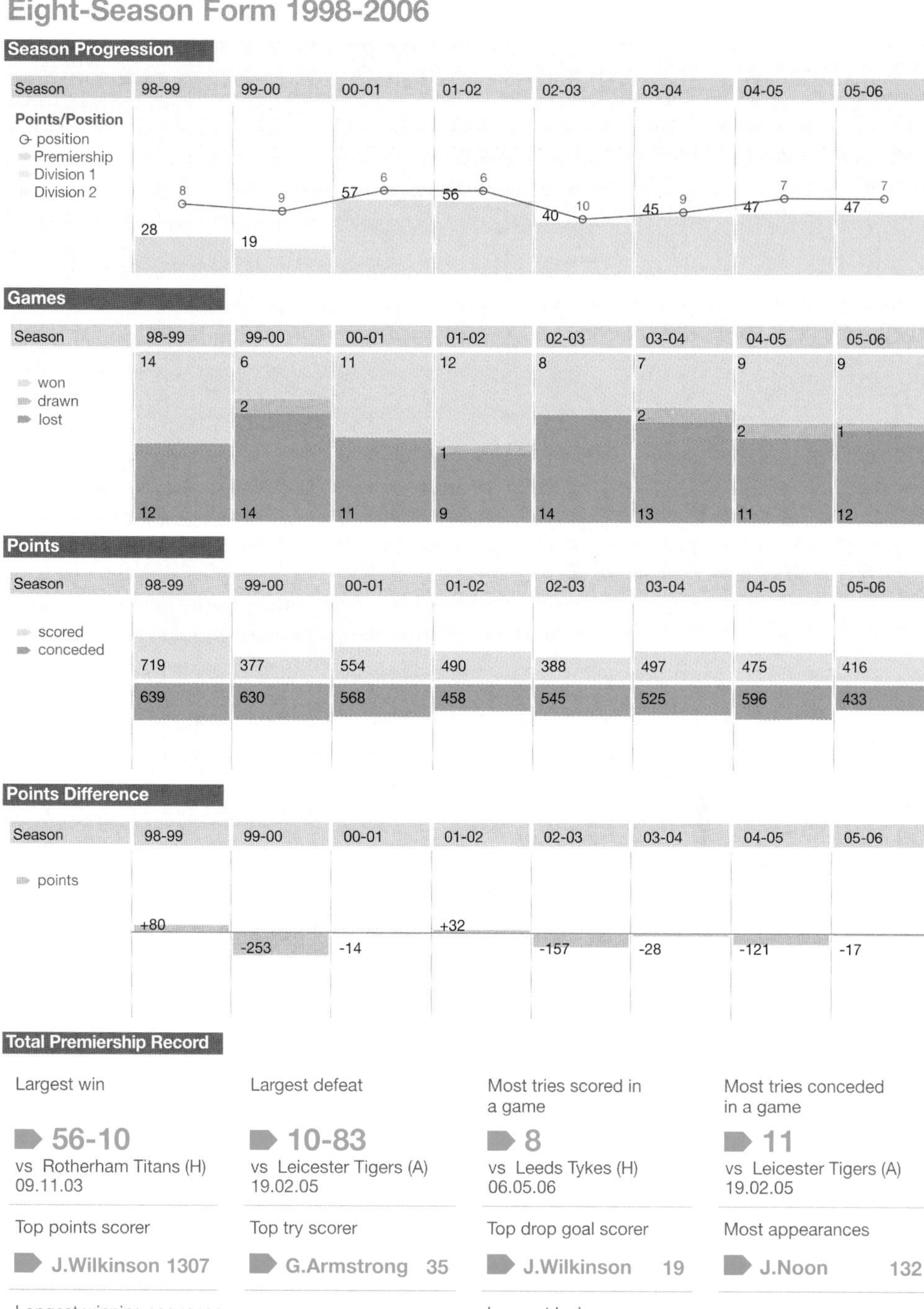

Total Premiership Record

Largest win
56-10
vs Rotherham Titans (H)
09.11.03

Largest defeat
10-83
vs Leicester Tigers (A)
19.02.05

Most tries scored in a game
8
vs Leeds Tykes (H)
06.05.06

Most tries conceded in a game
11
vs Leicester Tigers (A)
19.02.05

Top points scorer
J.Wilkinson 1307

Top try scorer
G.Armstrong 35

Top drop goal scorer
J.Wilkinson 19

Most appearances
J.Noon 132

Longest winning sequence
12 wins from 23.08.97 to 10.03.98

Longest losing sequence
7 defeats from 03.11.02 to 03.01.03

Newcastle Falcons EFL

ENHANCED FIXTURE LIST

[does not include play-off data]

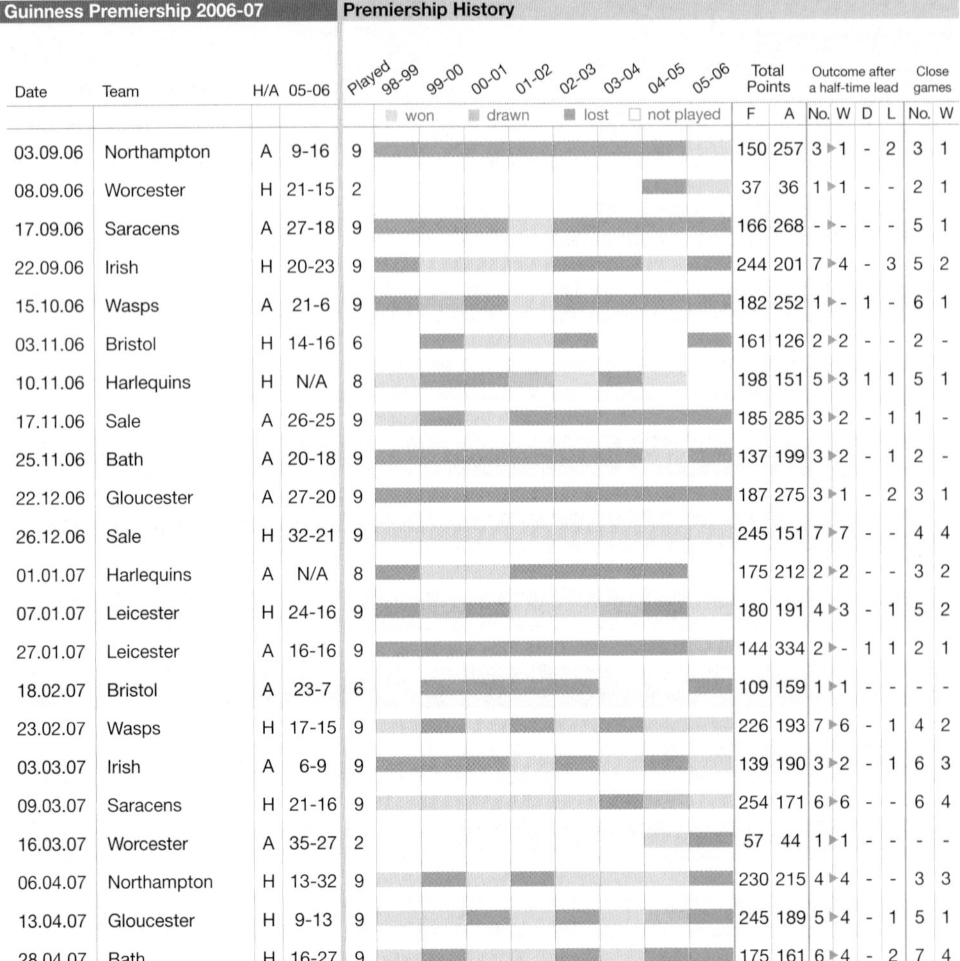

Guinness Premiership 2006-07				Premiership History								
Date	Team	H/A	05-06	Played	Total Points F	Total Points A	Outcome after a half-time lead No.	W	D	L	Close games No.	W
03.09.06	Northampton	A	9-16	9	150	257	3	1	-	2	3	1
08.09.06	Worcester	H	21-15	2	37	36	1	1	-	-	2	1
17.09.06	Saracens	A	27-18	9	166	268	-	-	-	-	5	1
22.09.06	Irish	H	20-23	9	244	201	7	4	-	3	5	2
15.10.06	Wasps	A	21-6	9	182	252	1	-	1	-	6	1
03.11.06	Bristol	H	14-16	6	161	126	2	2	-	-	2	-
10.11.06	Harlequins	H	N/A	8	198	151	5	3	1	1	5	1
17.11.06	Sale	A	26-25	9	185	285	3	2	-	1	1	-
25.11.06	Bath	A	20-18	9	137	199	3	2	-	1	2	-
22.12.06	Gloucester	A	27-20	9	187	275	3	1	-	2	3	1
26.12.06	Sale	H	32-21	9	245	151	7	7	-	-	4	4
01.01.07	Harlequins	A	N/A	8	175	212	2	2	-	-	3	2
07.01.07	Leicester	H	24-16	9	180	191	4	3	-	1	5	2
27.01.07	Leicester	A	16-16	9	144	334	2	-	1	1	2	1
18.02.07	Bristol	A	23-7	6	109	159	1	1	-	-	-	-
23.02.07	Wasps	H	17-15	9	226	193	7	6	-	1	4	2
03.03.07	Irish	A	6-9	9	139	190	3	2	-	1	6	3
09.03.07	Saracens	H	21-16	9	254	171	6	6	-	-	6	4
16.03.07	Worcester	A	35-27	2	57	44	1	1	-	-	-	-
06.04.07	Northampton	H	13-32	9	230	215	4	4	-	-	3	3
13.04.07	Gloucester	H	9-13	9	245	189	5	4	-	1	5	1
28.04.07	Bath	H	16-27	9	175	161	6	4	-	2	7	4

98-99, 99-00, 00-01, 01-02, 02-03, 03-04, 04-05, 05-06 — won / drawn / lost / not played

Club Information

Useful Information

Founded
1995
(Gosforth formed in 1877)

Address
Kingston Park
Brunton Road
Kenton Bank Foot
Newcastle NE13 8AF

Capacity
10,000

Main switchboard
0191 214 5588

Website
www.newcastle-falcons.co.uk

Travel Information

Car

From South:
Take the M1 and turn right onto the M62 at junction 42, towards the A1. Follow the A1 all the way into Newcastle, heading for the junction for Newcastle Airport. When you reach that junction, take the Kingston Park exit then continue straight ahead over two mini roundabouts. After passing under a bridge, turn right into Brunton Road then continue until you see the ground on your left.

From West:
Follow the A69 until it joins the A1, and follow signs for the Newcastle Airport junction. Then as route for South.

Train

GNER and Virgin Trains run services to Newcastle Central. From there, catch the Tyne and Wear Metro to Kingston Park station.

Air

Newcastle International Airport is a short cab ride from the stadium.

Maps

Area Map

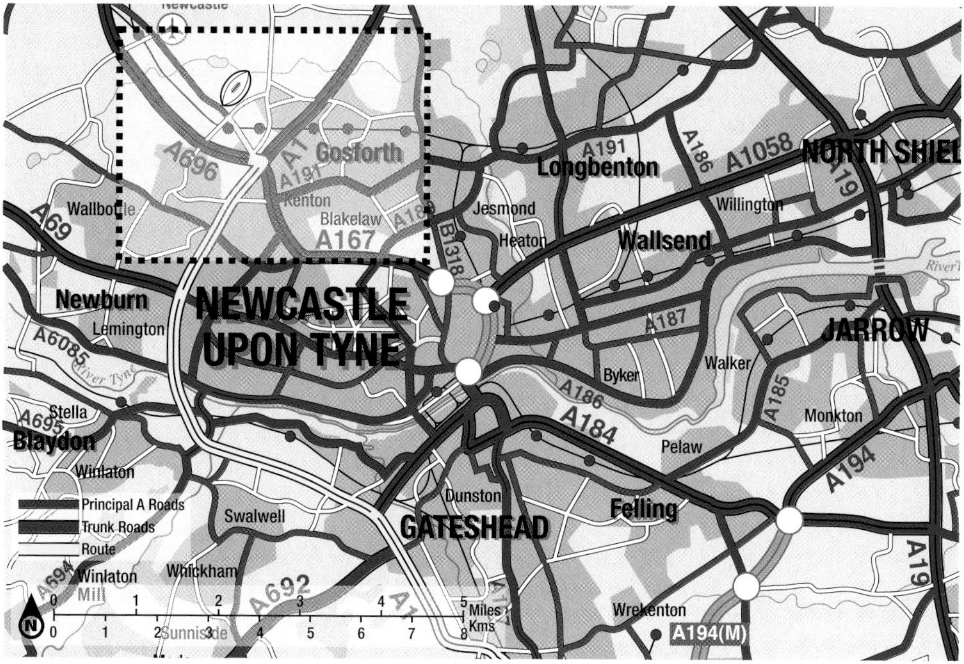

Local Map

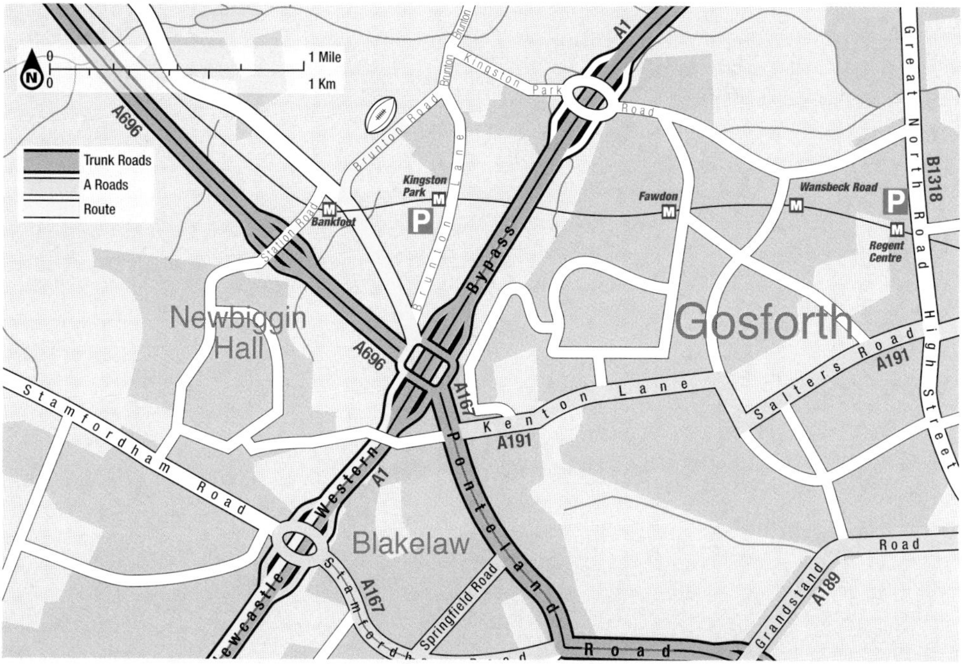

Northampton Saints

Season Summary 2005/06

Position	Won	Drawn	Lost	For	Against	Bonus Points	Total Points
6	**10**	**1**	**11**	**464**	**488**	**11**	**53**

Saints fans waited in anticipation for All Black Carlos Spencer to pull on a Northampton shirt and they certainly weren't disappointed, as Spencer wowed the Franklin's Gardens crowd with his electric pace and breathtaking skills, ensuring he was voted Saints Player of the Year. Despite inconsistent form in the Premiership, Saints rose to the occasion with perhaps the performance of the season against Saracens in February, where they put on an outstanding display of rugby. Northampton fans will enjoy Heineken Cup rugby at Franklin's Gardens next season and Saints will face French Champions and last season's beaten finalists Biarritz in the quest for European glory.

Head Coach: Budge Pountney

Club Honours
Heineken Cup: 1999-2000

Season Squad

Stats 2005-06

Position	Player	Height	Weight	Apps	Rep	Tries	Points
P	P.Barnard	6'0"	17st 8lb	9	1	1	5
L	S.Boome	6'3"	17st 0lb	1	2	-	-
8	D.Browne	6'5"	16st 3lb	39	-	2	10
P	C.Budgen	5'8"	17st 10lb	11	8	1	5
FB/W	J.Clarke	6'3"	14st 1lb	22	-	6	30
W	B.Cohen	6'2"	15st 10lb	13	1	7	35
C	R.Davies	5'9"	14st 0lb	3	4	2	10
W	P.Diggin	5'8"	13st 2lb	3	1	-	-
BR	M.Easter	6'3"	16st 0lb	4	2	2	10
P	S.Emms	5'11"	17st 8lb	1	7	-	-
FL	D.Fox	6'0"	15st 10lb	11	7	2	10
L	D.Gerard	6'6"	19st 0lb	5	11	-	-
H	M.Grove	6'3"	17st 2lb	-	1	-	-
P	L.Harbut	5'10"	17st 7lb	-	3	-	-
FL	S.Harding	6'1"	16st 4lb	10	7	1	5
H	D.Hartley	6'1"	17st 11lb	4	8	-	-
SH	J.Howard	5'9"	12st 7lb	4	9	-	-
C/FH	R.Kydd	5'11"	14st 3lb	3	3	-	-
W	S.Lamont	6'2"	15st 0lb	12	2	6	30
FL	B.Lewitt	6'3"	15st 0lb	6	7	-	-
L	M.Lord	6'4"	17st 2lb	17	5	-	-
C	S.Mallon	6'3"	14st 11lb	4	1	2	10
FH	L.Myring	6'0"	14st 3lb	1	-	1	5
P	C.Noon	5'11"	18st 3lb	1	2	-	-
FB	J.Pritchard	5'9"	13st 5lb	1	1	-	4
C	D.Quinlan	6'4"	16st 2lb	14	1	1	5
L	A.Rae	6'5"	15st 8lb	1	1	-	-
FB	B.Reihana	6'0"	13st 7lb	21	-	5	206
H	D.Richmond	5'11"	15st 6lb	10	4	-	-
SH	M.Robinson	5'10"	13st 8lb	18	4	2	10
W	J.Rudd	6'2"	17st 0lb	11	3	1	5
BR/L	G.Seely	6'4"	17st 0lb	2	1	-	-
P	T.Smith	5'10"	16st 3lb	19	-	-	-
BR	M.Soden	6'2"	16st 4lb	2	2	-	-
FH	C.Spencer	6'1"	15st 0lb	21	-	4	34
P	B.Sturgess	6'1"	17st 10lb	3	3	-	-
H	S.Thompson	6'2"	18st 2lb	9	4	3	15
BR	P.Tupai	6'4"	17st 10lb	11	1	1	5
C	A.Vilk	5'11"	15st 6lb	3	4	1	5

Northampton Saints

Last Season Form 2005/06

Season Progression

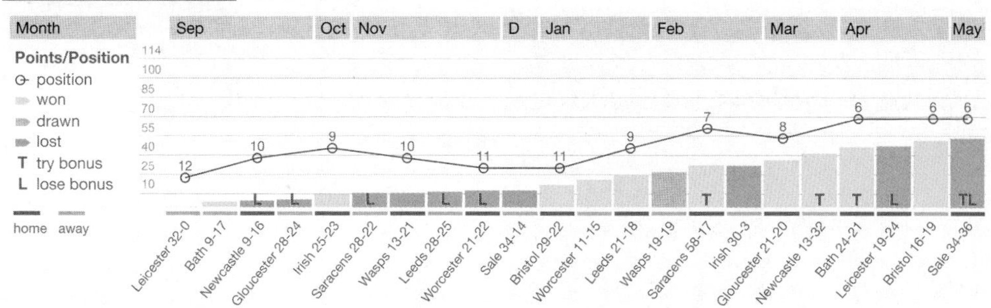

Home Matches

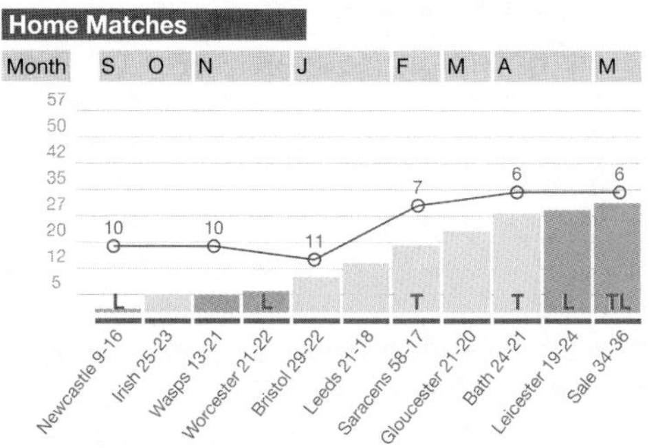

Away Matches

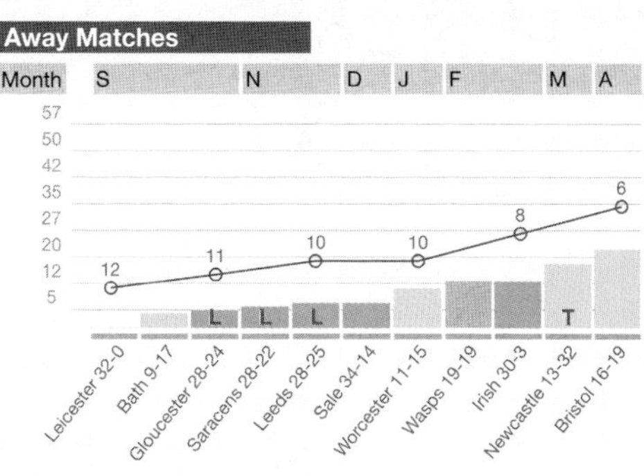

Premiership Statistics

Premiership Statistics	Total	Home	Away
Tries	53	31	22
Coversions	35	22	13
Penalty goals	41	23	18
Drop goals	2	2	0
Kick %	61%	64%	57%
Yellow/Red cards	15/0	3/0	12/0
Powerplay tries	7	6	1
Shorthand tries	2	0	2

Powerplay tries are scored when your side are playing with a man or more advantage due to yellow or red cards.

Shorthand tries are scored when your side are playing with a man or more fewer due to yellow or red cards.

Team Performance

Position	Team	% total points won	% won at home	% won away
1	Sale			
2	Leicester	12%	21%	0%
3	Irish			
4	Wasps			
5	Gloucester	19%	18%	19%
6	**Northampton**			
7	Newcastle			
8	Worcester	35%	21%	55%
9	Bath			
10	Saracens			
11	Bristol	34%	40%	26%
12	Leeds			

Northampton Saints

Top Scorer

Bruce Reihana

Points Facts

Total points	% team points	Home	Away
206	45	131	75

Points by Time Period

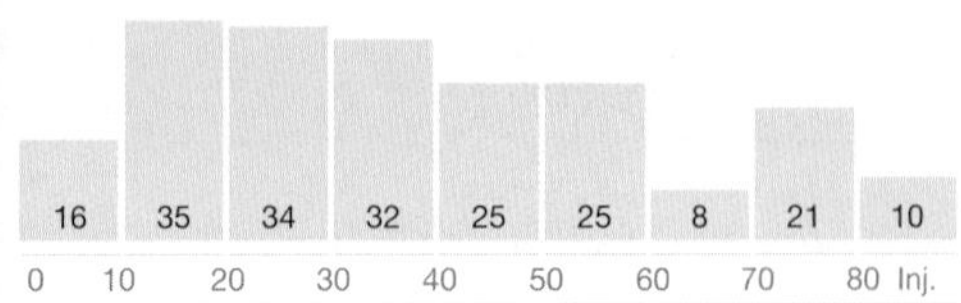

Team Tries and Points

Tries by Time Period

	0–10min	10–20min	20–30min	30–40min	40–50min	50–60min	60–70min	70–80	Injury time
scored	7	4	6	7	3	8	7	10	1
conceded	7	7	8	6	5	4	6	6	1

Tries by Halves

	Total	1st half	2nd half	1st half %	2nd half %
scored	53	24	29	45%	55%
conceded	50	28	22	56%	44%

How Points were Scored

- tries: 265
- conversions: 70
- pen goals: 123
- drop goals: 6

How Points were Conceded

- tries: 250
- conversions: 64
- pen goals: 162
- drop goals: 12

Tries Scored by Player

- backs: 38
- forwards: 14

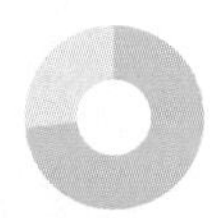

Tries Conceded by Player

- backs: 37
- forwards: 12

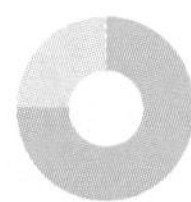

Northampton Saints

Eight-Season Form 1998-2006

Season Progression

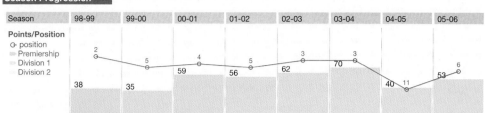

Season	98-99	99-00	00-01	01-02	02-03	03-04	04-05	05-06
Points	38	35	59	56	62	70	40	53
Position	2	5	4	5	3	3	11	6

Points/Position: position; Premiership; Division 1; Division 2

Games

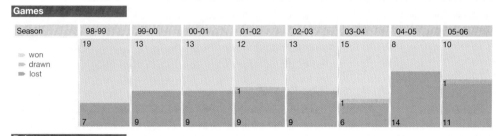

Season	98-99	99-00	00-01	01-02	02-03	03-04	04-05	05-06
won	19	13	13	12	13	15	8	10
drawn				1		1		1
lost	7	9	9	9	9	6	14	11

Points

Season	98-99	99-00	00-01	01-02	02-03	03-04	04-05	05-06
scored	754	551	518	506	512	574	410	464
conceded	556	480	463	426	376	416	473	488

Points Difference

Season	98-99	99-00	00-01	01-02	02-03	03-04	04-05	05-06
points	+198	+71	+55	+80	+136	+158	-63	-24

Total Premiership Record

Largest win

42-0
vs Rotherham (H)
10.02.01

Largest defeat

12-54
vs London Wasps (H)
09.05.00

Most tries scored in a game

9
vs Newcastle Falcons (H)
27.03.99

Most tries conceded in a game

7
vs London Irish (A)
18.11.01

Top points scorer

P.Grayson 1238

Top try scorer

B.Cohen 45

Top drop goal scorer

P.Grayson 9

Most appearances

G.Seely 133

Longest winning sequence

7 wins from 05.11.99 to 26.01.00

Longest losing sequence

9 defeats from 18.09.04 to 28.11.04

Northampton Saints EFL

ENHANCED FIXTURE LIST

[does not include play-off data]

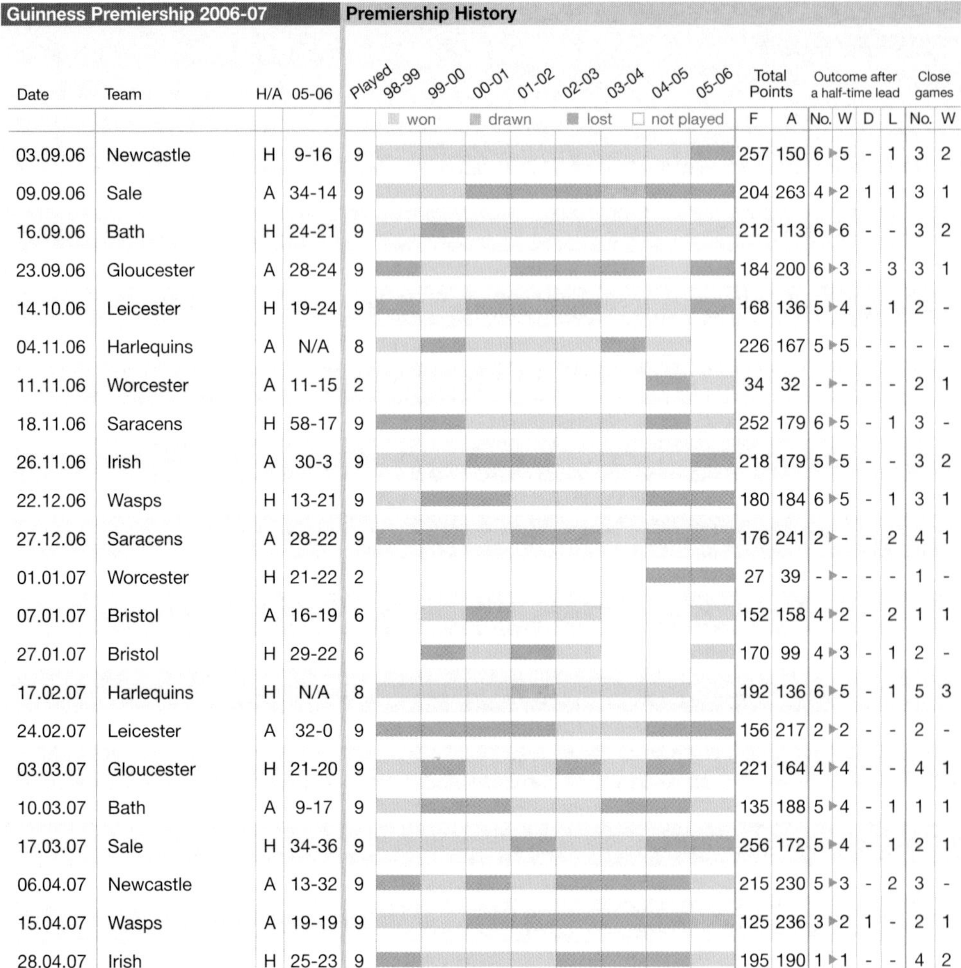

Guinness Premiership 2006-07				Premiership History									
Date	Team	H/A	05-06	Played	Total Points F	Total Points A	Outcome after a half-time lead No.	W	D	L	Close games No.	W
03.09.06	Newcastle	H	9-16	9	257	150	6	5	-	1	3	2
09.09.06	Sale	A	34-14	9	204	263	4	2	1	1	3	1
16.09.06	Bath	H	24-21	9	212	113	6	6	-	-	3	2
23.09.06	Gloucester	A	28-24	9	184	200	6	3	-	3	3	1
14.10.06	Leicester	H	19-24	9	168	136	5	4	-	1	2	-
04.11.06	Harlequins	A	N/A	8	226	167	5	5	-	-	-	-
11.11.06	Worcester	A	11-15	2	34	32	-	-	-	-	2	1
18.11.06	Saracens	H	58-17	9	252	179	6	5	-	1	3	-
26.11.06	Irish	A	30-3	9	218	179	5	5	-	-	3	2
22.12.06	Wasps	H	13-21	9	180	184	6	5	-	1	3	1
27.12.06	Saracens	A	28-22	9	176	241	2	-	-	2	4	1
01.01.07	Worcester	H	21-22	2	27	39	-	-	-	-	1	-
07.01.07	Bristol	A	16-19	6	152	158	4	2	-	2	1	1
27.01.07	Bristol	H	29-22	6	170	99	4	3	-	1	2	-
17.02.07	Harlequins	H	N/A	8	192	136	6	5	-	1	5	3
24.02.07	Leicester	A	32-0	9	156	217	2	2	-	-	2	-
03.03.07	Gloucester	H	21-20	9	221	164	4	4	-	-	4	1
10.03.07	Bath	A	9-17	9	135	188	5	4	-	1	1	1
17.03.07	Sale	H	34-36	9	256	172	5	4	-	1	2	1
06.04.07	Newcastle	A	13-32	9	215	230	5	3	-	2	3	-
15.04.07	Wasps	A	19-19	9	125	236	3	2	1	-	2	1
28.04.07	Irish	H	25-23	9	195	190	1	1	-	-	4	2

Key: won / drawn / lost / not played

Club Information

Useful Information

Founded
1880

Address
Franklin's Gardens
Weedon Road
Northampton
NN5 5BG

Capacity
13,591 (11,500 seated)

Main switchboard
01604 751543

Website
www.northamptonsaints.co.uk

Travel Information

Car

From North:
Approaching on the M1, exit at junction 16 and take the A45 onto Weedon Road, which is signposted 'Town Centre'. Turn left into Ross Road and follow signs for the car park.

From South:
Approaching on the M1, exit at junction 15a and follow signs for Sixfields. Turn left to join the A45 onto Weedon Road. Then as route for North.

Train

Silverlink trains run from Milton Keynes Central or Coventry to Northampton station.

Silverlink Trains also run directly from London Euston to Northampton station.

From Northampton station, turn right and continue walking until you pass the bus station and enter a shopping area. Turn left, then left again down Abbey Street into the Northampton Saints Car Park.

Maps

Area Map

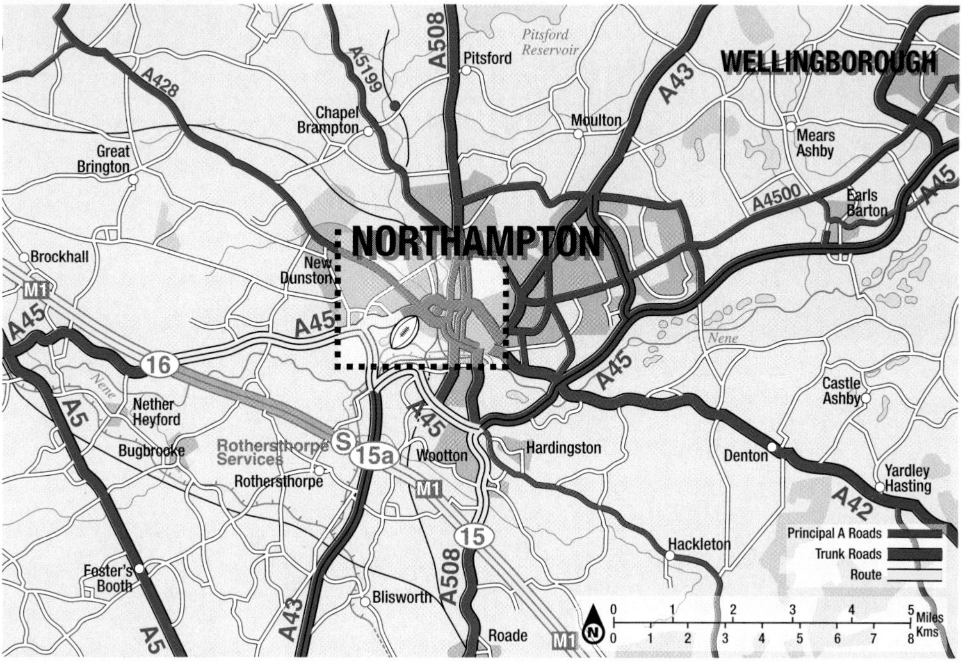

Local Map

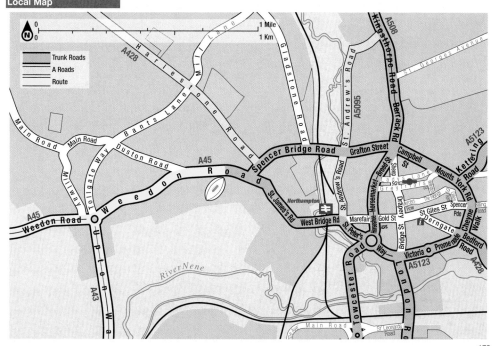

Sale Sharks

Season Summary 2005/06

Position	Won	Drawn	Lost	For	Against	Bonus Points	Total Points
1	**16**	**1**	**5**	**573**	**444**	**8**	**74**

An emphatic win over Tigers at Twickenham saw the north west side winning their first league title and making Premiership history finishing top of the league and going on to claim the Premiership title. Although Sharks were forced to play periods of the season without key players due to international commitments, they proved they had quality players to stand in for the likes of Charlie Hodgson and Mark Cueto, only losing five Premiership games throughout their campaign. Head Coach Kingsley Jones has retained all his key players and has recruited well for the coming season – including Newport Gwent's John Bryant and Leeds' Chris Bell – as he looks to emulate the success achieved in 2005/06.

Director of Rugby: Philippe Saint-Andre

Club Honours
Parker Pen Shield: 2002, 2005
Guinness Premiership Champions: 2006

Season Squad

Stats 2005-06

Position	Player	Height	Weight	Apps	Rep	Tries	Points
BR	P.Anglesea	6'3"	16st 4lb	-	4	-	-
8	N.Bonner-Evans	6'4"	18st 0lb	7	4	-	-
H	N.Briggs	5'10"	14st 13lb	-	1	-	-
H	S.Bruno	5'9"	16st 9lb	6	9	1	5
FL	J.Carter	6'3"	17st 0lb	2	1	-	-
8	S.Chabal	6'3"	17st 0lb	17	1	3	15
SH	V.Courrent	5'9"	13st 12lb	12	5	3	82
P	B.Coutts	6'3"	18st 0lb	9	2	-	-
W	M.Cueto	6'0"	14st 9lb	16	-	6	30
L	C.Day	6'6"	16st 10lb	9	10	-	-
P	L.Faure	6'1"	18st 0lb	6	4	-	-
L	I.Fernandez Lobbe	6'5"	17st 4lb	12	6	3	15
SH	B.Foden	6'0"	13st 7lb	1	7	1	5
W	S.Hanley	6'4"	15st 12lb	7	1	4	20
FL	M.Hills	6'1"	14st 7lb	-	2	-	-
FH	C.Hodgson	5'10"	12st 13lb	15	1	2	248
L/BR	C.Jones	6'7"	16st 1lb	19	1	2	10
P	M.Jones	5'7"	19st 0lb	-	1	-	-
FH	D.Larrechea	6'0"	14st 3lb	11	2	1	32
L/BR	B.Lloyd	6'5"	15st 13lb	-	1	-	-

Position	Player	Height	Weight	Apps	Rep	Tries	Points
FL	M.Lund	6'3"	16st 9lb	19	1	4	20
SH	S.Martens	5'11"	14st 7lb	14	2	3	15
C/W	C.Mayor	6'2"	15st 0lb	5	10	5	25
W	M.Riley	6'2"	14st 4lb	-	1	-	-
W	O.Ripol Fortuny	5'9"	12st 6lb	13	2	4	20
P	E.Roberts	N/A	N/A	1	2	-	-
FB	J.Robinson	5'8"	13st 4lb	23	-	4	29
L	D.Schofield	6'6"	18st 0lb	17	3	3	15
C/W	E.Seveali'i	5'10"	14st 0lb	14	-	3	15
P	A.Sheridan	6'5"	18st 10lb	8	2	-	-
P	B.Stewart	6'2"	18st 0lb	14	9	-	-
C/W/BR	E.Taione	6'4"	19st 6lb	1	4	-	-
C	M.Taylor	6'1"	15st 0lb	20	-	1	5
H/FL	A.Titterrell	5'8"	14st 9lb	19	5	2	10
C	R.Todd	5'11"	16st 0lb	11	4	1	5
P	S.Turner	6'0"	17st 9lb	10	12	-	-
W/C	N.Wakley	6'2"	15st 0lb	-	2	-	-
FL/L	J.White	6'5"	18st 6lb	16	2	-	-
SH	R.Wigglesworth	5'9"	13st 3lb	6	12	1	19

Last Season Form 2005/06

Season Progression

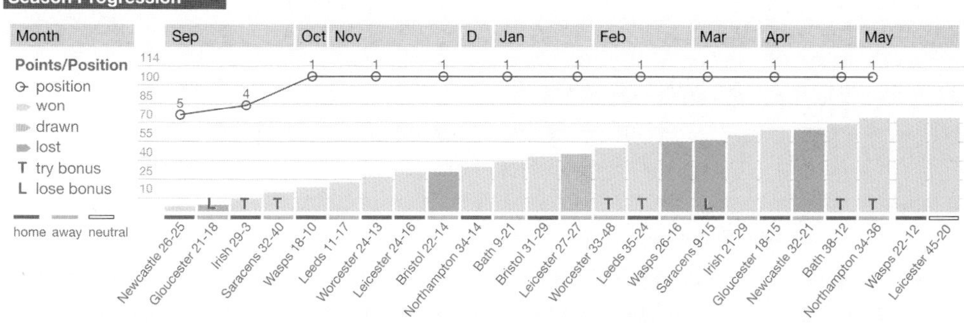

Home Matches

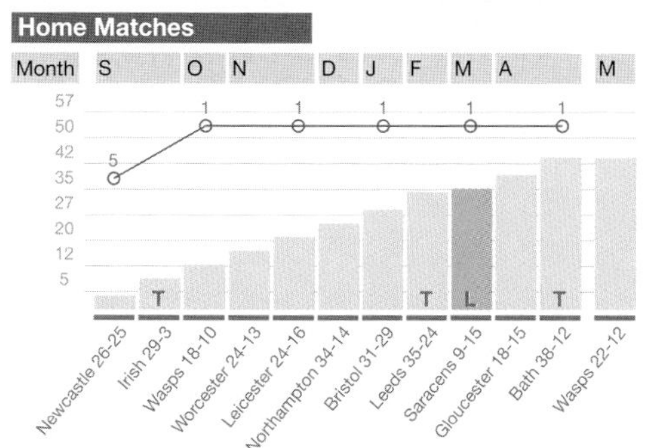

Away Matches

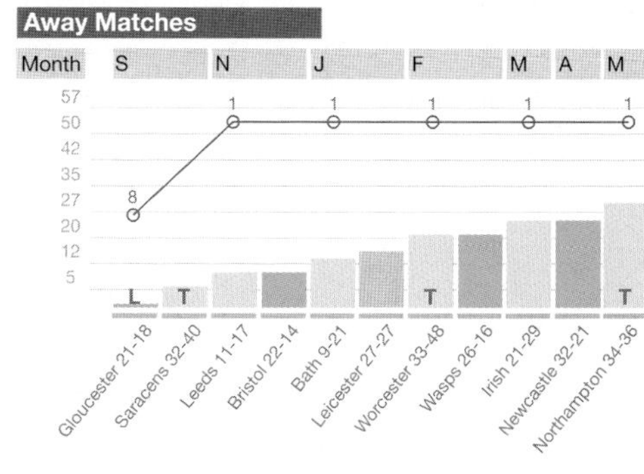

Premiership Stats

Premiership Stats		Home	Away	Neutral
Tries	57	23	30	4
Coversions	41	17	22	2
Penalty goals	84	50	28	6
Drop goals	7	3	3	1
Kick %	73%	77%	70%	73%
Yellow/Red cards	14/2	6/0	8/2	0/0
Powerplay tries	5	3	2	0
Shorthand tries	0	0	0	0

Powerplay tries are scored when your side are playing with a man or more advantage due to yellow or red cards.

Shorthand tries are scored when your side are playing with a man or more fewer due to yellow or red cards.

Team Performance

Position	Team	% total points won	% won at home	% won away
1	**Sale**			
2	Leicester	28%	28%	27%
3	Irish			
4	Wasps			
5	Gloucester	22%	25%	18%
6	Northampton			
7	Newcastle			
8	Worcester	27%	27%	27%
9	Bath			
10	Saracens			
11	Bristol	23%	20%	28%
12	Leeds			

Sale Sharks

Top Scorer

Charlie Hodgson

Points Facts

Total points	% team points	Home	Away	Neutral
248	39	157	68	23

Points by Time Period

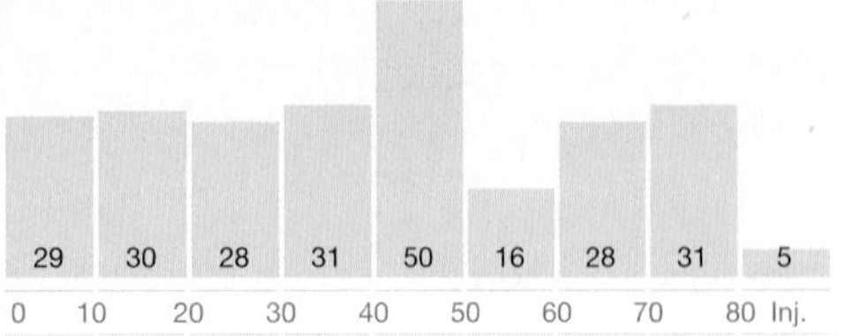

Team Tries and Points

Tries by Time Period

scored
conceded

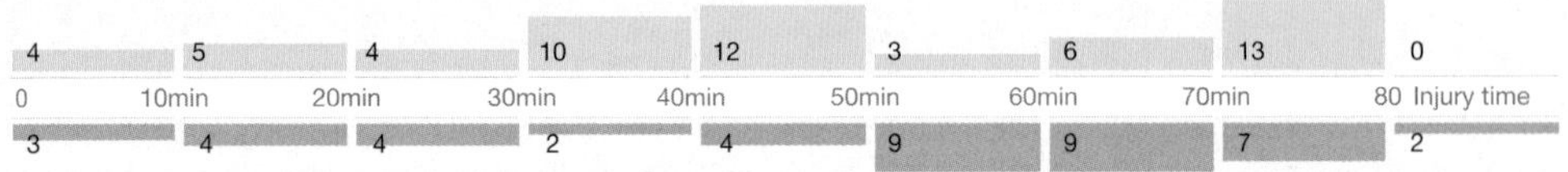

Tries by Halves

scored
conceded

	Total	1st half	2nd half	1st half %	2nd half %
scored	57	23	34	40%	60%
conceded	44	13	31	30%	70%

How Points were Scored

tries:	285
conversions:	82
pen goals:	252
drop goals:	21

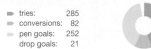

How Points were Conceded

tries:	220
conversions:	58
pen goals:	186
drop goals:	12

Tries Scored by Player

backs:	39
forwards:	18

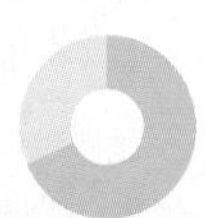

Tries Conceded by Player

backs:	33
forwards:	10

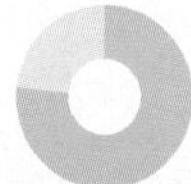

Eight-Season Form 1998-2006

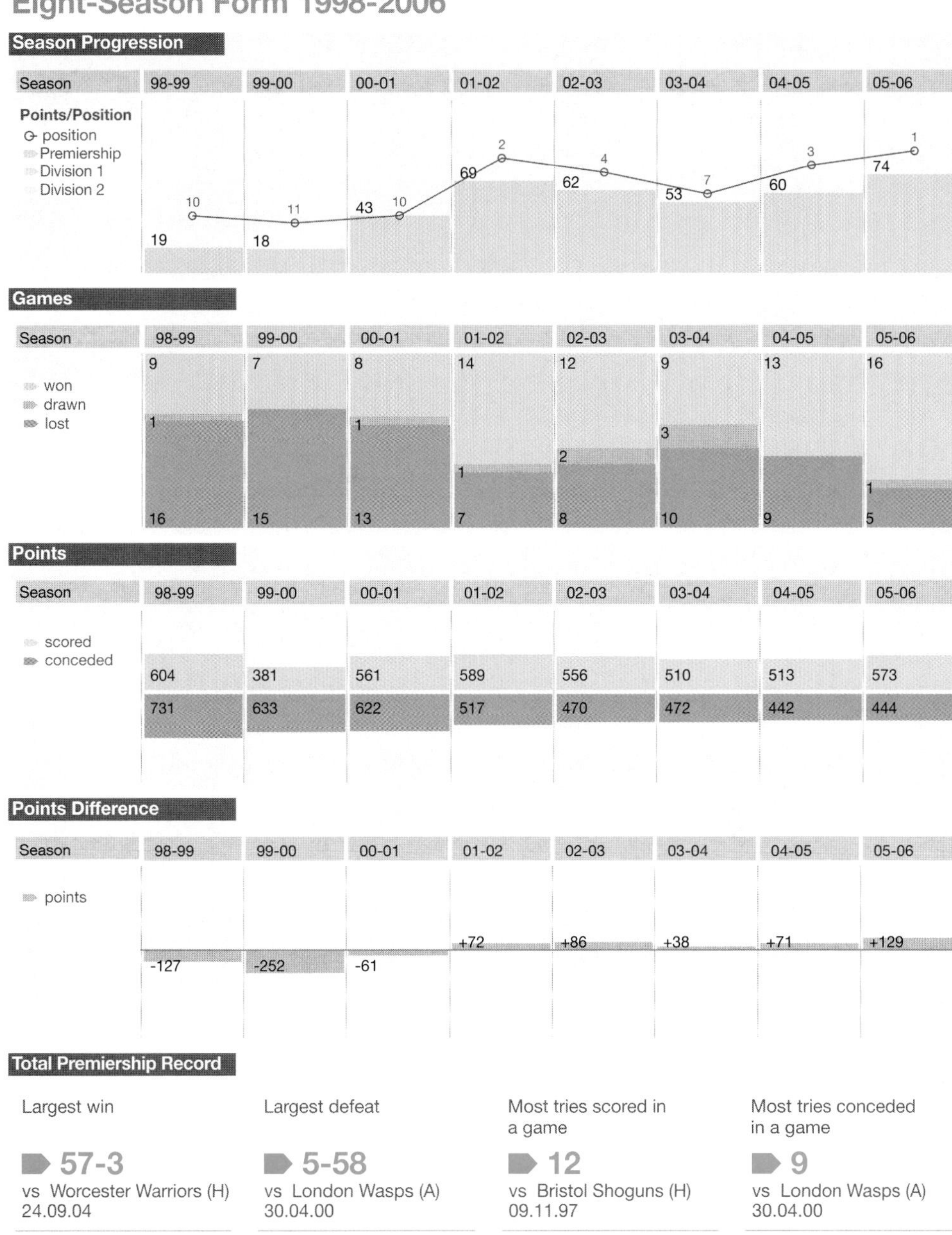

Total Premiership Record

Largest win
57-3
vs Worcester Warriors (H)
24.09.04

Largest defeat
5-58
vs London Wasps (A)
30.04.00

Most tries scored in a game
12
vs Bristol Shoguns (H)
09.11.97

Most tries conceded in a game
9
vs London Wasps (A)
30.04.00

Top points scorer
C.Hodgson 1088

Top try scorer
S.Hanley 75

Top drop goal scorer
C.Hodgson 14

Most appearances
J.Baxendell 131

Longest winning sequence
6 wins from 08.05.04 to 03.10.04

Longest losing sequence
7 defeats from 20.12.98 to 14.02.99

Sale Sharks EFL

ENHANCED FIXTURE LIST

[does not include play-off data]

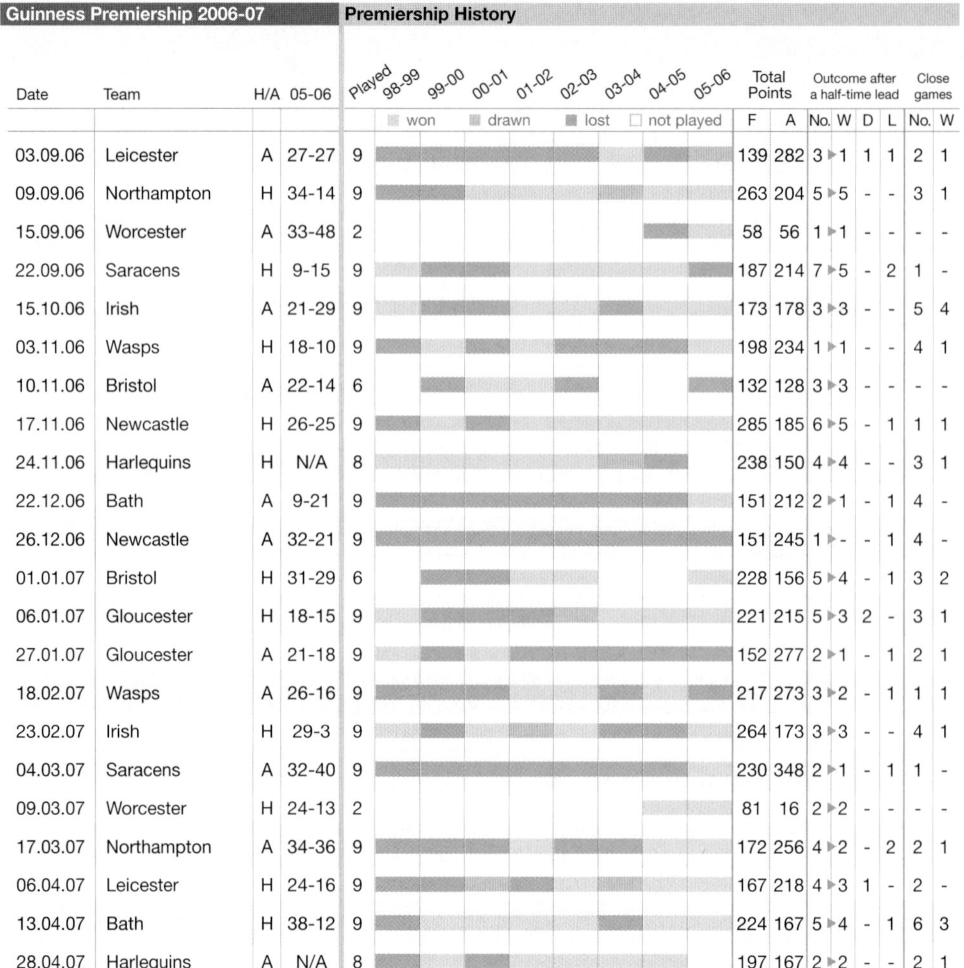

Guinness Premiership 2006-07 | **Premiership History**

Premiership History seasons: 98-99, 99-00, 00-01, 01-02, 02-03, 03-04, 04-05, 05-06 (won / drawn / lost / not played)

Date	Team	H/A	05-06	Played	Total Points F	Total Points A	Outcome after a half-time lead No.	W	D	L	Close games No.	W
03.09.06	Leicester	A	27-27	9	139	282	3	1	1	1	2	1
09.09.06	Northampton	H	34-14	9	263	204	5	5	-	-	3	1
15.09.06	Worcester	A	33-48	2	58	56	1	1	-	-	-	-
22.09.06	Saracens	H	9-15	9	187	214	7	5	-	2	1	-
15.10.06	Irish	A	21-29	9	173	178	3	3	-	-	5	4
03.11.06	Wasps	H	18-10	9	198	234	1	1	-	-	4	1
10.11.06	Bristol	A	22-14	6	132	128	3	3	-	-	-	-
17.11.06	Newcastle	H	26-25	9	285	185	6	5	-	1	1	1
24.11.06	Harlequins	H	N/A	8	238	150	4	4	-	-	3	1
22.12.06	Bath	A	9-21	9	151	212	2	1	-	1	4	-
26.12.06	Newcastle	A	32-21	9	151	245	1	-	-	1	4	-
01.01.07	Bristol	H	31-29	6	228	156	5	4	-	1	3	2
06.01.07	Gloucester	H	18-15	9	221	215	5	3	2	-	3	1
27.01.07	Gloucester	A	21-18	9	152	277	2	1	-	1	2	1
18.02.07	Wasps	A	26-16	9	217	273	3	2	-	1	1	1
23.02.07	Irish	H	29-3	9	264	173	3	3	-	-	4	1
04.03.07	Saracens	A	32-40	9	230	348	2	1	-	1	1	-
09.03.07	Worcester	H	24-13	2	81	16	2	2	-	-	-	-
17.03.07	Northampton	A	34-36	9	172	256	4	2	-	2	2	1
06.04.07	Leicester	H	24-16	9	167	218	4	3	1	-	2	-
13.04.07	Bath	H	38-12	9	224	167	5	4	-	1	6	3
28.04.07	Harlequins	A	N/A	8	197	167	2	2	-	-	2	1

Club Information

Useful Information

Founded
1861

Address
Edgeley Park
Hardcastle Road
Edgeley
Stockport
SK3 9DD

Capacity
10,641 (3,132 seated)

Main switchboard
0161 283 8888

Website
www.salesharks.com

Travel Information

Car

From South:
Leave the M6 at junction 19 (towards Manchester Airport, Stockport A55), then turn right at the roundabout onto the A556. After approx four miles you reach a roundabout, turn right onto the M56 (towards Manchester). After approx a further seven miles, exit the M56 and join the M60 (signposted Stockport, Sheffield). Leave the M60 at junction 1 and follow the signs to Cheadle and Stockport County FC at the roundabout. Continue straight ahead at the first set of traffic lights, then right at the next set (keep following signs for Stockport County FC). After a mile, turn left onto the B5465 Edgeley Road, then after another mile turn right into Dale Street. Take the second turning on the left into Hardcastle Road to reach the stadium.

From North:
From the M62 join the M60 and continue south. Leave the M60 at junction 1, then as route for South.

Train

Stockport station is approx half a mile from the stadium. Arriva Trains Northern run services from Sheffield to Stockport. From London, Virgin Trains run from London Euston to directly to Stockport.

Maps

Area Map

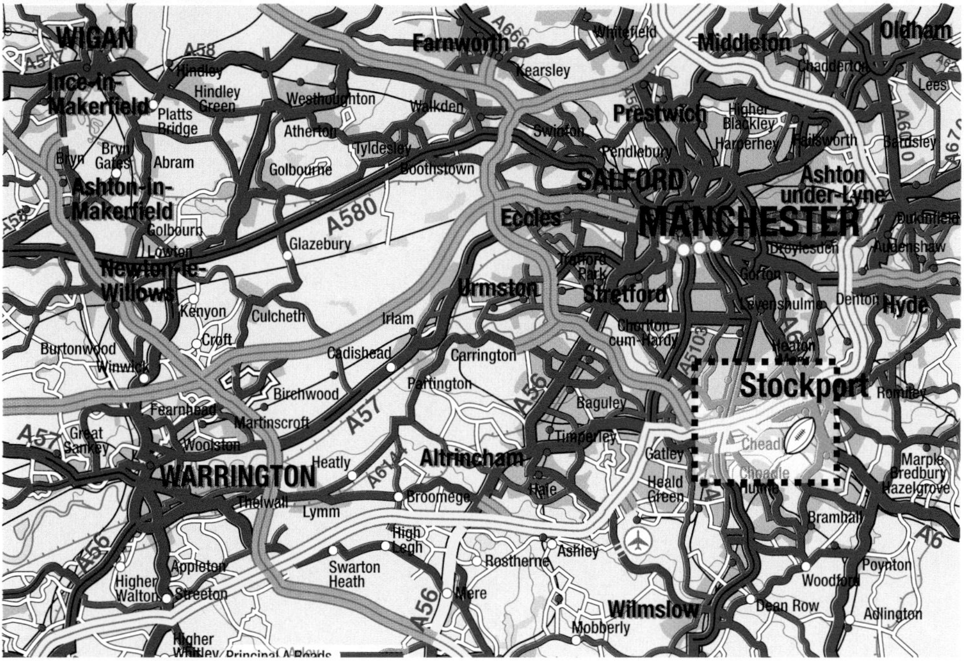

Local Map

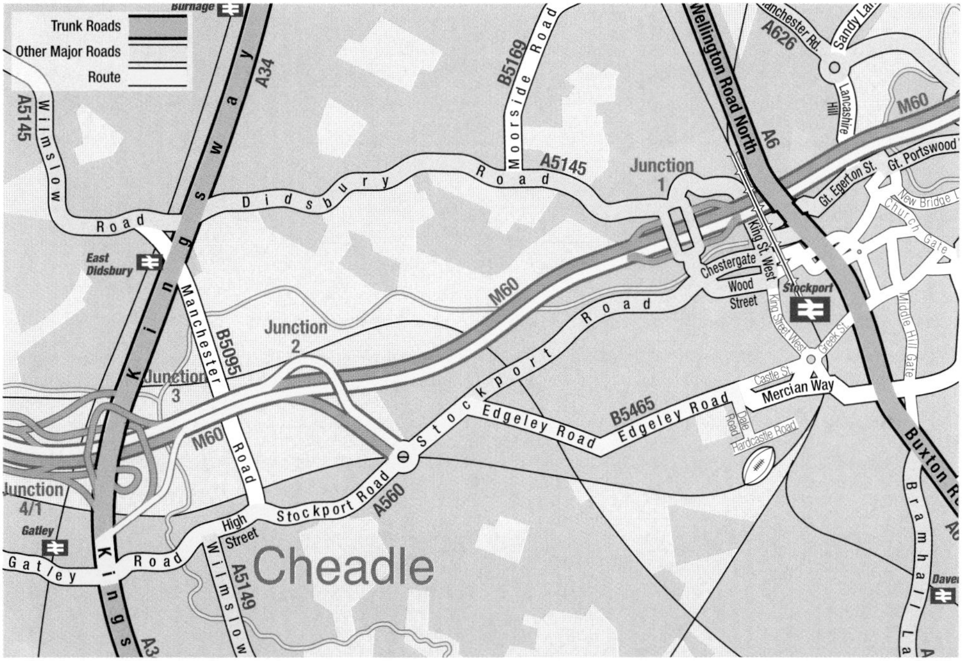

Saracens

Season Summary 2005/06

Position	Won	Drawn	Lost	For	Against	Bonus Points	Total Points
10	8	1	13	433	483	12	46

Eight successive Premiership defeats saw Saracens plunge to 11th in the league and only four points above bottom club Leeds in February, ending Steve Diamond's reign. However, thanks to the arrival of Australian coach Eddie Jones, the Vicarage Road side pulled themselves from the brink of relegation, finding some form during the latter part of the season. A memorable win against Sale marked a turning point in their campaign, triggering a run of four successive wins for the men in black, easing them into 10th place. The Watford side was boosted by the news that French international Thomas Castaignede had signed a one-year contract extension.

Director of Rugby: Alan Gaffney

Club Honours
Pilkington Cup: 1998

Season Squad

Stats 2005-06

Position	Player	Height	Weight	Apps	Rep	Tries	Points
FL	S.Armitage	5'9"	16st 8lb	2	1	3	15
C	P.Bailey	6'0"	12st 8lb	6	1	-	-
8	D.Barrell	6'4"	15st 0lb	-	1	-	-
C	M.Bartholomeusz	5'9"	13st 8lb	12	-	2	10
SH	K.Bracken	5'11"	13st 0lb	12	4	-	-
P	B.Broster	5'11"	16st 9lb	6	9	-	-
H	S.Byrne	5'10"	15st 6lb	12	5	-	-
H	M.Cairns	5'11"	16st 0lb	10	11	2	10
FH	T.Castaignede	5'9"	13st 3lb	9	1	4	20
L	K.Chesney	6'6"	18st 4lb	14	8	1	5
SH	A.Dickens	5'10"	12st 9lb	8	5	-	-
L	I.Fullarton	6'7"	16st 12lb	6	1	-	-
C	D.Harris	5'10"	15st 12lb	4	6	1	5
W	R.Haughton	6'2"	13st 7lb	9	2	3	15
FH	G.Jackson	5'11"	13st 6lb	22	-	3	238
C	B.Johnston	6'3"	16st 7lb	13	1	3	15
H	A.Kyriacou	5'11"	15st 2lb	-	3	-	-
FH	N.Little	6'0"	15st 0lb	-	1	-	-
P	N.Lloyd	6'0"	16st 9lb	4	10	-	-
P	H.Mitchell	N/A	N/A	2	2	1	5
C	A.Powell	5'11"	14st 4lb	2	5	2	10
L	S.Raiwalui	6'6"	18st 13lb	17	2	-	-
BR	T.Randell	6'2"	17st 4lb	7	5	-	-
SH	M.Rauluni	5'10"	13st 7lb	2	13	1	5
BR	B.Russell	6'3"	15st 10lb	9	9	1	5
L	T.Ryder	6'5"	16st 9lb	7	2	-	-
BR	A.Sanderson	6'2"	16st 1lb	4	1	-	-
FB	D.Scarbrough	6'1"	13st 3lb	19	1	7	35
BR	D.Seymour	5'11"	14st 2lb	9	7	-	-
BR	B.Skirving	6'4"	16st 12lb	14	1	2	10
C	K.Sorrell	5'11"	13st 8lb	21	-	2	10
W	T.Vaikona	6'2"	16st 2lb	15	1	2	10
P	C.Visagie	6'1"	18st 0lb	14	1	-	-
BR	H.Vyvyan	6'6"	16st 0lb	21	-	-	-
P	K.Yates	5'11"	17st 12lb	18	2	-	-

Last Season Form 2005/06

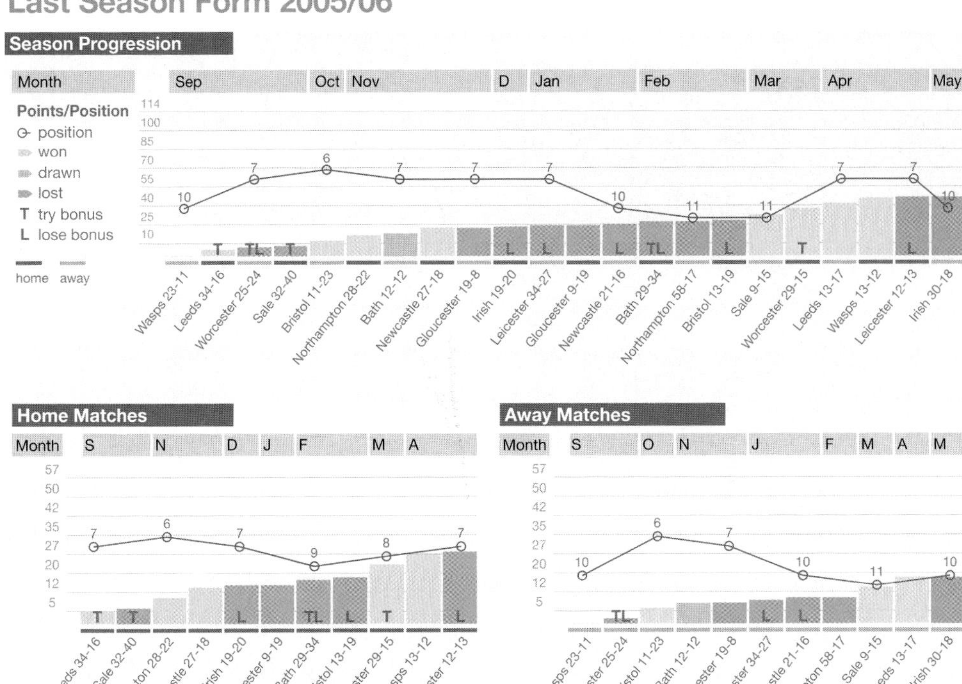

Premiership Statistics

	Total	Home	Away
Tries	42	23	19
Coversions	32	20	12
Penalty goals	51	30	21
Drop goals	2	0	2
Kick %	78%	85%	69%
Yellow/Red cards	12/0	4/0	8/0
Powerplay tries	4	3	1
Shorthand tries	2	1	1

Powerplay tries are scored when your side are playing with a man or more advantage due to yellow or red cards.

Shorthand tries are scored when your side are playing with a man or more fewer due to yellow or red cards.

Team Performance

Position	Team	% total points won	% won at home	% won away
1	Sale			
2	Leicester	15%	10%	23%
3	Irish			
4	Wasps			
5	Gloucester	15%	26%	0%
6	Northampton			
7	Newcastle			
8	Worcester	30%	35%	23%
9	Bath			
10	**Saracens**			
11	Bristol	40%	29%	54%
12	Leeds			

Saracens

Top Scorer

Glen Jackson

Points Facts

Total points	% team points	Home	Away
238	56	135	103

Points by Time Period

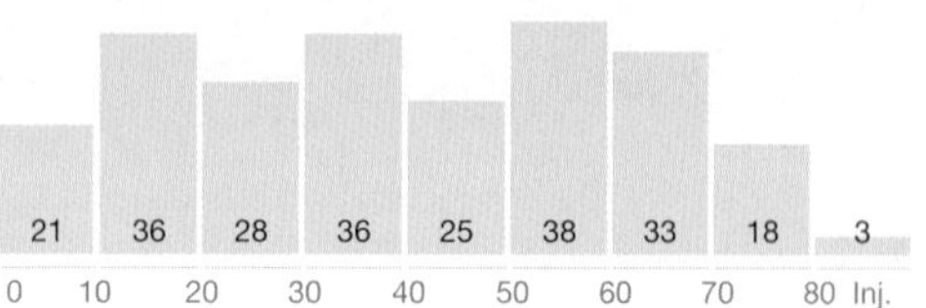

Team Tries and Points

Tries by Time Period

scored
conceded

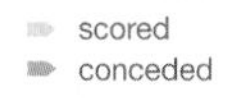

	0–10min	10–20min	20–30min	30–40min	40–50min	50–60min	60–70min	70–80	Injury time
scored	5	5	1	6	6	6	8	5	0
conceded	4	5	8	9	3	4	2	12	1

Tries by Halves

scored
conceded

	Total	1st half	2nd half	1st half %	2nd half %
scored	42	17	25	40%	60%
conceded	48	26	22	54%	46%

How Points were Scored

- tries: 210
- conversions: 64
- pen goals: 153
- drop goals: 6

How Points were Conceded

- tries: 240
- conversions: 60
- pen goals: 168
- drop goals: 15

Tries Scored by Player

- backs: 30
- forwards: 10

Tries Conceded by Player

- backs: 37
- forwards: 9

Saracens

Eight-Season Form 1998-2006

Season Progression

Season	98-99	99-00	00-01	01-02	02-03	03-04	04-05	05-06
Points	33	37	58	34	42	39	57	46
Position	3	4	5	10	8	10	5	10

Points/Position: position, Premiership, Division 1, Division 2

Games

Season	98-99	99-00	00-01	01-02	02-03	03-04	04-05	05-06
won	16	14	12	7	8	8	12	8
drawn	1					1	2	1
lost	9	8	10	15	14	13	8	13

Points

Season	98-99	99-00	00-01	01-02	02-03	03-04	04-05	05-06
scored	748	729	589	425	499	397	384	433
conceded	583	514	501	671	587	543	428	483

Points Difference

Season	98-99	99-00	00-01	01-02	02-03	03-04	04-05	05-06
points	+165	+215	+88	-246	-88	-146	-44	-50

Total Premiership Record

Largest win

59-5
vs Rotherham (H)
24.09.00

Largest defeat

13-55
vs London Irish (H)
22.11.01

Most tries scored in a game

9
vs Bedford Blues (A)
16.04.00

Most tries conceded in a game

7
vs Newcastle Falcons (A)
15.05.02

Top points scorer

G.Johnson 363

Top try scorer

T.Castaignede 25

Top drop goal scorer

A.Goode 9

Most appearances

K.Chesney 153

Longest winning sequence

7 wins from 29.04.98 to 11.10.98

Longest losing sequence

9 defeats from 26.11.05 to 26.02.06

ENHANCED FIXTURE LIST

[does not include play-off data]

Guinness Premiership 2006-07 / Premiership History

won | drawn | lost | not played

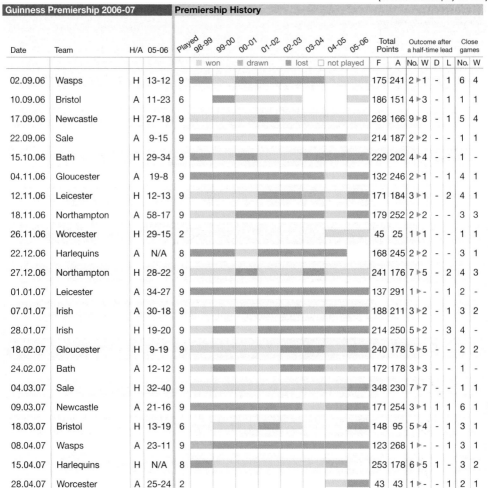

Date	Team	H/A	05-06	Played	Total Points F	Total Points A	Outcome after a half-time lead No.	W	D	L	Close games No.	W
02.09.06	Wasps	H	13-12	9	175	241	2	1	-	1	6	4
10.09.06	Bristol	A	11-23	6	186	151	4	3	-	1	1	1
17.09.06	Newcastle	H	27-18	9	268	166	9	8	-	1	5	4
22.09.06	Sale	A	9-15	9	214	187	2	2	-	-	1	1
15.10.06	Bath	H	29-34	9	229	202	4	4	-	-	1	-
04.11.06	Gloucester	A	19-8	9	132	246	2	1	-	1	4	1
12.11.06	Leicester	H	12-13	9	171	184	3	1	-	2	4	1
18.11.06	Northampton	A	58-17	9	179	252	2	2	-	-	3	3
26.11.06	Worcester	H	29-15	2	45	25	1	1	-	-	1	1
22.12.06	Harlequins	A	N/A	8	168	245	2	2	-	-	3	1
27.12.06	Northampton	H	28-22	9	241	176	7	5	-	2	4	3
01.01.07	Leicester	A	34-27	9	137	291	1	-	-	1	2	-
07.01.07	Irish	A	30-18	9	188	211	3	2	-	1	3	2
28.01.07	Irish	H	19-20	9	214	250	5	2	-	3	4	-
18.02.07	Gloucester	H	9-19	9	240	178	5	5	-	-	2	2
24.02.07	Bath	A	12-12	9	172	178	3	3	-	-	1	-
04.03.07	Sale	H	32-40	9	348	230	7	7	-	-	1	1
09.03.07	Newcastle	A	21-16	9	171	254	3	1	1	1	6	1
18.03.07	Bristol	H	13-19	6	148	95	5	4	-	1	3	1
08.04.07	Wasps	A	23-11	9	123	268	1	-	-	1	3	1
15.04.07	Harlequins	H	N/A	8	253	178	6	5	1	-	3	2
28.04.07	Worcester	A	25-24	2	43	43	1	-	-	1	2	1

Club Information

Useful Information

Founded
1876

Address
Vicarage Road Stadium
Vicarage Road
Watford
Herts
WD1 8ER

Capacity
22,100 (all seated)

Main switchboard
01923 475222

Website
www.saracens.com

Travel Information

Car

From North:
Leave the M1 at junction 5, taking the third exit from the roundabout and follow signs to Watford Town Centre. When joining the ring road get into the middle lane, before moving into the left lane after the second set of traffic lights. Follow signs for Watford General Hospital, which is next to Vicarage Road.

From West:
Leave the M25 at junction 19, and follow the A411 Hempstead Road, signposted Watford. Go straight over the first roundabout, then left at the second. Follow the signs towards Watford General Hospital, which is next to Vicarage Road.

Train

Watford High Street station is approx 10 minutes walk from the stadium. North London Railway trains run from London Euston station.

Tube

Watford tube station is approx 20 minutes walk from the stadium, on the Metropolitan Line.

Maps

Area Map

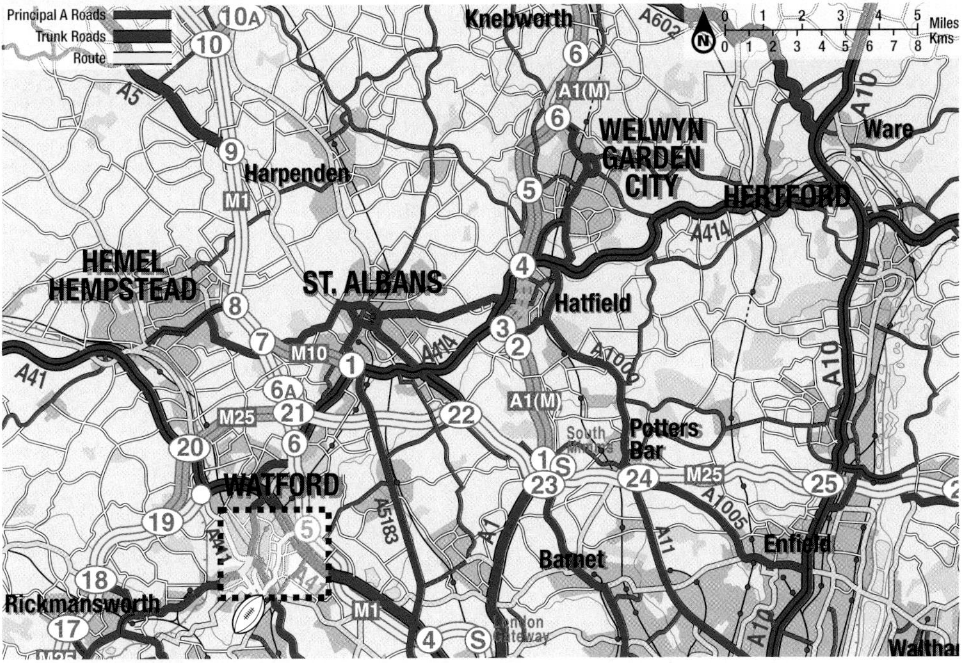

Local Map

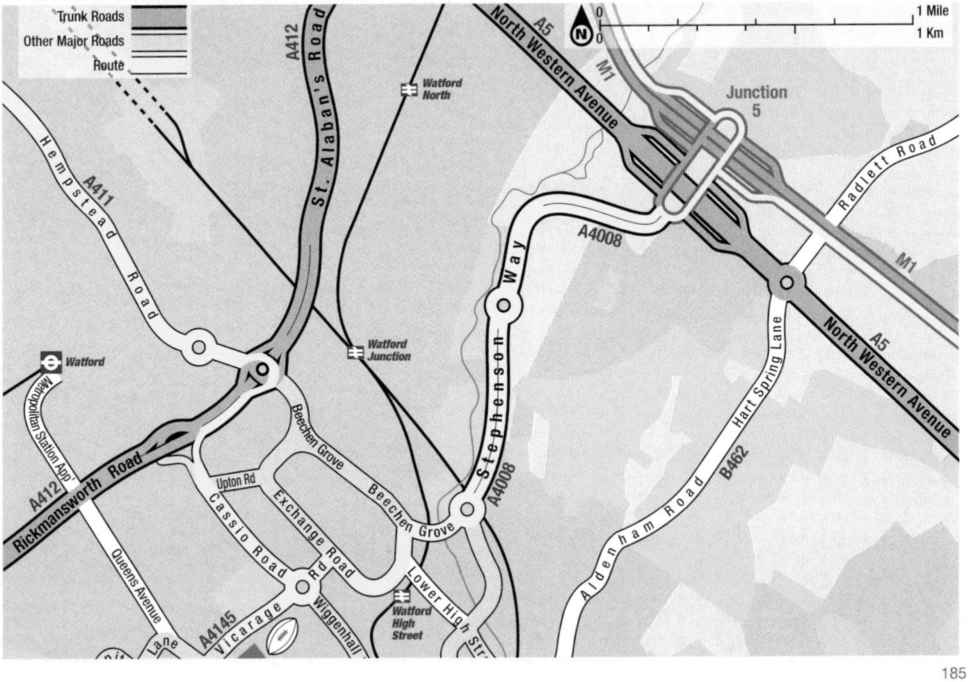

Worcester Warriors

Season Summary 2005/06

Position	Won	Drawn	Lost	For	Against	Bonus Points	Total Points
8	9	1	12	451	494	9	47

In their second season in the top flight and under the watchful eye of John Brain and new head coach Anthony Eddy, Worcester were fourth in the league at Christmas and on course for finishing in the top half. However, with Pat Sanderson sidelined for much of the season with a back injury, Warriors struggled to replicate that kind of form in the second half of the season, winning only three league games in 2006. Andy Gomarsall jostled for a place with Matt Powell to form the half back pairing with Shane Drahm, with Powell ending the season the favoured of the two. Warriors finished the season in a creditable eighth position, one place higher than their first year in the Premiership.

Head Coach: Anthony Eddy
Director of Rugby: John Brain

Club Honours
N/A

Season Squad

Stats 2005-06

Position	Player	Height	Weight	Apps	Rep	Tries	Points
P	C.Black	5'11"	17st 2lb	-	1	-	-
L	R.Blaze	6'7"	18st 0lb	1	2	-	-
FH	J.Brown	5'10"	11st 2lb	5	2	-	30
L	T.Collier	6'6"	21st 3lb	1	5	-	-
FB	T.Delport	6'2"	14st 6lb	16	2	4	20
FH	S.Drahm	5'9"	12st 10lb	17	3	3	233
H	C.Fortey	5'11"	17st 8lb	15	4	-	-
P	L.Fortey	5'10"	16st 3lb	2	6	-	-
L	C.Gillies	6'7"	17st 8lb	20	-	-	-
SH	A.Gomarsall	5'10"	14st 4lb	13	5	1	5
W	C.Hallam	N/A	N/A	-	1	-	-
FL	T.Harding	6'0"	15st 4lb	7	4	1	5
W	A.Havili	5'7"	15st 10lb	14	-	6	30
BR	D.Hickey	6'3"	15st 12lb	17	2	2	10
H	G.Hickie	5'10"	15st 10lb	1	8	-	-
C	B.Hinshelwood	6'2"	15st 10lb	7	-	-	-
P	C.Horsman	6'2"	17st 6lb	6	-	-	-
BR	K.Horstmann	6'3"	16st 9lb	19	2	3	15
W	J.Hylton	6'0"	13st 5lb	4	3	-	-
H	A.Keylock	N/A	N/A	-	-	-	-
FB/W	N.Le Roux	5'8"	11st 13lb	13	1	2	10
C	T.Lombard	6'2"	13st 5lb	21	-	2	10
P	M.MacDonald	6'1"	20st 5lb	1	3	-	-
W/C	M.Maguire	6'1"	14st 11lb	1	-	-	-
L	P.Murphy	6'7"	17st 6lb	21	1	1	5
L	E.O'Donoghue	6'6"	17st 4lb	1	8	-	-
W	U.Oduoza	6'3"	14st 4lb	3	-	-	-
SH	M.Powell	5'10"	13st 9lb	7	10	-	-
C	D.Rasmussen	6'2"	14st 12lb	17	2	2	10
SH	N.Runciman	5'9"	11st 11lb	2	-	1	5
BR	P.Sanderson	6'2"	14st 8lb	11	-	2	10
P	T.Taumoepeau	6'0"	18st 0lb	14	5	-	-
C	G.Trueman	6'0"	14st 2lb	4	4	1	5
BR	J.Tu'amoheloa	5'10"	14st 6lb	7	-	-	-
C/W	M.Tucker	6'0"	15st 10lb	7	-	-	-
BR	S.Vaili	6'4"	17st 6lb	5	11	2	10
H	A.Van Niekerk	5'10"	16st 12lb	6	3	-	-
FH/C	S.Whatling	5'10"	15st 0lb	3	6	-	3
P	T.Windo	6'0"	16st 12lb	21	-	3	15

Worcester Warriors

Last Season Form 2005/06

Season Progression

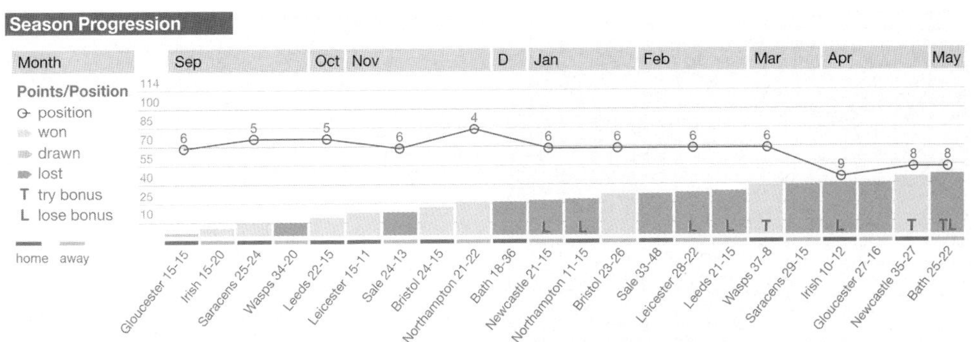

Home Matches

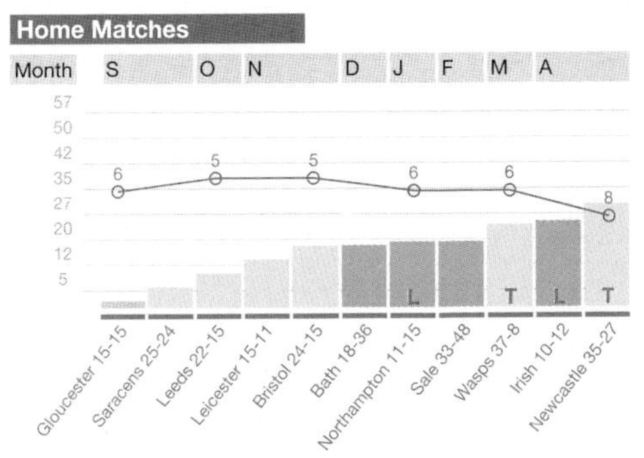

Away Matches

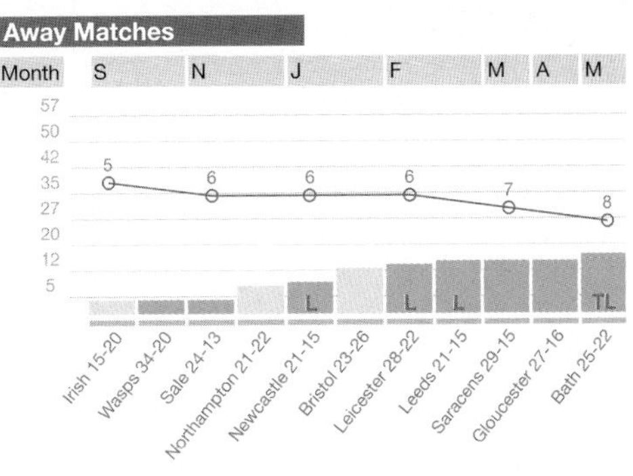

Premiership Statistics

	Total	Home	Away
Tries	40	22	18
Coversions	28	15	13
Penalty goals	61	35	26
Drop goals	4	0	4
Kick %	70%	69%	71%
Yellow/Red cards	15/2	6/1	9/1
Powerplay tries	8	5	3
Shorthand tries	0	0	0

Powerplay tries are scored when your side are playing with a man or more advantage due to yellow or red cards.

Shorthand tries are scored when your side are playing with a man or more fewer due to yellow or red cards.

Team Performance

Position	Team	% total points won	% won at home	% won away
1	Sale			
2	Leicester	20%	15%	27%
3	Irish			
4	Wasps			
5	Gloucester	24%	25%	22%
6	Northampton			
7	Newcastle			
8	**Worcester**	24%	23%	24%
9	Bath			
10	Saracens			
11	Bristol	32%	37%	27%
12	Leeds			

Worcester Warriors

Top Scorer

Shane Drahm

Points Facts

Total points	% team points	Home	Away
233	54	117	116

Points by Time Period

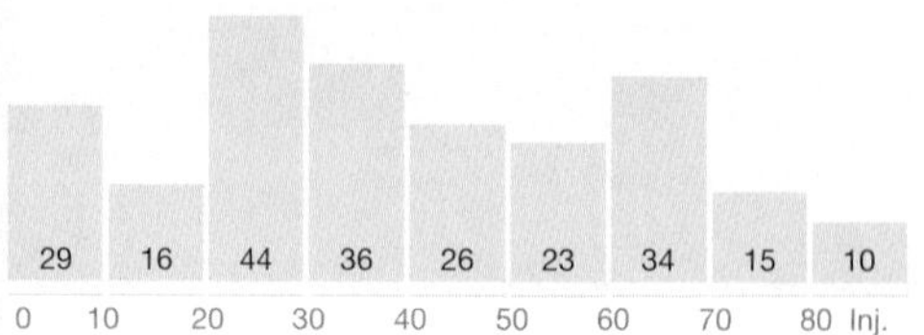

0–10	10–20	20–30	30–40	40–50	50–60	60–70	70–80	Inj.
29	16	44	36	26	23	34	15	10

Team Tries and Points

Tries by Time Period

scored
conceded

	0–10min	10–20min	20–30min	30–40min	40–50min	50–60min	60–70min	70–80	Injury time
scored	5	3	6	6	5	4	4	7	0
conceded	7	5	6	7	9	9	7	5	1

Tries by Halves

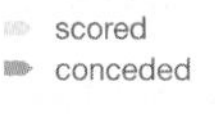

scored
conceded

	Total	1st half	2nd half	1st half %	2nd half %
scored	40	20	20	50%	50%
conceded	56	25	31	45%	55%

How Points were Scored

- tries: 200
- conversions: 56
- pen goals: 183
- drop goals: 12

How Points were Conceded

- tries: 280
- conversions: 64
- pen goals: 144
- drop goals: 6

Tries Scored by Player

- backs: 22
- forwards: 14

Tries Conceded by Player

- backs: 41
- forwards: 15

Worcester Warriors

Eight-Season Form 1998-2006

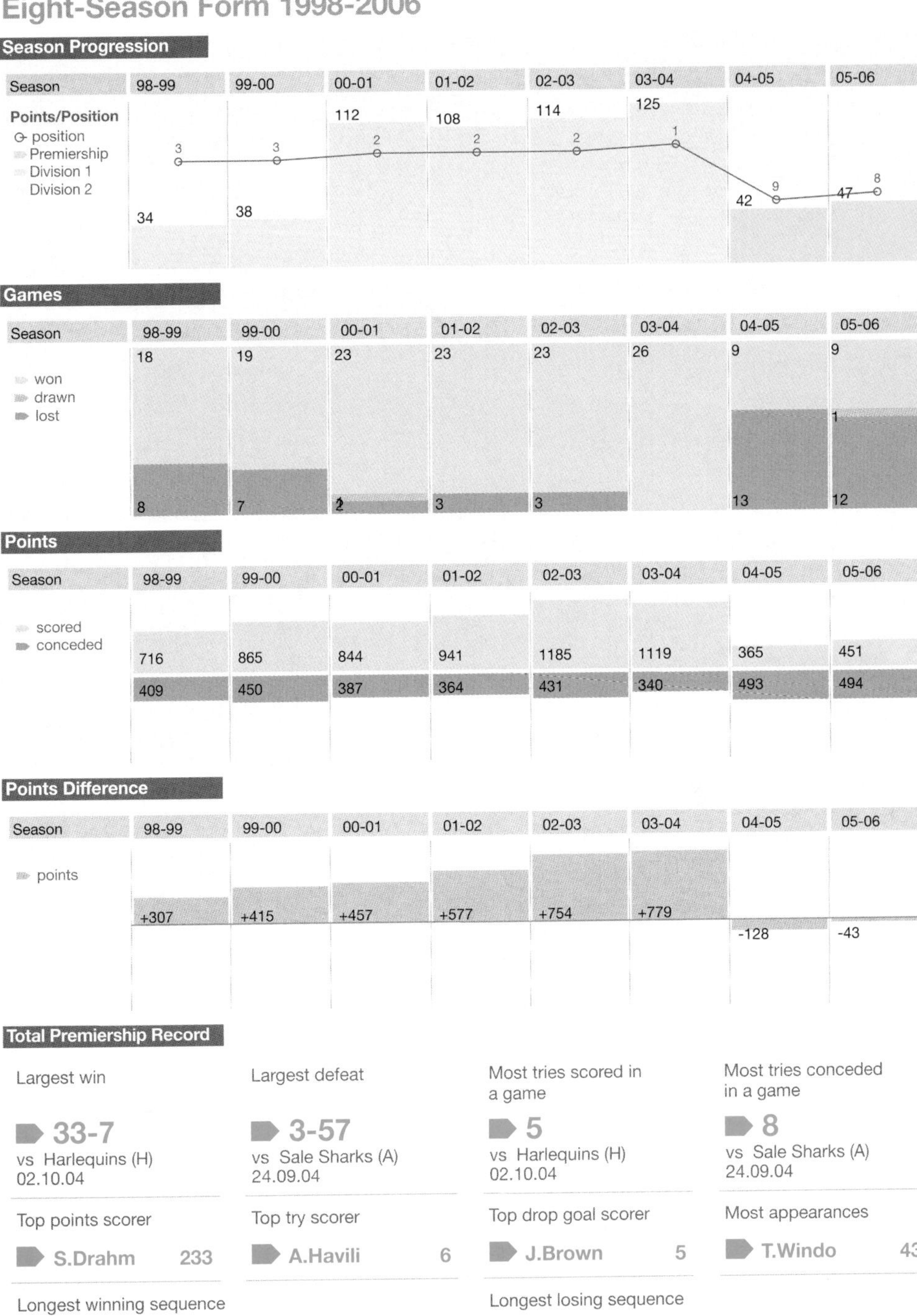

Total Premiership Record

Largest win
33-7
vs Harlequins (H)
02.10.04

Largest defeat
3-57
vs Sale Sharks (A)
24.09.04

Most tries scored in a game
5
vs Harlequins (H)
02.10.04

Most tries conceded in a game
8
vs Sale Sharks (A)
24.09.04

Top points scorer
S.Drahm 233

Top try scorer
A.Havili 6

Top drop goal scorer
J.Brown 5

Most appearances
T.Windo 43

Longest winning sequence
3 wins from 04.02.05 to 25.02.05

Longest losing sequence
4 defeats from 10.10.04 to 13.11.04

Worcester Warriors EFL

ENHANCED FIXTURE LIST

[does not include play-off data]

Guinness Premiership 2006-07				Premiership History																
Date	Team	H/A	05-06	Played	98-99	99-00	00-01	01-02	02-03	03-04	04-05	05-06	Total Points		Outcome after a half-time lead				Close games	
					won		drawn		lost		not played		F	A	No.	W	D	L	No.	W
02.09.06	Bristol	H	24-15	1									24	15	1	1	-	-	-	-
08.09.06	Newcastle	A	21-15	2									36	37	1	1	-	-	2	1
15.09.06	Sale	H	33-48	2									56	58	1	1	-	-	-	-
23.09.06	Bath	A	25-22	2									32	43	1	-	-	1	1	-
13.10.06	Gloucester	H	15-15	2									28	33	1	-	-	1	2	-
04.11.06	Leicester	A	28-22	2									29	78	-	-	-	-	1	-
11.11.06	Northampton	H	11-15	2									32	34	1	1	-	-	2	1
17.11.06	Harlequins	A	N/A	1									15	9	-	-	-	-	1	1
26.11.06	Saracens	A	29-15	2									25	45	1	-	-	1	1	-
22.12.06	Irish	H	10-12	2									26	18	1	1	-	-	1	-
27.12.06	Harlequins	H	N/A	1									33	7	1	1	-	-	-	-
01.01.07	Northampton	A	21-22	2									39	27	2	2	-	-	1	1
07.01.07	Wasps	A	34-20	2									37	66	1	-	-	1	-	-
26.01.07	Wasps	H	37-8	2									64	32	2	2	-	-	1	1
17.02.07	Leicester	H	15-11	2									26	49	1	1	-	-	1	1
24.02.07	Gloucester	A	27-16	2									32	55	-	-	-	-	-	-
03.03.07	Bath	H	18-36	2									40	62	1	-	-	1	1	-
09.03.07	Sale	A	24-13	2									16	81	-	-	-	-	-	-
16.03.07	Newcastle	H	35-27	2									44	57	1	1	-	-	-	-
08.04.07	Bristol	A	23-26	1									26	23	1	1	-	-	1	1
15.04.07	Irish	A	15-20	2									35	40	-	-	-	-	1	1
28.04.07	Saracens	H	25-24	2									43	43	1	-	-	1	2	1

Club Information

Useful Information

Founded
1871

Address
Sixways
Pershore Lane
Hindlip
Worcester
WR3 8ZE

Capacity
10,000 (3,700 seated)

Main switchboard
01905 454183

Website
www.wrfc.co.uk

Travel Information

Car

M5 Junction 7 (Worcester South) and follow AA signs for Park & Ride, County Hall (Countryside Centre). For a 15:00 kick off, buses start at 12:30 then every few minutes until 14:25. For a 20:00 kick off, buses start at 18:20 then every few minutes until 19:25.

M5 Junction 6 (Worcester North) and follow AA signs for Park & Ride, Blackpole (Blackpole East Trading Estate). For a 15:00 kick off, buses start at 12:30 then every few minutes until 14:25. For a 20:00 kick off, buses start at 18:20 then every few minutes until 19:25.

M5 Junction 6 (Worcester North) and follow AA signs for Park & Walk, Shire Business Park.

Train

Worcester Shrub Hill Station. Orange Bus Route 31 to City Bus station (every 10 minutes), then transfer to Rugby Special Service at frequent intervals (Stand F). A taxi to Sixways is about £8.00.

Worcester Foregate Street Station. Rugby Special Bus Service from outside the station every 10 minutes. For a 15:00 kick off, buses start to leave the station at 12:30 then every few minutes until 14:05 to the ground. For a 20:00 kick off, buses leave the station at 18:00 then every few minutes until 19:05.

Maps

Area Map

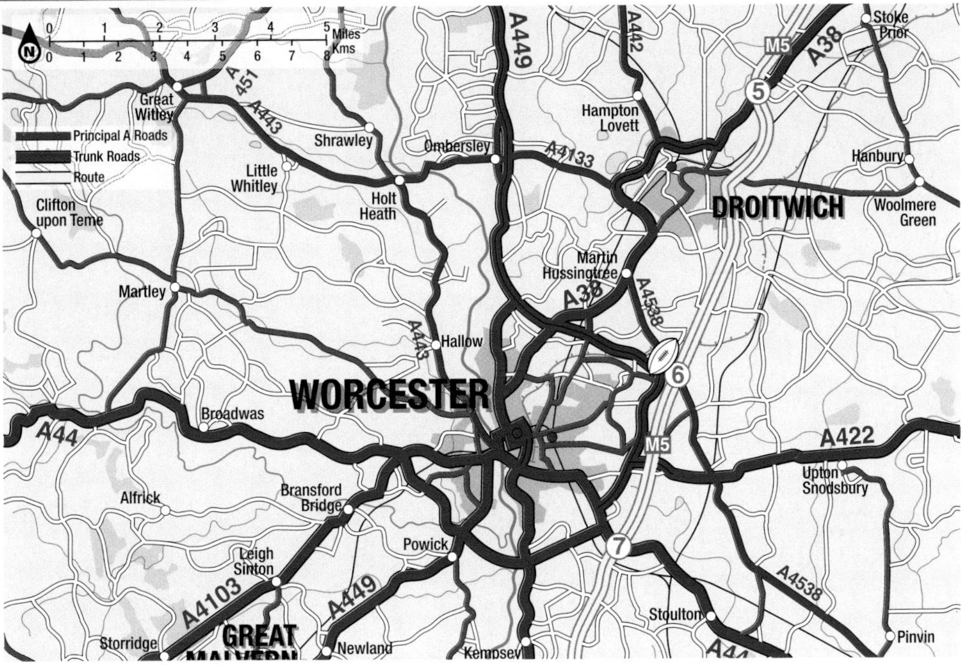

Local Map

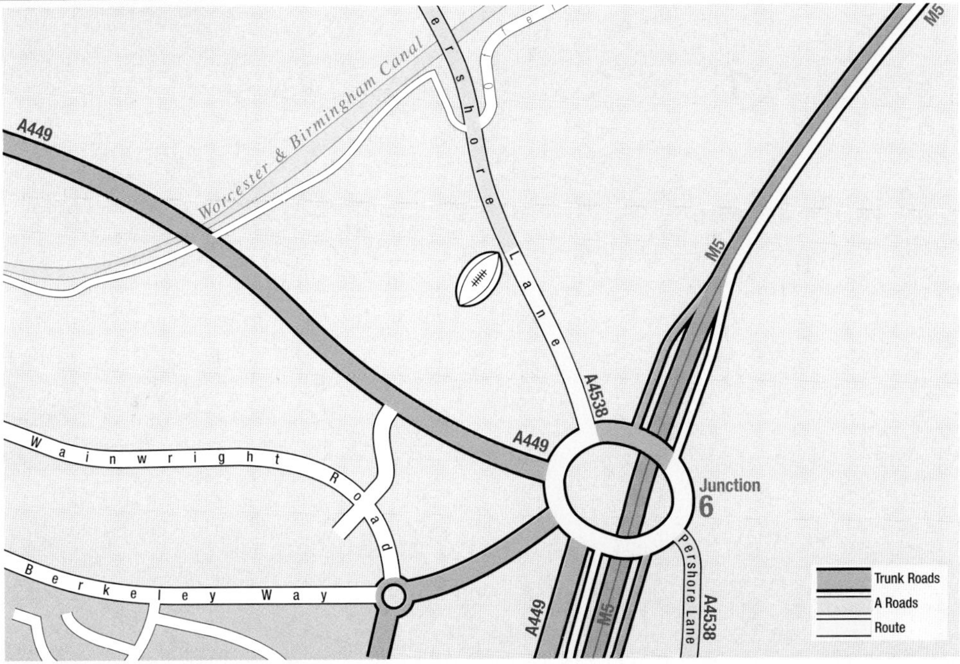

Premiership Fixture Grid 2006/07

HOME / AWAY	Bath Rugby	Bristol Rugby	Gloucester	Leicester Tigers	London Irish	London Wasps	NEC Harlequins	Newcastle	Northampton	Sale Sharks	Saracens	Worcester
Bath Rugby		17-Nov	7-Apr	9-Sep	4-Nov	1-Jan	27-Jan	25-Nov	10-Mar	22-Dec	24-Feb	23-Sep
Bristol Rugby	27-Dec		24-Nov	15-Apr	10-Mar	24-Sep	15-Oct	18-Feb	7-Jan	10-Nov	10-Sep	8-Apr
Gloucester	2-Sep	28-Apr		10-Mar	1-Jan	18-Nov	17-Mar	22-Dec	23-Sep	27-Jan	4-Nov	24-Feb
Leicester Tigers	17-Mar	22-Dec	16-Sep		18-Nov	28-Apr	3-Mar	27-Jan	24-Feb	3-Sep	1-Jan	4-Nov
London Irish	17-Feb	16-Sep	10-Nov	26-Dec		18-Mar	2-Sep	3-Mar	26-Nov	15-Oct	7-Jan	15-Apr
London Wasps	12-Nov	4-Mar	26-Dec	26-Nov	8-Sep		17-Sep	15-Oct	15-Apr	18-Feb	8-Apr	7-Jan
NEC Harlequins	6-Jan	24-Feb	9-Sep	23-Sep	7-Apr	10-Mar		1-Jan	4-Nov	28-Apr	22-Dec	17-Nov
Newcastle	28-Apr	3-Nov	13-Apr	7-Jan	22-Sep	23-Feb	10-Nov		6-Apr	26-Dec	9-Mar	8-Sep
Northampton	16-Sep	27-Jan	3-Mar	14-Oct	28-Apr	22-Dec	17-Feb	3-Sep		17-Mar	18-Nov	1-Jan
Sale Sharks	13-Apr	1-Jan	6-Jan	6-Apr	23-Feb	3-Nov	24-Nov	17-Nov	9-Sep		22-Sep	9-Mar
Saracens	15-Oct	18-Mar	18-Feb	12-Nov	28-Jan	2-Sep	15-Apr	17-Sep	27-Dec	4-Mar		26-Nov
Worcester	3-Mar	2-Sep	13-Oct	17-Feb	22-Dec	26-Jan	27-Dec	16-Mar	11-Nov	15-Sep	28-Apr